GREAT RECIPES
FROM
The New York Times

GREAT RECIPES
— FROM —
The New York Times

RAYMOND A. SOKOLOV

WINGS BOOKS
New York • Avenel, New Jersey

For Kathy Robbins, Elizabeth Mackey
and Kate Hartson, without whom...

Copyright © 1973 by Raymond A. Sokolov

This 1994 edition is published by Wings Books,
distributed by Random House Value Publishing, Inc.,
40 Engelhard Avenue, Avenel, New Jersey 07001,
by arrangement with the author.

Random House
New York • Toronto • London • Sydney • Auckland

Printed and bound in the United States of America

Library of Congress Cataloging-in-Publication Data
Sokolov, Raymond A.
    Great recipes from the New York Times / Raymond A. Sokolov.
        p.   cm.
    Includes index.
    ISBN 0-517-17758-7
    1. Cookery.   I. Title.
TX714.S613   1994
641.5—dc20   93-28785
                                                    CIP

8 7 6 5 4 3 2

Interior design: June Negrycz
Illustrations: Ron Kuriloff

Contents

Acknowledgments

The following friends and colleagues were of direct or indirect help in collecting these recipes: American National Cow Belles, Carolyn Anderson, Aragva Hotel (Moscow), Preston A. Barba, The Baroque (New York), Naomi Barry, James Beard, Simone Beck, Giuseppe Bellini, Fifi Bergman, Jane Berquist, Maurice Bonté, Jane Brown, Katherine Burton, Sharon Cadwallader, Teresa Candler, Carlton House (New York), Miriam Chau, Jane Chekenian, Anna and Alex Chen, Julia Child, Craig Claiborne, Wayne Culver, Elizabeth David, Avanelle S. Day, Dorothy Dean, Harriet de Onis, Susan Derecskey, Alexandre Dumaine, Eleanor Early, Mrs. David Felix, Michael and Frances Field, Gertrude Barnes Fiertz, Lynn and Wesley Fisher, Mrs. Morris Flexner, Pearl Byrd Foster, Phyllis Frucht, Pei-Mei Fu, Clarita Garcia, Elizabeth Gardner, Erica Gettinger, J. Paul Getty, Ed Giobbi, Anania Gitto, Richard Grausman, Mrs. Gardiner Green, Rebecca Greenberg, Jane Grigson, Albert Grobe, Ann Hark, Lucy Horton, Government of India Information Service, Jewish Family Service, Judith and Evan Jones, Madeleine Kamman, Gertrude Katz, Diana Kennedy, Frances Parkinson Keyes, Klube's Restaurant (New York), Ernest Koves, George Kristidimas, Alice Laden, Alfred LaGrange, George and Karen Lang, Garibaldi Lapolla, V. La Rosa & Sons, Theresa Laudo, Philomène Le Douzen, Calvin Lee, Virginia Lee, Leah Lenney, Leah W. Leonard, Larry Lorenzo, Joan Lorring, Lüchow's Restaurant (New York), Lun Far's Restaurant (New York), Juanita Kirk Lynch, Odette Magen, Anita Malugani, Beryl Marton, Erich Matthes, Paul Mayer, Walter S. McIlhenny, Perla Meyers, Robert Jay Misch, Anand and Kusum Mohan, Piper Laurie, Louis Morino, Jack Nisberg, Patrick O'Higgins, Judi Ohr, George Ohsawa, William Olcott, Roger Parizot, Alice Peerce, Pierre Hotel (New York), Leena Pihkala, June Platt, Fernand Point, Pearl Primus, Albert Pucci, Chew Quan, Lily Joss Reich, Therese Reisner, Irma Rhode, Luise Rhode, Helmut Ripperger, Ann Roe Robbins, Mrs. B. G. Robinson, Claudia Roden, I. Rokeach & Sons, Richard Rosen, Dora Rosenberg, Elisabeth Rosenthaler, Naomi Rubinstein, Harrison E. Salisbury, Viviana Schetky, Ellen and John Schrecker, Rachel

viii   ACKNOWLEDGMENTS

Schwartz, Evelyne Sharpe, Eva Shaye, Carly Simon, Josephine E. Sokolov, Margaret G. Sokolov, Trudy Solin, André Soltner, William Spry, Deirdre Stanforth, Rudolph Stanish, Mabel Stegner, Ruth Steinberg, William Toet, May Trent, Ernest Treyvaud, Robert Tsang, Tatu Tuohikorpi, United States Department of Agriculture Bureau of Human Nutrition and Home Economics, United States Navy, Charles Virion, Sarah MacLeod Walker, George and Inger Wallace, Mrs. James K. Wallace, Andrew T. Weil, M.D., Caroline D. Weiss, Germaine Cazenave Wells, Eudora Welty, Carl Werner, Grandma Wertheimer, Jenny and Merry White, Mrs. John Bell Williams, Imogene Wolcutt, Henry Wong, T. T. Wong, Lou Hoy Yuen.

Introduction

When I came to the *New York Times* as food editor in the spring of 1971, American kitchens and restaurants were at a crossroads. There was a brave new world hatching from coast to coast, a world of sophisticated home cooks—trained by James Beard, Julia Child and my predecessor at the *Times,* Craig Claiborne—ready to appreciate and prepare the authentic traditional dishes of France, Italy and the rest of the world. Many of these people had also traveled abroad and learned firsthand what al dente pasta tasted like and just how the browned butter sizzled when the *truite meunière* was served.

At home, in the United States, however, they carried this knowledge around with them like armor in a hostile territory. Most of the restaurants, even (or perhaps especially) in New York, that represented their favorite gastronomic countries, were embarrassing holdovers from a simpler day. Just as virtually all American Chinese restaurants served grotesque adaptations of Cantonese food adulterated into chop suey, so too the European chefs had doctored their native menus to suit naive customers who had since become more sophisticated.

The proof that national food stereotypes were fading fast showed dramatically back then in a wave of restaurant closings. The most public failure was that of Le Pavillon. Established as a spinoff of the French pavilion restaurant at the 1939 New York World's Fair, Le Pavillon under its cunning and tyrannical founder Henri Soulé had defined *haute cuisine* for Americans for thirty years. The restaurant had acquired a prestige so great that its snobbery and its shrewdly chosen menu spread to almost all of the other luxury restaurants in New York.

Soulé had cleverly mixed together expensive ingredients, French home cooking (for example, the lamb stew called *navarin*) and regional specialties of his hometown Lyons (such as the pike dumplings called *quenelles de brochets*). There was, of course, much more to French food. The growing number of people who knew this from direct encounters with the real thing in France began to wish that they could find a broader choice of French dishes on U.S. restaurant menus than those offered by Le Pavillon and its clones, or by lesser places specializing in bistro recipes like duck with orange sauce and *coq au vin*. The discerning diner in those days could take refuge in the garden at Lutece, easily the most French of French restaurants then in North America, and the most accomplished.

In the constricted economic climate of the Nixon administration's wage and price controls, the old order crumbled. Le Pavillon folded, as did The Colony and the Cafe Chauveron. At the same time, cooking in France changed under the radical influence of chefs such as Paul Bocuse and the Troisgros brothers. This *nouvelle cuisine* soon came to our shores. And its methods—a simplicity of appearance borrowed from the Japanese, an inventive and witty approach to recipes and techniques borrowed from the past, and a lust for new ingredients borrowed from cultures all over the world—were soon applied to American traditions and regional foods.

In America, the arrival of *nouvelle cuisine* had the ironic effect of preserving local dishes that had barely survived from pioneer days and of glamorizing ingredients no one had cared about for generations. At the same time, a liberalized U.S. immigration law, combined with war and political turmoil in Asia, produced a new wave of refugees from all parts of China funneled through Taiwan, and from Vietnam, Thailand, Cambodia and the Philippines. The first sign of this was the rise of Szechuan cuisine, a bonanza that first struck with real force in the early 1970s.

This was also the time when the natural foods movement began to touch large numbers of mainstream people. You didn't have to be a vegetarian Buddhist to think that organic flour and tomatoes were a good idea.

All these revolutionary changes were filling the air when I took up my august post at the *Times*. I was a bit overwhelmed to be filling Mr. Claiborne's shoes and sitting next to the carefully tended wall of recipe files maintained by Velma Cannon. They were a true heritage. The office itself was an institution, including a test cook with a diploma in home economics from the University of London, a spacious and grandly equipped test kitchen, a photo studio and a clerical staff of two.

I particularly liked the way the secretaries answered the phone. "Food news," they would say. It made me smile inwardly, at first. But I rapidly concluded that we were, in fact, functioning like any other news bureau of the *Times*. And we had a major story to cover, for outside the *Times* building, in a thousand new restaurants, grand and humble, in millions of kitchens, and in farms and gardens across the country, Americans were changing the way they ate, at home and away from home.

My job was to cover this food news as it happened. So I interviewed Szechuan, Hunan and Fukien chefs, watched them cook in their steaming kitchens at their giant woks, and printed their recipes in the paper. I visited André Soltner of Lutece at his weekend home and brought back some of his new ideas about *his* tradition. I attended an informal summit of organic food suppliers in Hereford, Texas. In general, I roamed as widely as I could, trying to capture a pivotal moment in our food history.

I was also often at my desk, fielding questions from readers, especially readers who remembered a recipe they had failed to clip from the food page. These queries sent me to the files and helped me discover new favorites of my own in this wonderful archive.

The result of all the searching and reporting and hanging around in innovative kitchens at an exciting time is this book. It is an anthology without an ideology. The choice of dishes is intentionally diverse. No one country or style or mood is favored. There are quick recipes and familiar recipes, as well as lavish and difficult showpieces. Recipes from down-home and from remote cultures. Every one was tested at the *Times*. I love them all.

RAYMOND SOKOLOV
NEW YORK, N.Y.
SEPTEMBER 1993

APPETIZERS

Marinated Mushrooms

1 pound small mushrooms
¼ cup wine vinegar
2 teaspoons salt
1 bay leaf
6 peppercorns
4 whole cloves
1 1-inch piece cinnamon stick
½ teaspoon snipped dill

1. Cut off and discard ends of mushroom stems, wash mushrooms well, and drain thoroughly by shaking a portion at a time in a sieve.
2. Bring to a boil in a stainless steel, aluminum, or enamel saucepan the vinegar, salt, mushrooms, and ¼ cup water. Skim off froth, if any, and add remaining ingredients. Simmer, stirring often, 20 to 25 minutes or until mushrooms settle to bottom of saucepan. Turn into glass canning jars and seal. Store in refrigerator. Serve at any time after cooling has taken place.

Yield: 1 pint

Herbed Mushrooms au Gratin

1 pound mushrooms
⅓ cup olive oil
3 tablespoons wine or tarragon vinegar
1 small onion, grated
2 medium cloves garlic, minced
1 tablespoon minced parsley
1 tablespoon minced chives
⅛ teaspoon each dried chervil, tarragon, and thyme
Pepper
1 bay leaf, crumbled
Cayenne or Tabasco
½ teaspoon salt
2 tablespoons butter
1 cup buttered soft bread crumbs

3

1. Cut off tough ends of mushroom stems. Clean mushrooms with a damp paper towel and slice thickly.
2. Mix oil, vinegar, and seasonings.
3. Add mushrooms, stir to coat them with marinade, and let stand at least 2 hours, stirring occasionally.
4. Drain off marinade. (It may be used as a condiment to flavor salad dressing.) Sauté mushrooms in butter until tender and transfer to a greased shallow heatproof dish.
5. Sprinkle with buttered crumbs and brown under broiler.

Yield: 5 servings

Artichokes Croisette

8 large artichoke bottoms (see below)
8 poached eggs (see below)
1 cup rouille (see page 301)
4 sprigs parsley, chopped

Place a warm artichoke bottom on a small plate, top with a poached egg and spoon over the warm rouille. Garnish with chopped parsley.

ARTICHOKE BOTTOMS

8 large artichokes
2 lemons, halved
4 teaspoons flour
Salt

1. Trim off the tough outer leaves of the artichokes. Using a sharp kitchen knife, slice off the stems of the artichokes and rub cut surfaces with lemon halves.
2. Neatly slice through the vegetables, parallel to the base, leaving intact an artichoke bottom less than 1 inch thick. Again, rub cut surfaces with lemon halves. Place bottoms in a large skillet.
3. Squeeze lemon halves and combine juice with the flour and enough water to make a smooth paste. Whisk in enough extra water to make a mixture that will cover the artichoke bottoms. Add salt to taste.
4. Bring to a boil, cover, and simmer until bottoms are tender, about 25 minutes. Drain and when cool enough to handle, remove

the fuzzy choke from the center by pulling and scraping with a spoon. Reheat the bottoms in hot, salted water.

POACHED EGGS

2 tablespoons white vinegar or lemon juice
8 eggs

1. In 2 small skillets, heat enough boiling salted water to just cover 4 eggs. Add 1 tablespoon vinegar or lemon juice to each.
2. Create a whirlpool by stirring each skillet of water vigorously with a spoon and drop 4 eggs into each. Lower the heat and let eggs steep in water just below the boiling point until done, about 4 minutes.
3. Remove with a slotted spoon and trim neatly with a cooky cutter.

Yield: 8 servings

Artichokes with Eggs

6 medium to large artichokes
  Salt
  Butter
1 tablespoon flour
¾ cup milk
¾ cup grated mild cheese
  Pinch paprika
6 poached eggs (See above)

1. Preheat oven to 325 degrees.
2. Wash artichokes. Cut off leaf tips with scissors. Cook in boiling, salted water until tender—25 to 40 minutes. Drain. Pull off leaves and discard. Cut out choke. Place bottoms in buttered baking dish.
3. Melt 1 tablespoon butter in saucepan and stir in flour until blended. Stir in milk slowly. When sauce is smooth, add ½ cup cheese. Season with salt and paprika. Stir until sauce is smooth and cheese melted.
4. Place 1 poached egg on each artichoke bottom. Pour sauce over eggs and sprinkle with remaining cheese. Dot with remaining butter and bake until brown. Serve hot.

Yield: 6 servings

André Soltner's Bibeleskäs
(Alsatian Prepared Cheese)

2 cups small-curd cottage cheese, sieved
  Pepper
  Salt
3 cloves garlic, finely chopped
1 tablespoon chopped parsley
½ cup heavy cream

1. Combine all ingredients. Mix until smooth.
2. Refrigerate several hours before serving.
3. Serve as an appetizer or cheese course.

Yield: About 2½ cups or 8 to 10 servings

Karjalan Piirakat
(Karelian Pasties)

FILLING:
¾ cup raw medium-grain rice
½ teaspoon salt
1½ cups water
¾ cup milk
4 tablespoons butter
1 egg, slightly beaten
¼ teaspoon pepper

DOUGH:
½ cup rye flour
½ cup wheat flour
¼ teaspoon salt

9 tablespoons water
  Flour

BUTTER DIP:
4 tablespoons butter
½ cup water

EGG BUTTER:
4 hard-boiled eggs
4 tablespoons butter
¼ teaspoon salt
¼ teaspoon pepper

1. Preheat oven to 475 degrees.
2. Cook rice in boiling salted water until water has been absorbed. Add milk and simmer until milk is absorbed. Add butter, egg, and pepper, and stir. Adjust seasonings.
3. While rice is cooking, mix rye and wheat flours and salt in a bowl and stir in water gradually to make a stiff dough.

4. Flour surface well.
5. Roll dough with hands into a 15-inch bar. Cut bar into 25 pieces.
6. Roll out pieces into very thin circles. Sprinkle flour on circles.
7. Brush excess flour off before filling with rice porridge.
8. Place 1½ tablespoons of rice porridge lengthwise down center of dough circles, leaving sides empty.
9. Crimp edges together with fingertips, both sides at the same time, starting at center. Final shape is oval.
10. Place on ungreased cookie sheet and bake for 15 minutes.
11. For dip, heat butter and water until butter is melted.
12. Line a platter with cloth and wax paper.
13. As pasties are taken out of oven, dip in butter dip and place on wax paper. Cover with cloth until ready to eat.
14. While hard-boiled eggs are still warm, mash roughly together with softened butter. Blend in salt and pepper. Texture should be like scrambled eggs. Refrigerate only long enough to chill; in other words, make egg butter shortly before serving.
15. Serve pasties with egg butter on side.

Yield: 8 servings

Raclette

½ wheel Bagnes cheese
  Small or new potatoes boiled in their jackets (2 per person)
  Pickled onions
  Sour gherkins

1. Hold the cut side of the cheese against the heat of a wood or charcoal fire. Turn the cheese two or three times to prevent it dripping as it melts.
2. When the cheese begins to bubble, scrape it with a knife onto a very hot plate. Repeat for each serving.
3. Serve with the peeled potatoes, onions, and gherkins.

Yield: About 18 servings

Dill Dip

1 cup sour cream
11 ounces cream cheese, at
   room temperature
3 ounces Spanish olives, pitted
   and chopped
3½ tablespoons chopped fresh
   dill
1 teaspoon finely chopped
   shallots

½ teaspoon Dijon mustard
1 dash worcestershire sauce
2 dashes Tabasco
White pepper
¼ teaspoon paprika
⅛ teaspoon garlic salt
Juice of 1 lemon

1. Combine all ingredients and mix well in a blender. Correct seasoning. Refrigerate in a serving bowl for several hours.
2. Serve with raw broccoli flowerets, cauliflowerets, endive, radishes, or whatever you like.

Yield: Enough dip to serve a dozen guests generously

Hunanese Hacked Chicken

½ pound boned chicken breast
2 tablespoons sesame paste
   Sesame oil
1 tablespoon imported dark
   soy sauce
1 tablespoon white vinegar
1 teaspoon monosodium
   glutamate (optional)
1½ teaspoons cayenne
1½ teaspoons crushed red
   pepper

1½ teaspoons minced fresh
   ginger
1½ teaspoons finely chopped
   scallions
1½ teaspoons minced garlic
1½ teaspoons chopped fresh
   coriander (also called
   Chinese parsley or cilantro)
1 tablespoon brown Szechuan
   peppercorns
1 cup peanut oil

1. Remove skin from chicken and plunge into boiling water for 5 minutes. Remove, drain, cool, and pull into 3-inch strips with a cross section of roughly ¼ inch. Reserve in a mixing bowl.
2. In another bowl, combine sesame paste with 1 tablespoon sesame oil, mixing until smooth. Continue stirring, blending in soy sauce, vinegar, and monosodium glutamate, if used.
3. Combine cayenne and crushed red pepper and moisten

thoroughly with sesame oil. Add to sesame paste mixture along with ginger, scallions, garlic, and coriander. Mix.

4. Fry Szechuan peppercorns for 15 minutes in 1 cup peanut oil heated to 300 degrees. Strain and discard peppercorns. Add 1½ teaspoons prepared oil to sesame paste mixture. Reserve remaining oil for future use.
5. Mix sauce together with chicken and serve on a flat dish or plate.

Yield: 2 to 4 servings

Szechuan Bon Bon Chicken

2 medium cucumbers, peeled and thinly sliced
Salt
2 ounces bean threads (cellophane noodles)
1 teaspoon brown Szechuan peppercorns
2 cups julienne strips (1½ inches long) cooked chicken
1 tablespoon finely chopped fresh ginger

1 tablespoon finely chopped garlic
¼ cup sesame paste
⅓ cup imported soy sauce
2 tablespoons sesame oil
2 tablespoons white vinegar
2 tablespoons hot red-pepper oil
4 teaspoons sugar

1. Sprinkle the cucumber with salt and let stand 10 minutes. Rinse, squeeze out excess water, and arrange in serving dish.
2. Place the cellophane noodles in a bowl and cover with warm water. Let soak 10 minutes. Drain well and place on top of the cucumber slices.
3. Place the peppercorns in a small, dry skillet and heat slowly until they smell fragrant and turn a darker color.
4. Grind the peppercorns in a mortar with a pestle and sprinkle over the chicken. Sprinkle ginger and garlic over chicken pieces and toss to mix.
5. Arrange chicken over noodles.
6. Combine the remaining ingredients in a bowl. Mix well. To serve, pour the sauce over the chicken and toss just before serving.

Yield: 6 servings

Mrs. Trent's Chinese Cold Chicken

2 whole chicken breasts
1 8-ounce can sliced bamboo
shoots
3 tablespoons white wine
vinegar
1 tablespoon sugar
⅛ teaspoon salt
2 tablespoons peanut oil

4 tablespoons bottled Chinese
fish sauce
1 tablespoon hot red-pepper
oil (or to taste)
2 tablespoons sesame oil
Pepper
1 large handful fresh coriander
sprigs (also called Chinese
parsley or cilantro)

1. Put an inch of water in a medium saucepan, bring to a boil, and
   put in chicken breasts. Cover. After 6 minutes at medium heat,
   turn chicken breasts, cover again, and let cook another 6 minutes.
2. Remove chicken breasts from saucepan, drain, and let cool.
3. Meanwhile, soak bamboo shoots, drained of any can liquid, for
   1 hour in 2 tablespoons vinegar, sugar, and salt, mixed together.
4. Remove chicken from bone and shred into strips ¼ inch wide and
   3 inches long. Put strips in a bowl.
5. Add peanut oil, fish sauce, hot red-pepper oil, sesame oil, and
   remaining vinegar (less vinegar if you want a hotter taste) to the
   chicken strips. Mix well.
6. Drain bamboo shoots as much as possible and add to chicken
   mixture. Mix well.
7. Just before serving, grind pepper over top and toss chicken
   mixture again.
8. Arrange chicken mixture on a platter, cover generously with
   coriander sprigs, and serve.

Yield: 6 servings

Peking Chicken and Cucumber Salad

1⅓ cups dried agar-agar, cut
into 1-inch-long pieces
1⅓ cups julienne strips (2
inches long) peeled, seeded
cucumber
1 cup julienne strips (2 inches
long) cooked chicken
¼ cup julienne strips (2 inches
long) cooked ham

2 tablespoons prepared hot
mustard
¼ cup sesame paste
¼ cup imported soy sauce
3 tablespoons white vinegar
2 teaspoons salt
2 tablespoons sesame oil

1. Put the agar-agar in a bowl, cover with warm water, and let soak 15 minutes. Squeeze dry and arrange on a serving platter.
2. Arrange the cucumber pieces over the agar-agar. Place the chicken over the cucumber and top with the ham pieces.
3. Place the remaining ingredients in a small bowl and mix well. To serve, pour the sauce over the dish and toss well.

Yield: 6 servings

Pei-Mei's Smoked Chicken

2 tablespoons brown Szechuan peppercorns
2 tablespoons salt
1 2½-pound chicken
1 scallion
3 slices fresh ginger
2 pieces star anise

1 ½-inch piece cinnamon stick
1 cup imported soy sauce
½ cup sugar
½ cup flour
½ cup black tea leaves, such as lapsang souchong
Sesame oil

1. Heat peppercorns and salt in a dry skillet over low heat briefly until the peppercorns have darkened slightly and become fragrant.
2. Rub salt-peppercorn mixture into chicken skin and let sit in the refrigerator for 5 hours or overnight.
3. Boil 2 quarts of water in a large pot. Add chicken, scallion, ginger, star anise, cinnamon, and soy sauce. Simmer for 20 minutes or to desired degree of doneness.
4. Remove chicken from pot, drain, and let cool to room temperature.
5. Put sugar, flour, and tea leaves in the bottom of a heavy iron pot, with tea leaves on top of flour and sugar. Place a rack over tea leaves and put the chicken on its side on the rack.
6. Cover pot and put over low flame for 8 minutes. Turn the chicken and smoke for 5 minutes more.
7. Remove chicken from pot and cut into serving pieces. Brush with sesame oil, let cool and serve. (Save broth for future use.)

Yield: 4 to 6 generous servings

Mousse de Pigeon au Genièvre Lutèce
(Pigeon Mousse with Juniper Berries as Prepared at Lutèce)

1½ pounds pigeon with bones (2 small squabs)
  1 pound chicken livers
    Salt
    Pepper
  2 cups duck fat, reserved from roasting about 3 5 to 6 pound ducks, or 2 cups (1 pound) lard
 12 blue juniper berries (see note)
 ¾ cup dry white wine

1. Preheat oven to 250 degrees.
2. Put the pigeon, bones included, and the chicken livers through the fine blade of a meat grinder.
3. To the resulting mixture add salt and pepper to taste, about ⅓ of the duck fat or lard and the juniper berries. Work the mixture until smooth, with a wooden spoon or by hand.
4. Put the pigeon mixture in a saucepan. Set the saucepan in a pan of shallow water and place both at the middle level of the oven. Cook for 30 minutes.
5. Add the wine, blending well, and replace in the oven for another 15 minutes.
6. Push the cooked mousse through a tamis strainer. (If a tamis is unobtainable, one can be improvised by nailing a section of metal screening taut over a piece of plywood with a large circle cut in it. The point is to have a flat, strong sieving surface. An ordinary convex strainer would turn this into herculean labor because it would clog too quickly.)
7. Blend in the remaining duck fat or lard, which has been heated until soft.
8. Pack the mousse in an earthenware dish and refrigerate. For storage purposes, it is helpful to smear the top of the mousse with a thin layer of softened lard.
9. Serve with toast.

Yield: About 18 servings

NOTE: *Dried juniper berries are available at gourmet specialty stores and may be substituted for fresh berries, but they will be tougher and generally less satisfactory. Lard is not an especially good substitute for duck fat. The taste of the mousse will be much improved if you husband duck fat over a short period of time in preparation for this recipe. One big, duck dinner will get you there. The main problem is to find a fruiting juniper.*

Oysters Bienville

24 large oysters on half shell
Rock salt (optional)
 1 tablespoon chopped scallion
 1 tablespoon butter
½ cup béchamel sauce (see
  page 296)
½ cup coarsely chopped
  mushrooms

½ cup coarsely chopped
  fresh shrimp
¼ cup dry white wine
Salt
Cayenne
 2 tablespoons heavy cream
Buttered bread crumbs
Grated parmesan cheese

1. Preheat oven to 375 degrees.
2. Arrange oysters in shallow baking pan, on layer of rock salt, if desired.
3. Sauté scallion in butter. Stir in béchamel sauce, mushrooms, and shrimp, and cook 2 to 3 minutes. Stir in wine plus salt and cayenne to taste. Add cream.
4. Top each oyster with this sauce, then sprinkle with buttered crumbs and grated cheese. Bake about 10 minutes, or until oysters curl at the edges. Put pan under broiler just long enough to delicately brown the oysters. Serve at once.

Yield: 4 to 6 servings

Hot Crabmeat Appetizer

 8 ounces cream cheese
6½ ounces crabmeat, flaked
 2 tablespoons finely chopped onion
 1 tablespoon milk
½ teaspoon creamed horseradish
¼ teaspoon salt
Pepper
⅓ cup toasted, slivered almonds

1. Combine all ingredients except almonds until well blended.
2. Spoon mixture into an 8-inch pie plate or casserole.
3. Sprinkle with almonds.
4. Preheat oven to 350 degrees.
5. Just before serving time, bake for 15 minutes. Serve hot with raw vegetables and pumpernickel rounds.

Yield: 4 servings

Eva Shaye's Gravlax
(Swedish Cured Salmon)

1 2-pound center cut salmon
  steak, boned but with skin
  on, to produce 2 thick
  fillets of fish
4 tablespoons salt
2 tablespoons sugar

2 teaspoons coarsley ground
  white pepper
1 large bunch fresh dill
  Cognac (optional)
  Oil (optional)
  Dill-mustard sauce (below)

1. The salmon should be cut as one single section so that it can be divided into 2 matching fillets after boning. Dry the pieces in paper toweling.
2. In a small bowl, mix together salt, sugar, and white pepper. If you do not want to devote a separate pepper mill to white pepper, grind the peppercorns at high speed in a blender to desired coarseness.
3. With roughly ¼ of the dill, make a bed for the salmon on a double thickness of aluminum foil large enough to wrap both salmon fillets.
4. Take 1 fillet and rub it on all sides, including skin, with about ⅓ of the mixed seasonings. Lay it, skin side down, on the dill.
5. Apply another ⅓ of the seasonings evenly to the flesh (top) of the first salmon fillet. Then lay another ¼ of the dill on top of the salmon.
6. Rub the remaining salmon fillet with the rest of the seasonings. Lay it on top of the first fillet so that the edges match up but with the thinner long edge of the top piece over the thicker long edge of the bottom piece. Lay another ¼ of the dill over the top of the top piece. Reserve remaining dill for sauce (see below).
7. Wrap up the salmon tightly in the aluminum foil. Place the package on a deep plate and refrigerate for 48 hours.
8. Drain the prepared salmon (gravlax) once a day and turn the package over each time. It will be ready to serve, in thin long slices, with lemon wedges, black bread, or white toast and dill-mustard sauce, on the third day. A thin, very sharp knife is essential for making attractive slices. Gravlax will keep for 3 to 5 days, but must be drained and turned daily.

Yield: 6 to 8 servings

NOTE: *It is possible to reduce the process of curing to 10 hours by rubbing cognac and then oil into the salmon before applying seasonings. In buying dill, remember that you will need enough to make 3 layers plus 5 to 6 tablespoons, chopped, for the sauce, not to mention extra sprays as decoration for the serving platter.*

DILL-MUSTARD SAUCE

    3 tablespoons mild brown mustard
    1 tablespoon sugar
    2 tablespoons white vinegar
    ½ cup oil
    5 to 6 tablespoons chopped fresh dill
       Salt
       Pepper

1. Mix mustard, sugar, and vinegar well.
2. Into this mixture, blend oil in a slow dribble as for mayonnaise.
3. Stir in remaining ingredients.

Yield: About 1¼ cups

Fukienese Fried Fish Rolls

4–6 Chinese mushrooms
   1 pound filleted sole or sea
      bass
   1 teaspoon imported light soy
      sauce
   1 teaspoon dry sherry
   1 teaspoon salt
   1 teaspoon pepper
   1 teaspoon sugar

   4 scallions, chopped into 2-inch
      lengths
   1 teaspoon monosodium
      glutamate (optional)
   ½ pound caul fat
      Cornstarch
   1 egg, lightly beaten
      Fat or oil for deep frying

1. Soak mushrooms in cold water until softened, about 30 minutes.
2. Chop mushrooms into thin strips with roughly the cross section of a kitchen match. Chop fish into similar strips.
3. In a bowl, mix together mushrooms, fish, soy sauce, sherry, salt, pepper, sugar, scallions, and monosodium glutamate, if used.
4. Spread out a piece of caul fat about 8 by 8 inches and sprinkle with 1 teaspoon cornstarch. Spread ¼ of fish filling from Step 3 over it.
5. Fold caul fat around filling. Brush with egg and dust all over with cornstarch.

6. Deep fry in hot oil (375 degrees) until golden brown, about 4 minutes. Slice into chopstick-size segments and serve. Proceed in the same way with the remaining caul fat and filling.

Yield: 4 servings

Josephine's Danish Cucumbers with Smoked Chub

1 medium cucumber, peeled and thinly sliced
2 teaspoons salt
3 scallions, finely chopped
3 tablespoons finely chopped parsley
½ medium green pepper, chopped
Pepper
1 teaspoon lemon juice
1 cup sour cream
Bibb lettuce
4 fillets of smoked chub, skinned
Cherry tomatoes
Lemon slices

1. In a bowl, cover cucumbers with ice water. Add salt and refrigerate for 3 hours.
2. Prior to serving, mix together in another bowl the scallions, 2 tablespoons parsley, green pepper, black pepper to taste, lemon juice, and sour cream.
3. Drain cucumbers thoroughly and combine with sour cream mixture.
4. Cover individual plates with beds of Bibb lettuce. Place 1 fillet of chub on center of each lettuce bed. Surround fillets with cucumber–sour cream mixture and sprinkle with remaining parsley. Trim lettuce with tomatoes and lemon slices.

Yield: 4 servings

Quiche Lorraine

½ pound sliced bacon or a like amount of cooked shrimp, crabmeat, or lobster
½ pound Swiss cheese, sliced
1 unbaked 9-inch pastry shell
4 eggs
1 tablespoon flour
½ teaspoon salt
Cayenne
Nutmeg (optional)
2 cups milk or light cream
1 tablespoon butter, melted

1. Preheat oven to 375 degrees.
2. Fry or broil the bacon, if used, until almost crisp.
3. Arrange bacon or seafood in alternating layers with the cheese over the pastry in the plate.
4. Beat eggs until blended and combine with the flour, salt, cayenne, and nutmeg to taste. Add milk or cream and butter.
5. Pour custard over bacon and cheese.
6. Bake pie on the lower rack of the preheated oven about 40 minutes—until custard is set. Serve warm.

Yield: 6 to 8 servings as a main supper or luncheon dish or 16 servings as an hors d'oeuvre

Potato Kugel

  2 pounds (6 medium) potatoes
  2 eggs
  ½ teaspoon baking powder
  4 tablespoons chicken fat or shortening (approximately)
    Salt
    Pepper

1. Grate potatoes on a medium-size grater into a bowl of cold water. Wash grated potatoes thoroughly until snowy white. Drain in a fine mesh strainer. Squeeze out remaining water.
2. Preheat oven to 350 degrees.
3. Combine potatoes with all remaining ingredients and mix thoroughly.
4. Put mixture in a muffin tin (with a capacity of 8 2½-inch muffins) greased with shortening. Bake until golden brown and a toothpick comes out clean, about 45 minutes.

Yield: 8 individual kugels

Buckwheat Blini

2 cups lukewarm milk
1 cup lukewarm water
1 package dry-active yeast
2 cups sifted buckwheat flour
3 eggs, separated
2 tablespoons butter, softened
1 teaspoon sugar
1 teaspoon salt

1. In a bowl, combine ½ cup of the milk and ¾ cup of the water. Dissolve the yeast in the remaining water and add to the milk mixture.
2. Stir in about 1 cup of the flour to make a thick batter. Beat well. Cover and set in a warm place for 2½ to 3 hours.
3. Beat the egg yolks. Gradually beat in the remaining milk, butter, sugar, and salt. Stir into the yeast mixture along with the remaining flour.
4. Beat the egg whites until stiff, but not dry, and fold into the batter. Cover and let stand 45 minutes at room temperature without stirring.
5. Ladle the mixture onto a hot greased griddle, or heavy skillet, to make 3-inch pancakes. It will take about ¼ cup of batter for each blini. Cook until lightly browned on bottom, turn and brown second side. Keep warm while cooking remaining batter.

Yield: About 3 dozen blini

NOTE: *To serve these blinis, bring them warm to the table with sour cream, melted butter, and red caviar (or black, to be totally authentic and wildly extravagant), and let everyone mix and match as he likes.*

Liver Knishes

1 pound beef liver
4 eggs, at room temperature
Chicken fat
1 medium onion, roughly chopped
Salt
Pepper

DOUGH:

⅔ cup shortening (approximately)

2 cups flour

1. Broil beef liver until well done. Rare liver will not do.
2. Bring to a boil enough water to cover eggs. Add eggs and simmer for 10 minutes. Plunge eggs into cold water. Remove shells.
3. Heat 2 tablespoons of chicken fat in a skillet and sauté the onion until golden brown.
4. In a meat grinder, not a blender, grind together liver, eggs, and onions. Grind twice, first through the medium disc, then the fine. Put liver filling in a bowl and mix in enough chicken fat to reach desired smoothness. It is hard to use too much chicken fat. Three tablespoons are a minimum.
5. Add salt and pepper to taste. Chill.
6. Prepare a pastry dough: Cut the shortening into the flour with 2 knives or a pastry blender until the dough has the consistency of cornmeal. Add water, a tablespoon at a time, mixing it in with a wooden spoon, until the dough can be pressed into a ball. Very little water, about ⅓ cup, is necessary. Chill dough.
7. Preheat oven to 375 degrees.
8. On a lightly floured board or marble, roll out dough into a rectangle slightly larger than 16 by 12 inches. Cut into 4 strips, each 4 by 12 inches.
9. Spread about ¾ of a cup of the liver filling evenly down the center of each strip. There will probably be some filling left. If you think you can accommodate it and still seal the strips into tubes, add this excess. Otherwise, reserve for a snack.
10. Roll strips into tubes: Flour your fingers and pull one side over the other. Moisten edges and press gently until sealed. Seal ends.
11. Make a series of crosswise cuts an inch or so apart and halfway through each tube along the entire length of each tube to facilitate serving.
12. Bake tubes on a cookie sheet greased with shortening for 45 minutes or until golden brown.

Yield: 48 small knishes

NOTE: *Prepared knishes may be frozen after Step 10 and kept until needed.*

Insalata di Carne Cruda
(North Italian Raw Beef Salad)

2 pounds raw, ground top-quality beef
Juice of 4 lemons
2 cloves garlic, chopped
½ cup olive or salad oil
Salt
Pepper

Cover the raw beef with the lemon juice. Add the garlic, oil, salt and pepper to taste. Refrigerate for 3 to 4 hours before serving. Mix occasionally.

Yield: 6 servings

Jien Duy
(Sesame Balls)

½ cup brown sugar
⅔ cup boiling water
½ pound glutinous rice powder (naw muy fun)
½ pound shredded coconut or peanut butter
½ cup snow white sesame seeds (jien maah)
Oil for deep frying

1. Dissolve brown sugar in water and bring to swift boil. Remove from fire and carefully stir in glutinous rice powder until dough is formed.
2. Roll dough into sausage shape, about 1 inch in diameter, and cut off 1-inch sections. Roll each section into a ball with palms of hands.
3. Flatten each ball of dough between the hands and place ½ teaspoon or more of coconut or peanut butter on it. Envelop filling with the dough completely and reroll into a smooth ball.
4. Dip balls into sesame seeds until entire surface is covered, gently pressing seeds into surface.
5. Place balls gently in 3 inches hot oil (350 degrees) and fry until orange-gold in color. Serve hot.

Yield: 6 servings

SOUPS

Consommé

3 pounds beef shin, separated into meat and bones cut up as small as possible
2 chicken carcasses, preferably raw
6–8 carrots, chopped
2 white turnips, chopped
3 leeks, chopped
1 stalk celery, chopped
1 parsnip, chopped
3 pounds lean beef, diced
1 medium onion studded with 1 whole clove
1 teaspoon salt

1. Put beef bones, chicken carcasses, and half of each vegetable ingredient (except onion) in a stockpot with 7 quarts of water. Bring to a boil, reduce heat, and simmer slowly for 12 to 15 hours, skimming occasionally. This process may be interrupted and resumed the next day. Its purpose is to extract as much gelatin as possible from the bones.
2. Strain, cool, and remove surface fat from liquid.
3. Having washed the original stockpot, put in it the shin meat and beef, tied in muslin, salt, onion with the clove, and the liquid from the bones. Bring slowly to a boil over moderate heat. Stir meat occasionally during this time and remove scum that rises to the surface of the liquid.
4. When liquid boils, add remaining vegetables, skim again, wipe off scum that has collected on inside of pot, and remove pot to edge of heat. Cook slowly for 4 to 5 hours.
5. Remove pot from heat, add 1 cup of cold water, and let cool for a few minutes. Remove surface fat.
6. Strain consommé through a chinois or other fine strainer and chill.
7. You may stop at this point and serve what you need of the consommé, freezing the rest (it will keep without significant loss of flavor for several months) or work on it briefly to make it even clearer and richer in flavor.

Yield: About 4 quarts

Clarified Consommé

 4 quarts cold consommé
¼ pound very lean ground beef
 2 egg whites
 2 crushed egg shells (optional)

1. Beat 1 cup of consommé with the other ingredients in a heavy pot. Heat remaining consommé to boiling and gradually beat into the egg-meat mixture.
2. Bring to a boil over medium heat, stirring constantly. When boiling point is almost reached, stop stirring, move the pot to the corner of the burner and barely simmer for 10 minutes. Do not stir.
3. Strain consommé through a damp, flannel-lined strainer or colander into a clean saucepan. Allow to drain undisturbed for 5 to 10 minutes. Reheat.

Yield: About 3 quarts

Three Consommé Garnishes

Brunoise

 1 carrot
 1 turnip
1½ leeks (white part only)
 1 stalk celery
 1 small onion
1½ tablespoons butter
¼ teaspoon confectioners sugar
 1 quart plus 1 cup consommé

1. Dice all vegetables as finely as possible.
2. Melt the butter in a saucepan, coating the bottom well. Add all ingredients except consommé. Cook slowly, covered, until vegetables have improved in color. Add 1 cup consommé and continue cooking slowly until vegetables are done.
3. Just before serving combine brunoise with quart of consommé which has been heated.

Yield: 6 servings

Threaded Eggs

3 eggs
  Salt
  Pepper
1 quart plus 3 cups consommé

1. Beat eggs together with salt and pepper to taste.
2. Bring 3 cups consommé to a boil.
3. Pour egg mixture through a tea strainer into consommé, shifting strainer back and forth across the surface of the liquid.
4. As soon as egg has coagulated into threads, remove from liquid with a slotted spoon, drain, and combine with remaining quart of hot consommé just before serving. Strain and reserve for future use the 3 cups of consommé in which the eggs were prepared.

Yield: 4 servings

Tomato Royales

3½ tablespoons tomato paste
  4 tablespoons heavy cream
  1 egg
  3 egg yolks
  1 quart hot consommé

1. Combine well all ingredients except consommé. Poach in 4 buttered baba molds or custard cups placed on a rack in a pan with boiling water coming halfway up the molds or cups. Cover cups with foil and pan with lid and simmer about 15 minutes or until set.
2. Remove molds from water; cool, refrigerate.
3. Unmold royales when they have cooled completely. Slice and cut them into small discs, cubes, or other shapes, freehand or with small cutters. Combine with hot consommé.

Yield: 4 servings.

Pho
(Vietnamese Beef Soup)

4 pounds beef shin with bones or 2 medium oxtails, cut up
1 medium onion, unpeeled
5 slices fresh ginger
1 piece star anise
1 teaspoon salt
2½ tablespoons bottled Chinese fish sauce
1 bundle medium Chinese vermicelli
Boiling water
½ pound leftover cooked sirloin (or beef tenderloin or eye chuck), thinly sliced
3 scallions, chopped
Fresh coriander sprigs
Pepper
Fresh chilies, sliced

1. Boil beef (with bones) or oxtails in 3 quarts cold water. Skim off foam and fat. Cover and simmer for 4 hours.
2. Broil onion until flesh is soft, turning often. Peel.
3. Add onion, ginger, anise, salt, and fish sauce to beef broth just before it has finished simmering.
4. Also just before beef broth finishes simmering, drop vermicelli into a pot of boiling water. Cook 8 minutes, remove from water, rinse in cold water, and drain.
5. Divide vermicelli into 3 equal portions and place in 3 individual serving bowls.
6. Divide beef into 3 equal portions and place on top of vermicelli in the bowls. Garnish each bowl with scallions and 2 or 3 fresh coriander sprigs.
7. Strain broth, reserving beef and flavorings. Pour 1 cup broth over contents of each bowl. Sprinkle with pepper and chilies. Serve immediately. Reserved beef, flavorings, and extra broth can be eaten separately.

Yield: 3 servings

Jane Grigson's Venison Soup

1 pound stewing venison, plus
  bones
1 thin slice Canadian bacon
1 stalk celery, cut into 3 pieces
1 medium onion, quartered
1 6-inch carrot
  Bouquet garni (3 sprigs
  parsley, 1 bay leaf, and
  ¼ teaspoon dried thyme)

¾ teaspoon mace
6 cups water
1 tablespoon butter
1 tablespoon flour
½ cup port
  Salt
  Pepper
  Red currant jelly (optional)

1. Put everything, except butter, flour, port, and jelly into a large pan.
2. Simmer for about 2 hours until the venison is cooked (the time depends on the age of the venison).
3. Skim and strain the soup. Pick a few nice pieces of meat out of the strainer and keep them warm; put the rest of the meat, without skin, bones, etc., back into the soup and mash in a blender or push through a food mill.
4. Bring back to a boil, turn the heat down a little, and add the butter and flour, which should be mashed together, in little knobs. Keep stirring as you do this, and the soup will thicken smoothly after about 4 or 5 minutes; it should not boil hard, but simmer.
5. Add the port wine and the pieces of venison. Correct the seasoning with salt and pepper, adding a little red currant jelly if you like. As with all venison dishes, this soup should be served very hot, in very hot soup plates.

Yield: 6 servings

André Soltner's Soupe aux Abattis de Volaille à la Ménagère
(A Great Chef's Chicken Soup)

 4 chicken gizzards, peeled
16 chicken wings
 3 medium carrots, finely diced
 1 large stalk celery, finely diced
 2 leeks, finely diced
 2 tomatoes, blanched, peeled,
   and diced
   Bouquet garni (6 parsley
   stems, 1 bay leaf, and ½
   teaspoon dried thyme)

  Salt
  Pepper
½ cup raw long-grain rice, well
  washed
2 large potatoes, diced
2 thin slices lean smoked
  bacon, diced and blanched
6 parsley sprigs, leaves only
1 clove garlic, finely chopped
  Nutmeg

1. Cook gizzards for 30 minutes in simmering water. Drain, dice, and reserve.
2. Cook chicken wings in lightly salted boiling water for 2 to 3 minutes. Drain. Pull out bones. Chop into 2-inch-long pieces. Reserve.
3. Combine gizzard and wing pieces in a large pot in 3 quarts of cold water along with carrots, celery, leeks, and tomatoes. Add bouque garni to soup. Season with salt and pepper to taste.
4. Bring soup to a boil, lower heat, and simmer slowly for 1½ hours.
5. Add rice and potatoes to soup. Remove bouquet garni. Continue simmering for another 30 minutes.
6. Meanwhile, sauté diced bacon until browned. Then chop parsley leaves so fine that you almost have a paste.
7. As the soup finishes cooking, add drained bacon, parsley, and garlic.
8. Season with nutmeg to taste and add more salt and pepper if necessary.

Yield: About 3 quarts or 10 to 12 servings

Jenny's Soup

1 carrot, sliced
1 potato, cut into ½-inch chunks
1 pinch dried thyme
1 bay leaf
  Pinch salt
  Pinch pepper

1. Put 2 cups cold water and carrot and potato into saucepan.
2. Add seasoning.
3. Bring to boil and simmer over low flame for 30 minutes.

Yield: 2 child's servings

Vegetable Soup

3 leeks (white part only), cut
  into 2-inch pieces
2 potatoes, cubed
3 carrots, cut into 1-inch pieces
2 parsnips, cut in half
  lengthwise and then cut into
  1-inch pieces
3 turnips, cubed
1 10-ounce package fresh
  spinach
1 head boston lettuce
6 cups homemade chicken
  stock
4 tablespoons butter
4 tablespoons flour
  Salt
  Pepper
½ cup heavy cream
2 tablespoons minced parsley

1. Wash the leeks thoroughly under cold water, prepare all the vegetables, wash the spinach, and break the lettuce into 3 or 4 pieces.
2. Heat the stock in a large casserole, add leeks, potatoes, carrots, parsnips, and turnips and cook over low heat until tender. Be sure not to overcook.
3. Strain the stock and keep the vegetables warm.
4. Heat the butter in the casserole and when it is quite hot, add the flour and cook for 1 minute, stirring without browning
5. Add the reserved warm stock all at once and whisk until the soup gets slightly thicker and is quite smooth.
6. Add the reserved vegetables as well as the spinach and lettuce, season the soup with salt and pepper to taste and cook for exactly 5 minutes.
7. Just before serving, add the heavy cream and finely minced parsley. Just heat the soup through and serve with black bread.

Yield: 4 servings

NOTE: *You may add or omit several seasonal vegetables, as long as you maintain some kind of coordination, and keep in mind that some vegetables require more or less cooking time than others.*

Cold Cucumber Soup

¼ cup sliced onion
2 cups diced, unpeeled
  cucumber
2 sprays parsley leaves
11 ounces canned chicken broth
2 tablespoons quick-cooking
  rice cereal

⅛ teaspoon pepper
¼ teaspoon dry mustard
1 cup heavy cream
Paprika

1. Place onion, cucumber, parsley, and broth in a saucepan. Add cereal and seasoning. Bring to a boil and cook, covered, until cucumber is very soft—about 15 minutes.
2. Put the cooked mixture through a sieve or food mill. Or blend in an electric blender about a minute, until contents are smooth.
3. Add 1 cup cold water and cream to the sieved mixture. Correct seasonings, if necessary, then chill thoroughly. Sprinkle with paprika before serving.

Yield: 4 servings

Chilled Tarragon Soup

2 cups heavy cream
  (approximately)
Juice of 1 lemon
3 egg yolks
1–2 teaspoons grated lemon peel
6 cups homemade chicken
  stock
2 tablespoons finely minced
  fresh tarragon

Salt
White pepper
2 tablespoons finely grated
  parmesan cheese
1 cup fresh watercress
  (optional)

1. In a small mixing bowl, combine 1 cup heavy cream and lemon juice and let the mixture stand for 1 hour to thicken.
2. Beat the 3 yolks in another bowl and add the thickened heavy cream and the lemon peel. Reserve.
3. Heat the chicken stock in a large, heavy-bottomed casserole. When the soup is very hot but not boiling, add the egg yolk and cream mixture. Be sure not to let the soup come back to a boil or the yolks will curdle. Cook just until the soup lightly coats the spoon.
4. Pour the soup into a bowl and add the finely minced tarragon. Chill for 4 to 6 hours before serving.

5. Before serving, thin the soup with enough of the remaining cream to achieve the desired consistency. Season with salt and pepper to taste and add parmesan cheese. For a slightly green tint and a little different flavor, puree the watercress with a little of the chilled soup in an electric blender and add to the bowl.

Yield: 4 servings

NOTE: *For a stronger tarragon flavor, heat the chicken stock with 1 whole large sprig of tarragon in Step 3.*

Sorrel Soup

1 cup sorrel, shredded
2 tablespoons butter
1 tablespoon flour
4 cups hot water
½ teaspoon salt
2 cups milk
1 egg, lightly beaten
Toasted bread squares (optional)

1. Put sorrel in saucepan with butter, cover, and cook until butter melts and sorrel wilts.
2. Add the flour, stir until well mixed, then add water and salt and cook over low heat for 15 minutes.
3. Mix together milk and egg, and add to the soup. Bring just to the boiling point, stirring constantly, but do not allow to boil.
   Serve from a soup tureen with toasted bread squares floating on top, if desired.

Yield: 4 to 5 servings

Erwtensoep
(Dutch Pea Soup)

2 pounds dried green split peas
4 leeks, chopped
4 stalks celery, chopped
1 pound onions, chopped
2 pig's hocks
1 pound smoked bacon in whole piece or slices

12 ounces Gelderland sausage, sliced (see note)
Salt
Pepper
Pumpernickel slices

1. Wash peas. Soak in water overnight.
2. Drain peas and bring to a boil with the vegetables in 4½ quarts fresh water.
3. Add the hocks, bacon, and sausage. Cover pot and simmer slowly, stirring often, until hocks are tender, 2 to 3 hours.
4. Remove hocks and bacon. Cut meat from hocks into small pieces; return to soup. Season with salt and pepper to taste.
5. Slice the bacon and put on pieces of pumpernickel to serve with the soup.

Yield: 12 servings

NOTE: *Gelderland smoked pork sausage is obtainable in German and Dutch neighborhoods. Lacking it, the home cook can substitute Holsteiner mettwurst. In this country, Dutch cooks unable to buy either sometimes use fresh pork sausage, adding it to soup during last half-hour of cooking.*

U.S. Navy Bean Soup

1 cup dried navy beans
1 ham bone or piece of ham or salt pork
8 cups boiling water or ham stock
1 small onion, chopped
  Pinch of ground cloves
  Pepper

1. Pick over, wash, and soak beans in water to cover for 3 or 4 hours.
2. Drain and add bone, stock, onion, and cloves. Heat to boiling point and let simmer 2 to 3 hours, or until tender. Remove bone; serve unstrained.

Yield: Approximately 12 servings

Succotash Chowder

1 large onion, chopped	1 teaspoon salt
3 tablespoons butter	Pepper
1 cup fresh or frozen corn	3 cups milk
1 cup fresh or frozen lima beans	2 tablespoons flour
2 cups cubed potatoes	Parsley

1. Sauté onion in butter in a saucepan until soft.
2. Add vegetables, 1 cup water, salt, and pepper. Simmer, covered, until potato has softened.
3. Add milk and heat to boiling.
4. Blend flour with a little water to make a smooth paste. Stir into soup and cook, stirring, until thickened, about 1 minute. Adjust seasonings. Serve sprinkled with parsley.

Yield: 4 large servings

Puerto Rican Potato and Avocado Soup

6 tablespoons butter
3 tablespoons flour
1 medium onion, grated
2 teaspoons salt
½ teaspoon pepper
6 cups milk

2 cups mashed potatoes (about 4 medium potatoes)
1 tablespoon white rum
1 avocado, peeled and cubed or sliced

1. Melt butter in a saucepan, add flour and grated onion, and cook, stirring, until beginning to brown. Season with salt and pepper.
2. Scald milk in a double boiler. Add flour paste and mashed potatoes and cook over boiling water, stirring constantly until mixture becomes the consistency of cream.
3. Just before serving, add rum. Float an avocado section in each piping hot soup plate.

Yield: 6 servings

Zucchini Soup with Pistou

6 zucchini, unpeeled and chopped
2½ teaspoons salt (approximately)
2 medium onions, chopped
4 tablespoons butter
6 cups chicken stock

Pepper
2 cups fresh or frozen lima beans
1 cup fresh or frozen peas
2 tablespoons sour cream
½ cup pistou (see below)

1. Puree 3 zucchini in the blender with ½ teaspoon salt.
2. Sauté remaining zucchini and onions in butter until tender.
3. Drain pureed zucchini. Reserve liquid and add pulp to sautéed zucchini and onions.
4. Bring chicken stock to boil. Add remaining salt, pepper, lima beans, and peas. Simmer until vegetables have softened. Add zucchini and onion mixture. Simmer for 5 more minutes.
5. Puree soup in blender. Correct seasoning. Mix zucchini liquid from Step 3 with sour cream and whisk into the soup. Reheat, but do not boil.
6. Serve while still hot with pistou on the side.

Yield: 10 servings

PISTOU

2 egg yolks
2 cloves garlic
4 slices bacon, blanched
1 teaspoon dried basil
5 tablespoons grated parmesan cheese (approximately)
  Olive oil

1. Break egg yolks into blender jar. Add garlic, bacon, and basil. Puree.
2. Pour mixture into a dish. Stir parmesan cheese into it until it thickens to a moist paste the density of whipped cream. Add olive oil to taste, but only a small amount, about 1 teaspoon.
3. Pass the pistou with the soup at the time of serving. It should be spooned into each bowl. Figure about 1 tablespoon per bowl.

Yield: About ½ cup

Chestnut Soup I

1 pound chestnuts
1 parsnip, peeled and finely diced
1 stalk celery, finely diced
1 carrot, finely diced
1½ pounds veal shank, with bone
2 tablespoons unsalted butter
1 leek, cut into 1-inch pieces
1 pound chicken backs, gizzard, or neck, with skin and fat removed
1–1½ tablespoons salt
¼ teaspoon pepper
1 cup heavy cream
2 egg yolks

1. Cook chestnuts: Without slitting, start them in enough cold water to cover; boil 15 to 25 minutes, until flesh is tender.
2. Remove chestnut shells and inner skins while nuts are still hot. Remove 1 nut at a time from hot water.
3. Run peeled chestnuts through a food mill. Reserve.
4. Sauté parsnip, celery, carrot, and veal in butter until vegetables have improved in color and meat has turned grey. Do not brown.
5. Add 6 cups cold water, leek, chicken parts, salt, and pepper to sautéed vegetables and veal. Bring to a boil and simmer, covered, until veal is soft, about 1½ hours.
6. Remove veal from pot, cut meat from bone, remove membranes, and slice into small pieces. Return sliced meat to pot. Discard membranes and bone.
7. Add ground chestnuts to pot. Simmer another 10 minutes.
8. Blend cream with yolks. Add to soup. Heat until very hot, but do not boil. Serve.

Yield: 10 servings

Chestnut Soup II

4 cups chestnuts
4 teaspoons oil
8 tablespoons butter
2 quarts chicken stock
2 cups heavy cream
1 teaspoon sugar
  Salt
  Pepper

1. Preheat oven to 450 degrees.
2. Cut a cross in flat side of each nut, coat nuts with oil, and bake for 20 minutes. Cool. Shell, and with a sharp knife, remove brown skins.
3. Heat butter in a 3-quart saucepan. Sauté nuts in it for 1 minute, stirring constantly to avoid burning. Add stock. Bring to a boil, cover, reduce heat, and simmer until chestnuts are tender (about 20 minutes).
4. Strain. Return stock to pot. Put chestnuts through a food mill.
5. Add pureed nuts to stock and bring to a boil. Stir in cream, sugar, salt, and pepper to taste. Reheat; serve.

Yield: 8 to 10 servings

Icelandic Cauliflower Soup

1 medium head cauliflower
   Beef stock or milk
8 tablespoons butter
½ cup flour
2 egg yolks

1. Remove the leaves from cauliflower and soak it in cold water, head down, for 30 minutes.
2. Boil cauliflower in salted water until tender—about 20 minutes. Remove cauliflower; cool. Cut into flowerets. Reserve cooking water.
3. Measure the water; add enough stock or milk to make 6 cups. Melt the butter in a separate pan and blend in the flour. Stir in the liquid slowly and heat to boiling.
4. Before serving, slowly add 1 cup of the soup to the lightly beaten egg yolks. Stirring constantly, add this mixture to pot of soup. Do not let the soup boil after the eggs have been added. Serve hot and garnish each plate with cauliflowerets.

Yield: 6 servings

Cream of Cauliflower Soup

1 small head cauliflower
¼ cup chopped onion
1 small potato, cubed
3 tablespoons butter
2 cups chicken stock
2 cups milk

1 cup light cream or
   evaporated milk
Salt
Pepper
Chopped parsley or paprika

1. Break cauliflower into flowerets. Peel the hard core and slice.
2. Sauté onion and potato in butter until just tender. Add 1 cup water and the cauliflower. Cover and cook until cauliflower is tender. If desired, reserve 6 cauliflowerets for garnishing.
3. Turn the cooked vegetable mixture, including cooking liquid, into a blender. Add ½ cup of stock and run until smooth. Or press vegetables with cooking liquid through a sieve.
4. Add remaining stock, milk, and cream. Heat to simmering. Season with salt and pepper to taste.

5. Serve hot with a garnish of reserved cauliflowerets and either parsley or paprika.

Yield: 6 servings

Puree of Artichoke Soup

  6 small, or 4 medium, or 3 jumbo artichokes
  1 lemon, halved
  6 tablespoons butter
6½ cups chicken stock (approximately)
  3 cups boiling water
  2 cups thickly sliced potatoes
    Salt
    Pepper

1. Wash the artichokes very well. Cut the small or medium artichokes in half vertically and the jumbo ones in quarters. Brush all cut surfaces with the lemon halves. With a small, sharp knife, remove the chokes, brush cut surfaces with lemon.
2. Melt the butter in a heavy kettle. Add the artichokes and turn to coat with the hot butter.
3. Heat 3 cups of the stock to boiling and add to the kettle. Add the water, bring to a boil, cover, and simmer 30 minutes or until artichokes are barely tender.
4. Add the potatoes, and salt and pepper to taste, and cook about 20 minutes longer or until potatoes are tender. With a slotted spoon, remove artichokes to one bowl and pieces of potato to another. Strain and reserve the cooking liquid.
5. Using a silver or stainless steel spoon, scrape all the edible material from each artichoke leaf, adding it to the potatoes. Add the artichoke bottoms to potato mixture.
6. Pass the scraped artichoke and potatoes through an electric blender in batches, using the reserved liquid to assist the blending. Add any leftover reserved liquid and pass the mixture through a chinois (conical) strainer or other fine mesh strainer.
7. Chill mixture several hours or overnight. Whisk enough of the remaining chicken stock into the chilled puree to reach desired consistency. Check the seasoning and add more salt and pepper if needed. Serve in cold bowls.

Yield: 4 servings

NOTE: *The soup can be served hot. After straining, it should be reheated and chicken stock added until it is desired consistency.*

Puree of Asparagus Soup

1½–2 pounds asparagus (1 average bundle)
   4 tablespoons butter
  ½ onion, finely chopped
3½–4 cups chicken stock
    Salt
    Pepper
  ⅛ teaspoon grated nutmeg

1. Break the asparagus where it breaks easily and discard tough ends. Wash very well. Cut off tips and set aside.
2. Slice stalks on a diagonal into ½-inch pieces.
3. Heat the butter in a skillet. Add the onion and cook 3 minutes. Add the sliced stalks, cook 1 minute. Add 2½ cups stock, salt and pepper to taste, and nutmeg. Bring to a boil, cover, and simmer until stalks are barely tender. Add the tips and cook until tender, about 3 minutes.
4. Blend the cooked asparagus and cooking liquid in an electric blender until smooth. Chill the soup several hours.
5. Whisk enough of the remaining stock into the pureed asparagus mixture to make the desired consistency. Serve in chilled bowls.

Yield: 3 to 4 servings

Green Soup

5–6 tablespoons butter
  3 large onions, finely sliced
  2 large potatoes, sliced
10½ ounces canned chicken broth
2½ cups milk
    Salt
  1 small bay leaf
  3 small sprigs fresh tarragon or ½ teaspoon dried
1 10-ounce package frozen chopped spinach
2 teaspoons imported soy sauce or more to taste
¼ teaspoon curry powder or more to taste
1 cup heavy cream
  Chopped fresh mint or green onion for garnish

1. Melt the butter in a heavy-bottomed dutch oven. Sauté the onions until wilted. Add potatoes, broth, milk, salt, bay leaf, and tarragon. Simmer, covered, until potatoes are tender.
2. Add the package of spinach and continue to simmer until spinach is fully defrosted and just cooked. Whirl the mixture in the blender, taking care not to puree the soup to a mechanical smoothness.
3. Return the soup to the rinsed-out pot and add the soy sauce and curry powder. Taste the soup for seasoning. The soy and curry should be so subtle that you can barely detect them. Serve hot or chill overnight. If served cold, again correct the seasonings, since chilling deadens the taste a bit. Stir in the cream just before serving (hot or cold). Garnish with mint or green onion.

Yield: 6 to 8 servings

Onion Soup

2 tablespoons butter
5 large onions, sliced into rings
2 quarts chicken stock
  Salt
  Pepper
1 large loaf Italian white bread
16 thin slices Swiss cheese double the area of slices of Italian bread (see note)
  Grated parmesan cheese

1. Melt butter in a large skillet.
2. In a skillet, sauté onions until slightly browned.
3. Transfer onions to large pot, add stock and salt and pepper to taste. Heat to a slow boil and simmer for 10 to 15 minutes.
4. Meanwhile, butter 16 bread slices or enough to cover the 8 ovenproof soup bowls you will use. Fold over Swiss cheese slices and place on top of bread slices.
5. Preheat oven to 500 degrees.
6. Under the broiler, toast tops of cheese-covered slices until cheese has melted completely.
7. Ladle soup into ovenproof bowls, leaving enough room in each bowl for cheese-covered bread slices.
8. Cover surface of soup in each bowl with cheese-covered bread slices. Sprinkle each bowl liberally with parmesan cheese.

9. Place bowls on a cookie sheet and bake in oven for 15 minutes.
10. Remove from oven and brown tops of bowls under broiler. Serve
    as soon as possible.

Yield: 8 servings

NOTE: *The yield, the amount of bread, and the quantity of Swiss
cheese necessary will vary somewhat according to the size of bowls, of
the loaf of bread, and the cross section of the original piece of
cheese.*

Fresh Corn Soup

5 ears corn
5 cups milk
1 slice onion
⅛ teaspoon pepper
5 tablespoons flour
  Salt
  Suger, if necessary
1 tablespoon butter

1. Shuck corn, removing silk. Cut off stalks.
2. Heat 4 cups milk over low flame in a saucepan with onion slice
   and pepper. Continue heating until milk steams, but do not boil.
3. While milk heats, slit corn kernels down the middle with
   the point of a knife, slicing down each lengthwise row of kernels.
4. Use back of knife to press out contents of kernels into a bowl,
   leaving the holes (the bases of the kernels) attached to the cob.
5. Remove onion slice from steaming milk and discard.
6. Scrape corn mush into hot milk, which remains on the fire. Cook
   corn and milk mixture over moderate heat for 10 minutes. Do not
   boil.
7. While corn and milk mixture cooks, blend 1 cup milk into the flour
   in a bowl, stirring out all lumps of flour.
8. Add a cup of the hot soup to the blended flour mixture, stirring
   vigorously. Return to bulk of soup in the saucepan. Heat, stirring,
   until mixture thickens, but do not allow to boil. To cook the flour
   fully will take at least 5 minutes.

9. Salt soup to taste and add sugar to taste if corn is not naturally very sweet.
10. Swirl butter into soup and serve as soon as butter has melted.

Yield: 6 to 8 servings

Pearl Primus's African Ground Nut Soup

1½ cups (1 pound) smooth peanut butter	Salt
	Black pepper
2 cups water (approximately)	¼ teaspoon ground allspice
1½ pounds stewing beef, cut into chunks	¼ teaspoon white pepper
	1 10-ounce package frozen okra
1 tablespoon oil	
2 medium onions, sliced into thirds	Sweet red pepper flakes

1. Put peanut butter in a saucepan. Add a small amount of water—1 tablespoon should be enough—to loosen the peanut butter to the consistency of library paste. Place mixture over moderate heat. Stir occasionally until oil begins to pool on top.
2. Meanwhile, brown beef in the oil. Add remaining water, onion, salt, black pepper, allspice, and white pepper. Bring to a boil, cover, and simmer until tender.
3. Cook okra according to package directions, drain, and mash.
4. When oil collects on top of the peanut butter mixture, keep pouring it off (and discarding) until it stops appearing in appreciable amounts.
5. Add okra to cooked beef. Gradually whisk in the peanut butter mixture and enough water to make it the consistency of a thick soup. Add pepper flakes and heat, stirring.

Yield: 6 servings

Macrobiotic Wakame Soup

1 large handful wakame, about 1 cup (See note)
5 cups boiling water
⅓ cup bonita flakes
1 tablespoon miso (soybean paste)

1. Soak wakame 10 to 15 minutes. Wash well.
2. Chop to noodle length or smaller and add to boiling water.
3. Add bonita flakes, cover, and cook 5 minutes.
4. Add miso, stir well, and cook 5 minutes more before serving.

Yield: 7 servings

NOTE: *Wakame is an edible seaweed available at natural food and macrobiotic stores, as is Miso.*

Fish Soup

2 pounds potatoes, cut into chunks
2½ cups milk
Salt
Pepper
1 medium onion, sliced
1 bay leaf
1 pound whiting, skinned, boned, and cut into large pieces

1 pound scrod, skinned, boned and cut into large pieces
1 pound salmon or flounder, skinned, boned, and cut into large pieces
½ cup heavy cream
4 tablespoons butter
1 generous handful fresh dill

1. Boil potatoes in milk until done. Add salt and pepper to taste.
2. Place onion in casserole with bay leaf. Add fish and cover almost entirely with water. Bring to a boil and simmer until fish becomes flaky.
3. Transfer fish pieces to potatoes and milk. Strain fish cooking liquid and add this, too. Adjust seasoning.
4. Add cream, butter, and chopped dill while soup is still hot. Cover. Do not reheat before serving.

Yield: 6 to 8 servings

Union Oyster House Fish Chowder

3 pounds haddock, including head, tail, and backbone
1 2-inch cube salt pork, diced
½ cup thinly sliced onions
4 cups diced potatoes
Salt
Pepper
1 quart milk, heated

1. Have dealer remove skin and cut fish into 2-inch pieces.
2. Put fish head, tail, and backbone (broken in pieces) into a pot. Cover with cold water and bring to a boil. Simmer for 5 minutes. Strain. Reserve stock; discard head, tail, and bone.
3. Fry salt pork 5 minutes. Add onions and let cook to a golden brown. Strain fat into a large pot. Discard onions and pork scraps.
4. Put a layer of potatoes in the fat in the pot, then a layer of haddock. Alternate until all has been used. Season with salt and pepper.
5. Add reserved fish stock and enough water so that liquid covers solid ingredients. Bring to boil and let simmer about 20 minutes. Add the hot milk.

Yield: 4 to 6 servings

Oyster Bisque

1 tablespoon butter
1 tablespoon flour
4 cups milk, scalded
½ cup finely chopped celery
1 small green pepper, seeded and finely ground
Salt
Pepper
1 quart oysters, ground through a meat grinder with the liquid included
Worcestershire sauce

1. Melt the butter in a saucepan and blend in the flour. Gradually whisk in the milk and bring the mixture to a boil, stirring constantly.
2. Add the celery, green pepper, salt, and pepper.
3. Add the ground oysters and heat through, but do not boil. Add Worcestershire sauce to taste.

Yield: 4 servings

Guadeloupean Soupe de Palourdes

2 pounds littleneck clams, well
  scrubbed
4 tablespoons butter
3 carrots, cut into large dice
3 leeks, sliced
1 stalk celery, sliced
2 potatoes, cut into large dice
1 cup roughly diced green
  cabbage
2 white turnips, cut into large
  dice

1 teaspoon dried chervil, or to
  taste
3 tablespoons chopped parsley
Salt
Pepper
3 canned hot chili peppers,
  chopped
1 quart hot water
4 cups cooked rice

1. Heat the clams in a small amount of water (about ¼ cup). When
    the shells open, remove the clams and reserve them and the
    cooking liquid, as well as 4 or 5 half shells for decoration.
2. Heat the butter in a large skillet and brown the carrots, leeks,
    celery, potatoes, cabbage, and turnips with the chervil, parsley,
    salt, pepper, and hot pepper.
3. Add hot water to the browned vegetables and cook over low heat
    for 5 minutes or until vegetables are crisp but tender. Add the
    clams and their cooking liquid. Garnish with the reserved shells.
    Serve hot with rice on the side.

Yield: 4 servings

Shrimp Bisque

5 tablespoons butter
1 tablespoon salad oil
24 medium shrimp in shells,
  washed
1 shallot or onion, finely
  chopped
2 tablespoons brandy

1 cup dry white wine
2 tablespoons flour
1 cup heavy cream
Salt
Pepper
Cayenne

1. Melt 3 tablespoons butter in a deep, heavy saucepan. Add oil,
    then shrimp, still in shells. Sauté, shaking pan lightly, until shells
    turn red. Add shallot or onion. Add brandy, heat, and ignite. Shake
    pan until flame dies away. Add white wine and allow shrimp
    to cook 5 minutes. Remove shellfish from pot. Add 1 cup water to
    cooking liquid.

2. Shell shrimp and return shells to saucepan. Simmer shells 10 minutes. Strain, reserving cooking liquid.
3. Pound shells in a mortar or put them through a meat grinder twice, using coarse blade. Add only 2 or 3 shells at a time to avoid clogging grinder.
4. Melt remaining butter in second saucepan. Add the flour and blend in over low heat. Gradually add to this mixture the cooking liquid. Stir until slightly thickened. Add the ground shells and cook over low flame about 20 minutes.
5. Add cream. Season to taste with salt, pepper, and cayenne. Add shrimp and heat, but do not boil. Serve at once.

Yield: 4 servings

Mussel Soup

2 large onions, coarsely chopped
6 stalks celery, coarsely chopped
½ green pepper, coarsely chopped
4 tablespoons olive oil
1 bottle dry white wine
Bouquet garni (¼ teaspoon dried thyme, ¼ teaspoon dried basil, few celery leaves, 3 sprigs parsley, 6 peppercorns, and ½ bay leaf)
2 large cloves garlic, crushed
1 16-ounce can stewed tomatoes
Salt
5 pounds mussels or 4 pounds mussels and 18 little neck clams
2 tablespoons finely chopped Italian parsley

1. Sauté the onions, celery, and green pepper in olive oil in a heavy 5-quart dutch oven until they begin to soften. Add the wine, bouquet garni, garlic, and tomatoes. Bring to a boil and simmer, uncovered, for 15 minutes. Taste for salt, remembering that the shellfish will impart a degree of saltiness to the finshed product.
2. Meanwhile, prepare the shellfish, rinsing them in several changes of water and scrubbing them with a steel brush. Debeard the mussels.
3. Bring the wine mixture again to a rapid boil, add the mussels, cover securely, and boil furiously for 7 minutes or until the shells open. Discard bouquet garni. Toss in the parsley.

Yield: 6 servings

Cream of Mussel Soup

1½ pounds debearded mussels,
    steamed
  2 small onions, minced
  3 tablespoons butter
  2 tablespoons flour
1½ cups milk
  1 pimiento, minced

1 egg yolk, lightly beaten
Salt
Cayenne or Tabasco
2 tablespoons dry sherry
  (optional)
Parsley, paprika, or nutmeg
  (optional)

1. Remove mussels from shells and strain broth. Set aside meat and broth.
2. Sauté onion in butter until soft, add flour, and blend well. Add milk and cook, stirring, until thickened.
3. Add mussel meat, 1½ cups broth, pimiento, and egg yolk. Season to taste and add sherry.
4. Heat, stirring, but do not boil. Serve plain or sprinkled with minced parsley, paprika, or nutmeg.

Yield: 4 servings

Vietnamese Asparagus and Crabmeat Soup

  4 cups chicken stock
1½ tablespoons cornstarch
  1 tablespoon bottled Chinese fish sauce
    Salt
1½ cups canned white asparagus, chopped into 2-inch chunks
  1 egg, lightly beaten
  1 6-ounce package frozen Alaskan king crabmeat, flaked

1. Heat stock over medium flame.
2. Dissolve cornstarch in 2 tablespoons of water and add to stock. Stir until mixture thickens slightly and comes to a boil.
3. Add fish sauce to broth and salt to taste.
4. Add asparagus to broth and when it reaches the boiling point again, add egg, letting it drip into the broth in a slow stream.
5. Add crabmeat to soup, stir, reheat, and serve.

Yield: 6 servings

Shanghai Country Soup

1 tablespoon preserved turnip
¼ pound smoked cooked ham
½ chicken breast
1 bamboo shoot
2 slices fresh ginger
½ stalk celery
½ green pepper, seeds and
  fiber removed
1 tablespoon thinly sliced
  carrot slivers
1 small onion, sliced

1½ cups chicken stock
1 tablespoon imported soy
  sauce
  Seasoned salt
½ cup crabmeat, or more,
  if desired
1½ tablespoons cornstarch
  dissolved in 2 tablespoons
  water
1 egg, beaten

1. Slice turnip, ham, chicken, bamboo shoot, ginger, celery, and
   green pepper into slivers, about 2 inches long whenever possible.
2. Combine ingredients in Step 1 with carrot, onion, chicken stock,
   and 3 cups water in a saucepan.
3. Bring soup to a boil, add soy sauce and salt. Continue at full boil
   for 3 minutes. Reduce to a fast simmer, add crabmeat, and
   cook for 3 minutes.
4. Stir in dissolved cornstarch gradually. Then remove from heat and
   stir in beaten egg.

Yield: 6 to 8 servings

MEATS

Beef

Entrecôte Bordelaise

1 2–2½-pound boned rib
  steak
2 tablespoons unsalted butter
3 shallots, finely chopped
¾ cup dry red wine
¼ teaspoon crushed black
  peppercorns
¾ cup plus 3 tablespoons veal
  stock (see page 291)
1¼ teaspoons potato starch or
  arrowroot

1 tablespoon madeira
3 ounces beef marrow,
  cubed, poached in water
  for 2 minutes, and drained
  (Some butchers will sell
  marrow; others will estimate
  marrow yield and sell you
  the bones. You do the
  scooping with marrow at
  room temperature.)

1. Sauté meat in a sauté pan or skillet, in butter.
2. When it is almost done, transfer it to another pan over slow heat
   so that it can finish cooking. Remove all but 2 tablespoons fat from
   the first pan and add the shallots, wine, and pepper. Reduce by ⅔.
3. While reduction is going on (or beforehand, if you wish), heat
   ¾ cup of veal stock in a small saucepan and add to it the potato
   starch mixed with remaining 3 tablespoons cold stock. Leave over
   low heat, stirring, until mixture thickens. Off heat, add Madeira.
   Strain the red wine–shallot reduction through a fine strainer and
   combine with thickened stock.
4. Bring to a boil, add poached marrow cubes, remove from heat,
   salt if necessary, and pour over steak when ready to serve.

Yield: 2 large or 4 medium servings

Steak au Poivre Vert

1 3-pound sirloin steak, 1–1½ inches thick
  Salt
1 tablespoon cognac or whiskey
1 tablespoon poivre vert (green peppercorns), drained and coarsely
  crushed in a mortar with a pestle (see note)
¼ cup heavy cream
½ teaspoon Dijon mustard

1. Cut off a piece of fat from the steak and render it in a heavy
   skillet. Pan fry the steak to desired degree of doneness. Transfer to
   a warm platter, season with salt to taste, and keep warm.
2. Remove any excess fat from the skillet. Add the cognac or whiskey
   and heat, stirring. Add the green peppercorns and cream. Bring
   to a simmer, stirring. Stir in the mustard and pour sauce over the
   steak.

Yield: About 3 servings

NOTE: *Poivre vert or green peppercorns are sold in specialty stores.*

Country Fried Steak

1⅓ pounds round steak, ¾ inch thick
½ cup flour
1½ teaspoons salt
½ teaspoon pepper
3 tablespoons fat or drippings
2 cups milk

1. Cut round steak into individual servings. Pound into meat ⅓ cup
   flour that has been seasoned with salt and pepper.
2. Brown meat on both sides in fat. Cover and cook slowly for
   1 hour or until tender. Remove steaks from pan, stir remaining
   flour into drippings, and add milk. Stir until smooth. Serve gravy
   over steaks.

Yield: 3 to 4 servings

Zrazy
(Polish Rolled Beef)

1 salted herring in brine
1 1-ounce stale hard roll
2 ounces fresh pork fat
2 ounces lean, boneless veal,
cut from the leg
1 clove garlic, finely chopped
½ lightly beaten egg

1 2-pound slice beef round,
pounded into a thin, flat
rectangle
Salt
3 tablespoons flour
¼ cup oil or lard
Boiled potatoes

1. Soak the herring overnight in water to cover, in the refrigerator, changing the water twice.
2. Next day, clean, skin, and bone the fish and chop finely.
3. Preheat oven to 375 degrees.
4. Soak the roll in water and then squeeze out excess water.
5. Grind the pork fat and veal through the fine blade of a meat grinder. Place in a bowl with the herring, roll, garlic, and egg. Mix well.
6. Spread the filling over the surface of the beef. Roll like a jelly roll and secure with string. Season with salt and coat with the flour.
7. Heat the oil or lard in a skillet and quickly brown the beef roll on all sides. Transfer to a shallow roasting pan. Pour over the skillet drippings and enough water to cover the bottom of the pan.
8. Bake, uncovered, about 1 hour or until the meat is tender, basting every 10 minutes. Add water, if necessary, to prevent drying on the bottom of the pan.
9. Remove string and serve roll sliced with potatoes.

Yield: 4 servings

Skillet Pot Roast

3 medium onions, chopped
3 pounds California roast of beef chuck with bone in
1 10¾-ounce can vegetable soup
1 soup-can full of California mountain red wine
½ teaspoon summer savory

1. Divide chopped onions roughly in half and spread half of them in a skillet with a close-fitting lid.
2. Score the meat at the edges and place on top of onions in skillet. Spread rest of onions on top of meat.
3. Pour soup and wine over meat in equal amounts until liquid just covers meat. Sprinkle summer savory on meat.
4. Bring to a boil, cover and simmer for 2 hours. After first hour, turn meat and continue simmering uncovered.
5. Remove from heat, drain excess liquid from meat back into skillet and reserve meat on a carving board.
6. Put skillet liquid in a heavy casserole or saucepan.
7. Cut meat into ¼-inch strips, removing any large pieces of bone, gristle, or fat.
8. Return meat to liquid in casserole or saucepan, heat over moderate flame and serve.

Yield: 6 servings

Anita Malugani's Stracotto con Maccheroni

3 pounds top round or eye round of beef	½ teaspoon dried sage leaves, crumbled
Salt	¼ teaspoon grated nutmeg
Pepper	2 cups dry red wine
Ground allspice	1 can (1 pound 10 ounces) Italian peeled tomatoes (3 cups)
Garlic powder	
1 small onion, minced	
1 tablespoon olive oil	1 8-ounce can tomato sauce
1 tablespoon butter	1 recipe maccheroni (see below)
2 bay leaves	

1. Buy meat in one solid piece, which is not fatty, and have the butcher tie it up well. Sprinkle all over with salt, pepper, allspice, and garlic powder. Let rest 15 minutes on work board.
2. In a heavy skillet, sauté minced onion in oil and butter. When onion has turned golden, add meat, bay leaves, sage, and nutmeg. Cook meat over high heat until it is well browned on all sides.
3. Transfer meat to an unglazed terra-cotta casserole. Add wine and simmer uncovered for about 20 minutes, thus allowing the alcohol in the wine to evaporate slowly. The casserole should be protected by an asbestos mat over the flame.

4. Add tomatoes (with liquid from can) and tomato sauce. Correct
   seasoning. Cover and continue to simmer for 3 to 3½ hours.
   It may be necessary to cook uncovered for last half-hour in order to
   thicken sauce. There should be about 5 cups.

Yield: 6 servings

NOTE: *Stracotto may be prepared in advance and refrigerated with
great success. Refrigeration also permits you to remove fat that comes
to the top of the sauce and forms a solid layer.*

MACCHERONI

  1 pound maccheroni (preferably mezzani #3)
     Stracotto sauce from above recipe
  ¼ pound parmesan cheese, grated

1. Preheat oven to 350 degrees.
2. Cook maccheroni according to package directions.
3. Drain maccheroni carefully. Place a layer in a 2-quart casserole.
   Then pour some of sauce from previous recipe over maccheroni
   layer. Then sprinkle a generous layer of cheese over sauce.
   Continue alternating layers in this order until maccheroni is used
   up. End with a cheese layer. Cover and heat in oven for
   15 minutes, until cheese is melted. Serve with sliced meat and
   remaining sauce.

Yield: 6 servings

Carbonnade à la Flamande

  4 pounds lean beef round, cut
     into 3-by-½-inch strips
  ¼ cup lard or rendered
     salt-pork fat
  8 medium onions, thinly sliced
  3 cloves garlic
     Salt
     Pepper
  2 cups beef stock
  3 cups domestic beer

  3 tablespoons brown sugar
 10 sprigs parsley
  2 whole cloves
  ⅛ teaspoon dried basil
  2 bay leaves
  ¼ teaspoon dried thyme
  2 tablespoons arrowroot
  ¼ cup wine vinegar
     Parslied potatoes

1. Preheat oven to 350 degrees.
2. Brown the meat strips a few at a time in the lard or salt-pork fat, heated in a skillet. Transfer to a casserole.
3. Add the onions to the skillet and cook slowly until lightly browned. Add to the casserole.
4. Add the garlic, salt, and pepper to the casserole and set aside.
5. Pour the beef stock into the skillet and bring to a boil, stirring to loosen all the browned pieces. Pour into the casserole with the beer and brown sugar.
6. Tie the parsley sprigs, cloves, basil, bay leaves, and thyme in a muslin bag and add to the casserole. Bring to a boil on top of the stove, cover, simmer 5 minutes. Place in the oven and bake 2¼ hours.
7. Mix the arrowroot with the vinegar. Remove the bag of herbs and discard. Stir the arrowroot mixture into the casserole and heat briefly on top of the stove until it comes to a boil.
8. Serve with parslied potatoes.

Yield: 8 servings

Hunanese Beef with Watercress

10 ounces flank steak
1 egg white
½ teaspoon salt
2 teaspoons cornstarch dissolved in 2 tablespoons water
1 teaspoon peppercorn-flavored oil (see Step 4, page 9)
1 teaspoon finely chopped fresh ginger
1 tablespoon finely chopped garlic
1 tablespoon chopped scallion
1 tablespoon chopped fried red chilies

4½ tablespoons dry sherry
1 tablespoon imported dark soy sauce
2 tablespoons monosodium glutamate (optional)
1½ teaspoons white vinegar Sesame oil
¼ teaspoon white pepper
1 teaspoon cayenne
1 teaspoon crushed red pepper
2 tablespoons plus 2 cups peanut oil
¼ pound watercress, cut into 3-inch lengths

1. Cut flank steak into 3- to 4-inch strips like carrot sticks. In a bowl, using hands, mix beef well with egg white, ¼ teaspoon salt, 1½ teaspoons cornstarch mixture, and peppercorn oil.

2. Collect prepared ginger, garlic, scallion, and chilies near the cooking surface.
3. In a bowl, combine 3½ tablespoons sherry, soy sauce, 1½ teaspoons monosodium glutamate, remaining cornstarch, vinegar, 1½ teaspoons sesame oil, and white pepper.
4. Combine cayenne and crushed red pepper with enough sesame oil to drench thoroughly and place near cooking area.
5. Heat 2 tablespoons peanut oil until very hot but not smoking in a wok or a skillet. Add watercress. Quickly stir in 1 tablespoon sherry, remaining salt and monosodium glutamate. Stir quickly 2 or 3 times and remove to serving dish.
6. In a clean wok or skillet, heat 2 cups peanut oil to approximately 300 degrees. Add beef strips. Stir in oil for about 15 seconds, until strips are gray all over and remove from oil with a slotted spoon or skimmer.
7. In same oil, cook dried red chilies until browned. Then return beef to wok with all prepared ingredients, dry and liquid, except cayenne–crushed red pepper mixture and watercress. After counting to two (while stirring), add pepper mixture and continue stirring until done. The meat should be quite rare inside and barely browned outside. The oil should not be extremely hot or this will be impossible to achieve.
8. When meat is done, remove from wok with slotted spoon or skimmer and place next to watercress on serving dish. Serve immediately.

Yield: 2 to 4 servings, depending on number of other courses in meal

Stifado
(A Greek Stew)

3 tablespoons salad oil
3 pounds beef chuck, cut into 1½-inch cubes
3 pounds small white onions, peeled
4 cloves garlic, peeled
⅓ cup dry red wine
1 tablespoon dark brown sugar
2 tablespoons red wine vinegar
1 6-ounce can tomato paste

1 bay leaf
1 cinnamon stick, broken into 2 pieces
4 or 5 whole cloves
¼ teaspoon ground cumin
¼ teaspoon whole dried rosemary
1 teaspoon salt
½ teaspoon pepper

1. In a large skillet, heat the oil to the smoking point. Quickly cook the beef cubes in it and, when they are evenly browned, remove them with a slotted spoon to a flameproof casserole.
2. Add the onions and garlic to the casserole and mix to distribute the ingredients evenly.
3. In a bowl, combine the wine, brown sugar, vinegar, and tomato paste. Stir until they are thoroughly blended, then add the bay leaf, cinnamon, cloves, cumin, and rosemary; pour the mixture over the contents of the casserole. Add the salt and pepper and mix well so that the meat is evenly coated.
4. Cover the casserole, bring the liquid to a boil, then lower the heat and simmer for 2 hours, or until the meat is tender Stir occasionally, redistributing onions and meat.

Yield: 6 servings

Puchero
(A Mexican Stew)

1 pound boneless lean round of beef, cubed
2 pieces marrow bone
1 large onion, chopped
1 clove garlic, minced
12 peppercorns
1 2½–3-pound chicken, cut into serving pieces
½ pound smoked ham, cubed
½ pound chorizo, sliced
2 teaspoons salt
4 large carrots, cut into 1-inch lengths
1 cup green beans, cut into sections

1 cup whole-kernel corn
4 zucchini, unpeeled and cut into 1-inch pieces
4 medium boiling potatoes
2 tablespoons oil
2 tablespoons butter
3 large firm bananas
Chicken stock (optional)
2 tablespoons cornstarch
2 pounds or 1½ cans (1 pound 4 ounces) garbanzo beans, drained
2 avocados, peeled and diced
⅓ cup fresh coriander or parsley, chopped

1. Put beef, marrow bone, onion, garlic, and peppercorns in a large pot; cover with water, about 2 quarts, and simmer slowly for 45 minutes.
2. Add chicken, ham, chorizo, salt, and water, if needed, to keep the meat covered. Bring to a boil, then simmer slowly for 25 minutes.

3. Add carrots and green beans. Simmer 15 minutes more, then add corn and zucchini. Cook 5 minutes more.
4. While meat is cooking, boil the potatoes. Then peel, slice, and fry them in hot oil and butter. Brown both sides and keep warm in a covered casserole.
5. Slice the bananas diagonally and fry them in the same pan until both sides are slightly browned. Place in casserole with potatoes.
6. Drain broth from the meat for soup and gravy—adding water or chicken stock, if necessary, to make 12 cups. Put the meats and vegetables in another casserole to keep warm.
7. For gravy, mix cornstarch with a little cold water. Add 2 cups broth, bring to a boil, stirring, and cook 2 minutes. Serve with meats, vegetables, and potato-banana mixture.
8. For soup, add garbanzos to remaining broth, boil 5 minutes, pour into bowls, and garnish with avocado and coriander or parsley.

Yield: About 8 servings

Russkoe Zkarkoe
(Lynn Fisher's Russian Stew)

4 medium potatoes, cubed	¾ cup beef stock, heated
6 tablespoons butter (approximately)	1 bay leaf
	6 tablespoons dry red wine
2 medium onions, cut into rings	1 cup sour cream, at room temperature
1 pound beef chuck	
Salt	1 tablespoon chopped fresh dill
Pepper	1 tablespoon chopped parsley

1. Preheat oven to 350 degrees.
2. Sauté potatoes lightly in 2 tablespoons butter. Add more butter if necessary, to keep potatoes from burning.
3. In a separate pan, sauté onions in 2 tablespoons butter until golden.
4. Cut meat into very small cubes and brown a few at a time in 2 tablespoons butter.
5. Arrange the meat in a layer at the bottom of an ovenproof casserole. Arrange potatoes on top of meat and onions on top of the potatoes. Sprinkle with salt and pepper to taste. Add hot stock and bay leaf.

6. Bake, covered, for 40 minutes. Pour in the wine and bake for another 10 minutes. Test meat for doneness.
7. Just before serving, dollop sour cream over the casserole, sprinkle with dill and parsley (which should be mixed together) and return to oven briefly to warm sour cream.

Yield: 6 to 8 servings

Hutspot Met Klapstuck
(A Dutch Stew)

    1   teaspoon salt
1½ pounds boneless chuck
    3   pounds carrots, sliced
    3   pounds potatoes, quartered
    1   pound onions, quartered
    2   tablespoons bacon fat (optional)
        Salt
        Pepper

1. In a large pot, bring 3 cups water and the salt to a boil. Add the meat, cover pot tightly, reduce heat, and simmer slowly for about 2 hours.
2. After meat has simmered for 2 hours, add the carrots. Continue simmering 15 minutes. Add the potatoes and onions, and, if meat is lean, the bacon fat. Continue simmering for approximately 30 minutes. Add water, if needed, but only enough to prevent burning. Mixture should not be souplike.
3. When all ingredients are tender, remove meat and keep warm. Mash vegetables together. Season with salt and very generously with pepper. Serve slices of meat along with the mashed vegetables.

Yield: 4 to 6 servings

Boeuf Stroganov
(From the 1954 edition of *The Soviet Cookbook*)

1 pound beef (fillet, sirloin tips, or rump)	Pepper
2 onions, chopped	1 tablespoon flour
3 tablespoons butter	¾ cup sour cream
Salt	1 tablespoon chili sauce
	Tabasco

1. Remove any gristle from meat and cut into slices ½ inch thick. Pound with cleaver, rolling pin, or the edge of a plate. Cut meat into 1-inch strips.
2. Sauté onions in butter about 2 minutes. Add meat, sprinkle with salt and pepper, and sauté for 5 or 6 minutes, turning so that meat browns evenly.
3. Sprinkle meat with flour and sauté for 2 or 3 minutes longer. Add sour cream and heat, but do not boil. Add chili sauce and Tabasco and salt to taste.

Yield: 4 servings

NOTE: *Fried potatoes usually accompany the meat and both may be sprinkled with finely chopped dill or parsley.*
   The quantity of sour cream in this formula is larger than that customarily used for boeuf Stroganov in this country. If a less "saucy" dish is desired, the amount of sour cream may be reduced.

Beef Miroton

2 small onions, minced	thinly sliced, or 1 pound
1 tablespoon butter	boiled beef, cut somewhat
½ tablespoon flour	thicker than the roast beef,
3 tablespoons dry white wine	hot
1 cup stock	Chopped parsley, if roast
Salt	beef is used
Pepper	Bread crumbs, if boiled beef
Few drops vinegar	is used
1 pound cooked roast beef,	

1. Sauté onions in butter until golden, sprinkle with flour, blend, and cook, stirring, 1 minute.
2. Add wine, stock, salt and pepper to taste. Simmer 7 or 8 minutes.
3. Arrange slices of hot roast beef on a hot platter. Add vinegar to onion sauce and pour over meat. Sprinkle with parsley and serve.
4. If boiled beef is used, combine it with the sauce and simmer gently until meat is very tender. Sprinkle with crumbs and bake in a 400-degree oven just long enough for a crust to form.

Yield: 4 servings

Boeuf à la Mode

4–5 pound boneless brisket	1 clove garlic
¼ pound pork fat, cut into larding strips	Pinch dried thyme
1 tablespoon salt	½ bay leaf
Pepper	Bouquet garni (few sprigs parsley, 1 stalk celery, and
2 cups dry red wine	1 leek)
2 tablespoons bacon fat	5–6 carrots, chopped
2 tablespoons flour	12 small onions, browned in
Veal knuckle bone	a little butter
1 quart beef stock or water	
1 cup drained, canned tomatoes	

1. Lard roast with pork fat, season with salt and pepper, and let soak in wine in a refrigerator for 6 hours, turning the meat over several times.
2. Drain meat, reserving the wine. Dry meat well and brown in bacon fat. Drain off fat when roast is golden. Sprinkle flour in bottom of pot and mix with the brown juice from the roast. Add wine, bone, stock, tomatoes, garlic, herbs, and bouquet garni. The meat should be just covered with liquid, but no more.
3. Bring to a boil, cover pot, reduce heat, and cook slowly 3 to 4 hours, or until roast is almost tender.
4. Remove meat and bone from gravy. Skim off all fat from gravy and strain. Clean pot and put back meat with carrots,

onions, and gravy. Simmer 20 to 30 minutes or until vegetables and meat are tender. Correct seasoning of gravy, which should have reduced to about half the original quantity.

5. Serve roast hot the first day. Slice remainder, pack in loaf pan, pour gravy over it, and refrigerate. Gravy will jell (as result of gelatin extracted from veal bone) and meat may be served in the aspic the second day.

Yield: 8 to 10 servings

New England Boiled Dinner

3 pounds corned beef brisket
4 medium onions
1 turnip, cubed
4 carrots, halved
4 potatoes, quartered
1 small head cabbage, cut into wedges

1. Cover corned beef with water and simmer until tender, about 3½ hours. Remove meat to a hot platter and keep hot in a low oven.
2. Boil onions, turnip, carrots, and potatoes in the broth for 30 minutes or until done.
3. Add cabbage during last 15 minutes of cooking.
4. Arrange vegetables around the corned beef on platter or, to allow room for carving, serve separately. (If corned beef has not been kept hot, return it to the pot for a few minutes.)

Yield: 6 servings

VARIATIONS:

CORNED BEEF AND CABBAGE: *Simmer corned beef in water to cover until tender with 1 sliced onion, ½ green pepper cut into rings, 5 cloves, 1 bay leaf, and ¼ teaspoon pepper. Fifteen minutes before meat is done, add 1 small head cabbage, cut into wedges, and cook, covered, until cabbage is tender-crisp, no longer.*

GLAZED CORNED BEEF: *Cook corned beef as directed above. Remove it from water, score the fat, stick with cloves, and cover lightly with brown sugar. Bake in a 400-degree oven until glazed, about 15 minutes.*

Cider Stew

3 large onions, sliced	2 teaspoons salt
3 tablespoons shortening or drippings	¼ teaspoon pepper
	½ teaspoon dried thyme
2 pounds stew meat (neck or shank) cut into large cubes	1 cup cider
	1 tablespoon ketchup
3 tablespoons flour (approximately)	3 large potatoes, quartered
	4 medium carrots, quartered

1. Brown onions in a large skillet in hot shortening or drippings.
2. Push onions to one side of skillet, add meat, and brown over high heat. Sprinkle meat with flour that has been seasoned with salt, pepper, and thyme. Stir to blend flour with meat drippings. Add cider and ketchup.
3. Cover skillet and cook until meat is tender, about 2 hours.
4. Add potatoes and carrots to meat and cook slowly 30 minutes longer. Remove meat and vegetables to platter and thicken cooking liquid with a small amount of flour to make gravy.

Yield: 6 servings

Boeuf Bourguignon

2 pounds round steak, cut into 2-inch cubes	1⅓ cups good red burgundy
	1 tablespoon brandy
½ teaspoon salt	¼ pound lean salt pork, diced
½ teaspoon pepper	1 tablespoon butter
Pinch dried thyme	12 small white onions
2 sprigs parsley	¼ pound mushrooms, sliced
½ bay leaf	1 beef bouillon cube
1 tablespoon salad or olive oil	1 clove garlic, mashed

1. Place steak in a bowl. Add salt, pepper, thyme, parsley, bay leaf, oil, wine, and brandy. Marinate in refrigerator 2 to 3 hours, turning meat once. Drain and dry meat; reserve marinade.
2. Preheat oven to 350 degrees.
3. Cover salt pork with cold water and boil 5 minutes. Drain.

4. Melt butter in a dutch oven. Add blanched salt pork and onions and cook until onions are lightly browned. Remove pork and onions and set aside. Brown mushrooms in fat in pan. Remove and add to onions and salt pork.
5. Brown steak cubes in same pan. Pour off fat and add bouillon cube dissolved in 1 cup water. Add garlic and strained marinade. Bring to a boil. Bake, covered, in preheated oven for 2 hours. Skim off fat.
6. Add mushroom, onions, and salt pork. Bake, covered, 30 minutes or longer, until tender.

Yield: 6 servings

Scotch Meldrum Potted Hough

3 pounds beef shin
1 marrow bone
1 veal knuckle bone
2 teaspoons salt
½ teaspoon pepper
½ teaspoon ground allspice
3 bay leaves

1. Have the butcher cut the meat into 2-inch pieces.
2. Put the meat and bones in a heavy aluminum or metal pan and cover with water (about 4 cups).
3. Add salt, pepper, allspice, and bay leaves.
4. Bring water to a boil, then lower heat and simmer until meat is tender, which will take at least 3 hours.
5. Remove bones and bay leaves and discard.
6. Take the meat from the pan and cut it into small chunks.
7. Put meat and cooking liquid into a large bowl.
8. Skim off the fat that floats to the top of the liquid.
9. Refrigerate bowl for an hour or so until its contents have molded firmly. This dish will mold without refrigeration if left overnight. It can also be removed from the bowl after Step 8 and left to set in smaller bowls for individual servings.

Yield: 8 servings

Fricadelles of Beef

3 large potatoes, baked
1 large onion, finely chopped
1 tablespoon butter
2 pounds cooked beef, finely chopped
1 egg, beaten
1 teaspoon chopped parsley

Salt
Pepper
Flour
Butter or fat
Piquant sauce (see page 299) or Tomato sauce (see page 298)

1. Cut baked potatoes in half and scoop out centers. Mash until smooth.
2. Sauté onion in butter until golden brown. Add to potatoes.
3. Add meat, egg, parsley, salt and pepper to taste. Mix well and shape into 6 flat cakes.
4. Roll in flour and fry in butter or other fat until brown on both sides. Serve with piquant or tomato sauce.

Yield: 6 servings

Chilean Pastel de Choclo Peasant Stock

1 cup raisins
1 pound ground beef chuck
2 teaspoons cumin
Salt
Pepper
¼ teaspoon paprika
3–4 medium onions, chopped
1 cup small black pitted olives
⅛ teaspoon ground or crushed dried chili peppers

1 3-pound chicken, quartered
4 tablespoons butter
½ cup dry white wine (approximately)
1 cup chicken stock (approximately)
1 10-ounce package frozen whole-kernel corn

1. Preheat oven to 350 degrees.
2. Leave raisins to soak in water for 10 minutes. Drain.
3. Lightly brown beef chuck in a skillet. Add cumin, salt, pepper, paprika, onions, olives, chili pepper, and drained raisins. Cook over low heat until onions are translucent. Remove from heat and reserve.
4. Brown chicken pieces lightly in the butter.
5. Put chuck mixture in a casserole. Place chicken pieces on top.

Add wine and stock to cover. Add corn. Put in oven, covered, and cook until done, about 30 minutes.

Yield: 4 to 6 servings

Hamburger Longchamps

1 small onion, chopped
1 tablespoon unsalted butter
½ bunch parsley, chopped fine
½ pound chopped sirloin or filet mignon
¼ teaspoon pepper
½ teaspoon salt
½ ounce beef marrow

Sauté onion in butter until golden brown. Cool and mix all ingredients with fingers. Form into a single hamburger and broil under a hot flame.

Yield: 1 serving

Barbecued Meat Loaves

3 strips bacon, cut into small strips
½ cup evaporated milk
1 egg, lightly beaten
2 teaspoons salt
1 cup dried coarse bread crumbs
2 teaspoons chopped onion
1½ pounds ground beef chuck
½ pound ground lean pork
½ cup ketchup
½ cup white vinegar
1 tablespoon worcestershire sauce
1 teaspoon chili powder

1. Preheat oven to 350 degrees.
2. Mix bacon, milk, egg, salt, bread crumbs, onion, and meat. Shape into 8 small loaves. Place in baking dish.
3. Mix together ketchup, vinegar, worcestershire sauce, and chili powder. Bring to a boil in a saucepan and simmer about 8 minutes.
4. Pour sauce over meat loaves and bake about 1 hour. Baste frequently.

Yield: 8 servings

Isis Wilson's Cuban Pot Roast

Half of a ½-inch thick center slice of cooked, smoked ham	3 bay leaves
5½–6 pound rump roast	2 cloves garlic
2 large onions, thinly sliced	2 tablespoons oil or 1 tablespoon lard
Juice of 3 limes	½ cup dry white wine
2 teaspoons oregano	Juice of 3 or 4 oranges
Black pepper	1 tablespoon salt

1. Cut ham into 1-inch squares.
2. With a small, pointed knife, cut holes 2- to 3-inches deep around the surface of the beef roast. Cut the same number of holes as you have ham squares and push one ham square all the way into each hole.
3. Lay half the slices from one onion along the bottom of a large glass bowl.
4. Make a marinade with the lime juice, 1 teaspoon oregano, ½ teaspoon black pepper, 2 crumbled bay leaves, and 1 clove garlic, chopped. Mix well.
5. Put rump roast in glass bowl on top of onions. Pour marinade over roast. Lay remaining slices from the first onion on top of the roast. Cover bowl with plastic wrap and refrigerate for 48 hours. Turn meat twice each day, basting with marinade, and rearranging onion slices.
6. When marination is finished, remove roast from bowl (discard marinade) and dry well with paper toweling.
7. Brown roast on all sides in hot oil or lard in a large pot. Remove roast from pot and reserve.
8. Put remaining onion slices and garlic (roughly mashed but still in one piece) into pot. Sauté them until onion slices are translucent. Remove garlic and discard.
9. Return roast to pot. Then add white wine, half the orange juice, salt, pepper to taste, remaining oregano, and bay leaf, crumbled.
10. Simmer roast over low heat, covered, for 3 hours or until meat is tender. Turn the roast occasionally during cooking and baste at the same time. Also, at half-hour intervals, pour small amounts of reserved orange juice over meat until all juice is used up.
11. To serve: Slice roast in fairly thick pieces. Strain the cooking liquid and pour over slices. The roast is normally accompanied with black beans, rice, and fried green plantains.

Yield: 6 to 8 servings

Veal

Veau des Gourmets

DUXELLES

4 tablespoons unsalted butter
2 tablespoons finely chopped shallots
½ pound mushrooms, very finely chopped
  Salt
  Black pepper
¼ cup dry white wine

1. To make duxelles: melt 4 tablespoons butter in a skillet. Add shallots, cover, and cook over moderate heat briefly until shallots have begun to give up their moisture.
2. Add mushrooms, salt, and pepper. Cook at a heat high enough to make the mushrooms yield up their liquid as steam. Keep stirring with a wooden spoon until all water has evaporated.
3. Add wine and cook, stirring, until it has completely reduced. Reserve finished duxelles.

MORNAY SAUCE

3 tablespoons butter
3 tablespoons flour
2 cups milk
  White pepper
¼ teaspoon grated nutmeg
2 egg yolks, lightly beaten
4 tablespoons grated gruyère cheese

1. To make mornay sauce: in a heavy nonaluminum saucepan, melt 3 tablespoons butter. Add flour all at once over medium low heat. Stir into butter until smooth and cook for 2 minutes, stirring continually. Let cool to body temperature. This is a roux.
2. Boil milk and stir into cool roux. Keep stirring over medium

heat. Let boil and add salt, white pepper, and nutmeg. Cook at
low heat for 5 minutes, stirring.
3. Stir in yolks and grated gruyère. Correct seasoning. Add 2
tablespoons sauce to duxelles and reserve the rest.

VEAL

4 tablespoons butter
2 pounds boned veal loin of cylindrical shape, tied with string
1 large carrot, coarsely chopped
1 large onion, coarsely chopped
  Bouquet garni (2 sprigs parsley, 1 bay leaf, and ½ teaspoon
  dried thyme)
⅓ cup dry white wine
  Veal stock (optional)

1. To prepare veal: preheat oven to 375 degrees. Melt 4 tablespoons
   butter in a small roasting pan as close to the size of the veal as
   possible. Put veal in pan and cook in oven for 15 minutes. Turn
   the veal so that it is coated with butter on all sides.
2. Make a bed of carrot and onion pieces in roasting pan. Add the
   bouquet garni. Put roast on vegetable bed and return to
   oven. Roast another 15 minutes. Pour wine in pan and
   roast for another 20 minutes or until veal drips clear, not pink,
   juice when pricked with a fork. If wine boils away, supplement
   with hot stock or water.
3. Let cooked veal rest for 20 minutes out of oven.

ASSEMBLING

8 thin slices prosciutto
8 thin slices gruyère cheese
1 tablespoon grated gruyère cheese
1 tablespoon butter

1. While veal is resting, reheat duxelles and mornay sauce, gently,
   to serving temperature. The mornay will lose its skin during
   heating. Also see that prosciutto and gruyère slices are at room
   temperature.
2. Preheat broiler.

3. Cut veal into 8 slices; reserve vegetables and cooking liquid.
4. Assemble the veau des gourmets on an ovenproof serving platter as follows: in an overlapping line, lay down a slice of veal, a bit of duxelles, a slice of prosciutto, more duxelles, a slice of cheese and still more duxelles. Repeat this pattern until veal, duxelles, prosciutto, and cheese slices are used up.
5. Pour all of the mornay sauce over the veau des gourmets. Sprinkle with grated gruyère.
6. Melt butter and drip over the top.
7. Brown lightly under broiler.
8. Push vegetables and cooking liquid through a fine strainer (discard bouquet garni first) and pour the resulting juice around the veal. Serve immediately.

Yield: 8 servings

NOTE: *It is very important to work quickly once you have sliced the veal. Otherwise this dish will come to the table cold.*

Swiss Veal

6 tablespoons butter	1 tablespoon sifted flour
1½ pounds tender veal, cut into thin strips about ½ inch wide	1 cup dry white wine
1 medium onion, chopped	1 tablespoon chopped parsley
2 large mushrooms, sliced	Salt
1 cup light cream	Pepper

1. Heat a heavy frying pan over high heat, add butter, and reduce heat to moderately high.
2. Mix veal, onion, and mushrooms and sauté in the butter, stirring often, until lightly browned, about 8 to 10 minutes.
3. Blend cream with flour and add to meat. Cook, stirring, until mixture boils. Turn heat low, cover, and simmer until veal is tender—5 to 6 minutes.
4. Mix wine and parsley. Add to meat with salt and pepper to taste and let come to a boil once, stirring constantly. Turn heat to very low, cover, and let simmer 2 minutes. Serve immediately.

Yield: 6 servings

Vitello Tonnato

5 tablespoons oil
1 large onion, sliced
1 stalk celery, sliced
2 carrots, sliced
5 bay leaves
3 whole cloves
5 sage leaves
2 teaspoons salt

3 cups dry white wine
3 pounds boned leg of veal or 3 pounds beef eye round
1 6½-ounce can tuna fish, drained
6 anchovy fillets
3 cups mayonnaise (see page 300)

1. Place 3 tablespoons oil in a saucepan and fry onion until golden. Add celery, carrots, bay leaves, cloves, sage, salt, and wine; boil for 10 minutes. Pour over meat and marinate the meat for 24 hours in the refrigerator.
2. Preheat oven to 350 degrees.
3. Drain the vegetables and meat; place in roasting pan with remaining 2 tablespoons of oil. Cover and bake 1 hour, basting occasionally with the marinade.
4. Cool the meat, cut into thin slices, and arrange on a serving platter.
5. Place tuna and anchovies in an electric blender. Blend until smooth and add mayonnaise sauce slowly. Pour the resulting sauce over meat and refrigerate for 24 hours before serving. If desired, garnish with hard-boiled eggs, capers, and lemon wedges.

Yield: 9 to 12 servings

Esterhazy Tokany

1½ pounds lean veal shoulder or chuck
½ onion, chopped
2 tablespoons butter
1–2 bay leaves
1 teaspoon salt
½ cup sour cream
¼ cup light cream
1 tablespoon flour

1. Cut veal into julienne strips ½ inch thick and 2 inches long.
2. Cook onion in butter until yellow. Add veal, bay leaves, and salt. Simmer, covered, 30 minutes.
3. Blend sour cream, light cream, and flour. Add to veal and simmer, stirring occasionally, until veal is tender. Adjust seasonings.

Yield: 5 servings.

Quaiette di Vitello con Piselli
(Veal Birds with Peas)

1 egg, lightly beaten
¼ teaspoon salt
¼ teaspoon pepper
¼ teaspoon ground allspice
1 tablespoon fine white bread crumbs
2 tablespoons grated parmesan cheese (approximately)
2 tablespoons chopped parsley

1½ pounds veal scallops, pounded to less than ⅛ inch thick and cut into 6 serving pieces
1 small onion, minced
1 tablespoon olive oil
1 tablespoon butter
2 8-ounce cans tomato sauce
1 10-ounce package frozen peas

1. To make the stuffing, combine in a bowl: egg, salt, pepper, allspice, bread crumbs, cheese, and parsley.
2. Spread each veal slice evenly with stuffing. Fold over sides and then roll up, starting from one end. Tie up with cooking twine.
3. In a saucepan, sauté onion in olive oil and butter until golden. Add veal birds and brown well on all sides.
4. Add tomato sauce, correct seasoning, and simmer, covered, for about 1½ hours. Remove cover during last 30 minutes to permit sauce to thicken.
5. Fifteen minutes before done, add frozen peas, cover again.
6. Before serving, remove twine. The dish may be accompanied by mashed potatoes.

Yield: 4 to 6 servings

Cima alla Genovese
(Stuffed Cold Veal)

1 4-pound boned breast of veal
1 pound sweetbreads
Juice of 1 lemon
½ calf's brain
Boiling salted water
1 cup dried Italian-style
mushrooms
6 tablespoons butter
¼ pound leg of veal, finely
diced
1 cup fresh, uncooked peas
2 tablespoons pine nuts

2 cloves garlic, finely chopped
½ teaspoon marjoram
¼ cup grated parmesan cheese
6 eggs, lightly beaten
Salt
Pepper
2 tablespoons oil
½ cup dry white wine
2 cups beef stock
1 carrot, quartered
1 stalk celery
1 onion, sliced

1. Pound the veal breast until it is about ¼ inch thick.
2. Soak the sweetbreads in ice water with lemon juice added for 15 minutes. Soak the brain in warm salted water to clean it well. Drain sweetbreads and brain and trim away membranes and filaments.
3. Drop sweetbreads and brains into boiling salted water to cover and simmer 5 minutes. Drain well. Chop finely.
4. Meanwhile, fold the veal breast in two across the length and sew up the sides with fine string to make a leakproof pocket.
5. Soak the mushrooms in warm water to cover 10 minutes. Drain and pat dry.
6. Heat 4 tablespoons of the butter in a skillet and sauté the leg of veal, chopped sweetbreads, and brain for about 5 minutes, stirring constantly.
7. In a large bowl, combine the peas, pine nuts, garlic, marjoram, cheese, sautéed veal mixture, eggs, and salt and pepper to taste. Mix well.
8. Set the veal breast pocket in a bowl to steady it and spoon, or pour, in the egg mixture. The pocket should be about ⅔ full.
9. Sew up the open end to make it leakproof.
10. Heat the remaining butter and oil in a heavy casserole or dutch oven and brown the stuffed veal breast on all sides. Add the wine and let it evaporate.

11. Add the stock and enough water to come about ⅓ the way up the meat. Add the carrot, celery, and onion. Bring to a boil, cover, and simmer one hour. Turn the meat, cover, and simmer another hour or until the meat is tender.
12. Remove meat from the casserole and allow to cool. Place a piece of plastic wrap or parchment paper over the meat and weight it with a heavy weight in the refrigerator, at least overnight.
13. Remove the strings, slice, and serve chilled, but not too cold.

Yield: 12 to 16 servings

Lamb

Lamb Chops Villeroi

  2 racks rib lamb chops (6–7 pounds, about 18 chops)
3½ cups soft bread crumbs (approximately)
  1 cup grated gruyère cheese
  3 eggs, lightly beaten
  6 cups villeroi sauce (see page 294)
    Butter
    Cooked rice

1. Preheat oven to 450 degrees.
2. Place racks of lamb on a rack in a roasting pan and put in oven. Reduce heat immediately to 350 degrees and cook until a meat thermometer inserted into the center of the meat in a middle chop registers 160 degrees, about 15 minutes.
3. When done, remove roasts from oven and let cool. Cut into chops, neatly.
4. Mix bread crumbs and grated gruyère. Beat eggs in another bowl.
5. Dip chops in lukewarm villeroi sauce. Coat well, let sauce set on chops a minute or so and then dip in bread crumb mixture, then in egg and again in bread crumb mixture to make as light a coating as possible. Heat enough butter in 2 skillets (preferably Teflon-coated) to just cover the bottom.
6. Brown chops on both sides in butter in the skillet. Drain.
7. Arrange chops in a crown around a mound of cooked rice on a serving platter. Serve immediately.

Yield: 12 to 14 servings

Shashlik, Kars-Style

1 pound lamb chops, cut into
   4 servings
2 lamb kidneys
Salt
Pepper
1 onion, finely chopped

Chopped parsley
1 tablespoon white vinegar or
   lemon juice
1 lemon
1 chopped scallion
Hot sauce (see Step 3)

1. Wipe lamb riblets and make shallow cuts across fibers. Cut kidneys in half lengthwise and remove center tubes and fat. Place in a bowl and season with salt and pepper.
2. Add onion, parsley, and vinegar or lemon juice and let marinate 2 to 3 hours.
3. Arrange ribs and kidneys alternately on skewers and broil over coals, turning frequently until brown. Remove skewers and serve with sliced lemon, chopped scallion, and parsley. Pass hot sauce. (As a substitute for commercial Russian hot sauce, season A-1 sauce with mustard, Tabasco, and a bit of sugar.)

Yield: 4 servings

Shish Kebabs

3 pounds shoulder lamb
   chops cut 1 inch thick
1 teaspoon salt
1 large clove garlic, mashed
½ cup chopped onion
1 teaspoon dried oregano
   or marjoram
¼ teaspoon pepper

¼ cup olive or salad oil
⅓ cup dry sherry or 1–2
   tablespoons white vinegar
   or lemon juice
8–10 small white onions,
   parboiled
½ pound small mushrooms

1. Remove bones and excess fat from lamb chops and cut meat into 1½-inch squares.
2. Place salt in a large bowl or casserole and mix with garlic. Add lamb chops and toss.
3. Add chopped onion, oregano or marjoram, pepper, oil, and sherry. Mix thoroughly. Store in refrigerator, covered, several hours or overnight. Turn meat a few times in marinade.

4. When ready to cook shish kebabs, drain off marinade, pour it over onions and mushrooms, and toss them in it.
5. To cook shish kebabs outdoors: have ready 4 or 5 long metal skewers or pointed strong slender green sticks. When fire has burned down to glowing coals, push lamb, onions, and mushrooms, alternating them, onto skewer or stick. Allow a bit of space between each piece for thorough cooking.
6. Hold skewers over the hot coals, turning to brown all sides. Be careful that the exposed portions of green sticks do not burn. The shish kebabs should be done in 12 to 15 minutes.
7. Remove each skewer and empty a serving of meat, onions, and mushrooms in a buttered frankfurter roll. Good accompaniments are tomatoes, cucumbers, and assorted relishes.
8. To cook shish kebabs indoors: alternate lamb, onions, and mushrooms on metal skewers. Place on hot, greased broiler rack or over a shallow pan with ends of skewers resting on sides of pan. Broil about 3 inches from source of heat 12 to 15 minutes, turning to brown all sides. Serve with rice cooked in broth, relishes, and salad vegetables.

Yield: 4 to 5 servings

Indian Mughal Biryani

1 1⅛-ounce jar cinnamon sticks (16 sticks)
2 tablespoons whole green cardamom
1 tablespoon whole cloves
3 tablespoons chopped fresh ginger
3 tablespoons chopped garlic
   Juice of 3 medium limes
4–5 fresh green chilies
2 tablespoons salt
4 tablespoons sour cream
½ pound fresh coriander with stalks, washed and finely chopped

¼ pound fresh mint leaves, finely chopped
4 pounds boned lamb shoulder cut into 1½-inch cubes
1¼ pounds unsalted butter (enough to make 2 cups ghee)
6 medium onions, thinly sliced
4 cups basmati rice, well washed and drained
1 tightly packed tablespoon whole saffron
1 cup milk

1. Puree in a blender the cinnamon, cardamom, cloves, ginger, and garlic. Combine with lime juice, chilies, salt, sour cream, coriander, and mint in a bowl. Add lamb cubes and let marinate at room temperature for at least 2 hours but not more than 3.
2. During marination, melt butter in a saucepan and continue heating over moderate heat until butter has turned a nut brown and milk solids have all burned and sunk to the bottom. Then strain the resulting clear ghee through voile or several layers of cheesecloth into a clean container.
3. Heat 1 cup ghee in a skillet and sauté onion slices until golden brown.
4. Combine sautéed onions and ghee from skillet with marinated mixture in a large ovenproof pot or casserole. Mix well and cook, uncovered, over high flame for 30 minutes, stirring occasionally.
5. In another pot, combine rice with 2 cups cold water. Bring to a boil and, after 2 minutes, reduce heat to moderate, cover and continue cooking until water has evaporated, but rice is still quite chewy, about 15 minutes.
6. Meanwhile, powder saffron in a mortar with a pestle and combine with milk, so that saffron dissolves as much as possible.
7. Preheat oven to 475 degrees.
8. When rice is ready and lamb mixture has cooked 30 minutes, spread rice in a layer over lamb mixture in large pot. Then distribute milk-saffron liquid over rice. Pour remaining ghee over surface. Cover pot, put in oven, and cook until all moisture is absorbed, 10 to 15 minutes.
9. Remove from oven, mix contents of pot well, and serve.

Yield: 12 servings.

Moussaka of Lamb

3 pounds boned lamb shoulder, roasted
2 medium onions
3 medium potatoes
1 quart strained lamb broth made from simmering 2 pounds lamb bones, trimmings, etc., in 2 quarts water and reducing liquid

Worcestershire sauce
Salt
Pepper
Grated nutmeg
6 slices eggplant
6 slices tomato
Olive or salad oil
⅓–½ cup bread crumbs

1. Preheat oven to 350 degrees.
2. Cut lamb, onions, and potatoes in ¼-inch cubes and place in a roasting pan with a cover. Bake, uncovered, stirring occasionally, until lightly browned.
3. Add lamb broth and seasonings to taste. Bake, covered, until lamb is very tender, 1 hour or longer. Transfer to a deep baking dish. Raise oven heat to 425 degrees.
4. Sauté eggplant and tomato slices in oil. Place eggplant on top of lamb and tomatoes on eggplant. Sprinkle crumbs over top of casserole.
5. Bake for 10 minutes.

Yield: 6 servings

Josephine's Lamb and Zucchini Casserole

6 medium or 3 large zucchini	1 clove garlic, finely chopped
Butter	1½ pounds ground leg of lamb
Salt	¼ cup converted rice
Pepper	1 teaspoon grated lemon peel
1 cup bread crumbs	2 tablespoons chopped fresh
2 tablespoons olive oil	mint or 1 teaspoon dried
¾ cup chopped onion	1 cup chicken stock

1. Preheat oven to 375 degrees.
2. Scrub zucchini and slice into thin discs. Arrange half the slices along the bottom of a buttered casserole. Dust with salt and pepper to taste.
3. Sauté bread crumbs over low heat in 4 tablespoons butter until browned.
4. Heat the oil in a skillet and sauté onion, garlic, lamb, and rice together until lamb is gray, not brown. Stir often.
5. Add to lamb mixture: 1 teaspoon salt, pepper to taste, lemon peel, and mint. Mix together and spoon evenly into casserole over zucchini. Cover lamb with remaining zucchini.
6. Pour chicken stock over top layer of zucchini. Sprinkle bread crumbs evenly over zucchini.
7. Bake in oven for 35 to 40 minutes.

Yield: 4 servings

Hunza (Lamb) Meatball Curry

2 pounds boned lamb shoulder or shank, finely ground
Salt
Pepper
1 tablespoon or more curry powder
2 tablespoons finely chopped parsley

2 medium onions, finely chopped
2 tablespoons safflower oil
1 pound mushrooms, sliced and sautéed
⅓ cup heavy cream

1. Combine ground lamb with 1 cup water, salt, pepper, curry powder, and parsley. Form meat into plum-size balls.
2. In a large saucepan, sauté onions in oil until transparent, but not browned.
3. Add 4 cups water to saucepan and bring to a boil. Add meatballs and cook over low heat for about 20 minutes.
4. Remove meatballs and reserve. Boil remaining contents of saucepan down to about 2 cups.
5. Return meatballs to saucepan. Add mushrooms and cream. Simmer until hot.

Yield: 6 to 8 servings

Pork

James Beard's Roast Loin of Pork

1 4–5-pound pork loin roast	1 cup dry white wine
1 clove garlic, chopped	Applesauce
Salt	Apple slices
Pepper	Brown sugar
2 tablespoons butter, melted	½ cup heavy cream

1. Preheat oven to 450 degrees.
2. Tie roast securely, stab it here and there and insert bits of garlic clove. Rub meat thoroughly with salt and pepper. Place fat side up in an open roasting pan. Sear in oven for 30 minutes, basting now and then with a mixture of the fat in the pan, butter, and white wine.
3. At the end of 30 minutes, reduce heat to 350 degrees and roast meat for another hour, basting often with pan drippings.
4. At the end of the hour, take roast out of oven. Pour off about ¾ of the fat in the pan, spread the roast with applesauce and arrange thin apple slices, sprinkled with brown sugar, around the roast. Return to the oven and cook for a few minutes, basting the apple slices until they are soft.
5. Just before serving, add heavy cream to the pan and let it cook up with the apples and pan juice. Remove the roast to a hot platter, cut the strings, and arrange the apples and sauce around it.

Yield: 8 to 10 servings

Pork Chops with Lirac

½ medium onion, chopped
4 teaspoons finely chopped
fresh tarragon
8 teaspoons finely chopped
parsley
¼ cup crumbled sharp
cheddar cheese
Salt

6 center-cut loin pork chops
about 1 inch thick
Flour
1 tablespoon butter
1½ cups Lirac or other dry rosé
wine
¾ cup chicken stock

1. Mix onion, tarragon, parsley, cheese, and ¼ teaspoon salt together in a bowl to make stuffing.
2. Cut pockets in the chops, cutting from the outside edge toward the bone and being careful not to let the point of the knife perforate the top or bottom of the chop. Make the opening of the pockets a little wider than the knife. Work the knife back and forth inside the chop to make the pockets as large as possible.
3. Fill pockets with stuffing (but not so full that they bulge) and close them up by pushing toothpicks through both lips of the opening. Put the toothpicks in at angles to each other so that they crisscross.
4. Dredge the chops in lightly salted flour.
5. Melt butter in a skillet over moderate heat. Add chops and brown them on both sides, pressing down with the end of a metal spatula along the inside of the rows of toothpicks to make sure that the underside of each chop next to the toothpicks browns.
6. While browning chops, preheat oven to 350 degrees.
7. Put browned chops in a shallow baking dish.
8. Deglaze skillet with enough wine to moisten the pan and pour resulting liquid into baking dish.
9. Add remaining wine and chicken stock (enough to make liquid in pan rise to just below the top of the chops).
10. Put baking pan in oven for 1 hour, turning chops after 30 minutes.
11. When chops are done, remove from oven. Drain them, discard liquid, and serve.

Yield: 6 servings

Fukienese Pork Chops with Scallion Sauce

10 thin pork chops
 1 teaspoon imported light
    soy sauce
 1 teaspoon sesame oil
 1 teaspoon five-taste spice
    powder
 1 teaspoon salt
 1 teaspoon sugar

 1 teaspoon monosodium
    glutamate (optional)
    Red food coloring (optional)
    Cornstarch
    Fat or oil for deep frying
 1 cup scallion sauce (see page
    299)

1. Cut meat away from bone of pork chops in one piece.
2. In a bowl, combine pork pieces with soy sauce, sesame oil, five-taste spice powder, salt, sugar, and monosodium glutamate. Mix well with hands. If desired, add enough red food coloring to achieve an overall shade roughly like that of a tomato. Let marinate in the refrigerator 1 hour, or longer for a more intense taste.
3. Dredge pork pieces lightly but thoroughly in cornstarch.
4. Deep fry in hot oil (375 degrees). Stir while frying with a skimmer and continue frying for 5 minutes or until meat has reached the desired degree of doneness.
5. Drain pork pieces, put on a serving platter, pour scallion sauce over them, and serve.

Yield: 4 to 5 servings

Lechoncito Asado
(Cuban Suckling Pig)

1 10–12-pound suckling pig, trussed
   Peanut oil
   Salt
1 small orange
1 recipe mojo (see below)

1. Rub salt generously into skin of pig. Wedge a dense ball of aluminum foil in its mouth and cover the ears and tail with aluminum foil.
2. Preheat oven to 450 degrees.
3. Pour enough oil into a roasting pan to create a thin film on the bottom. Put pig on its side in the pan and put in oven at middle level, with head turned toward front of oven.

4. After about 25 minutes, or as soon as the pig begins to smoke, turn oven down to 375 degrees. After 1¼ hours at 375 degrees, turn the pig on its other side, baste with additional oil, and return to the oven with the head toward the rear.
5. Continue roasting for 1¼ hours longer, or until the thigh joints move easily in their sockets, the skin is crisp and golden, and a meat thermometer registers 180 degrees.
6. During the last half of roasting, remove the aluminum foil from ears and tail. Set pig upright in pan. Baste with more oil and return to oven.
7. When done, turn off oven and leave pig in oven to rest with door ajar for 15 to 30 minutes before serving.
8. Remove aluminum ball from mouth, insert orange, and serve, along with mojo in a separate sauceboat.
9. To carve, first cut off trotters, then slice skin along backbone and separate from flesh. Cut skin in serving pieces and serve with meat cut from the rib section.

Yield: 8 to 10 servings

MOJO

1 small head of garlic
1 teaspoon salt
½ teaspoon pepper
½ teaspoon oregano
½ teaspoon cumin
 Juice of 2 limes or 2 naranjas agrias (sour oranges)
1½ cups pork fat, smoking hot

1. Pound garlic, salt, pepper, oregano, cumin, and juice into a paste. Add hot pork fat and stir well with a spoon.

Hot Glazed Ham

1 cooked ham
 Whole cloves
1 cup madeira or sherry
¼ cup light molasses

1. Preheat oven to 275 degrees.
2. If necessary, skin the ham. If the outside layer of fat seems too thick, remove some fat.

3. Place ham on a rack in an open roasting pan and bake until ham is
    heated throughout. Allow about 10 minutes per pound of ham.
    If ham is well browned on surface when purchased, bake it with
    the top covered with aluminum foil.
4. About 30 minutes before ham is done, score the fat in a
    diamond pattern with a sharp knife. Set a clove in the center
    of each diamond.
5. Pour madeira over ham and brush it lightly with the molasses.
    Continue baking, basting frequently with drippings in pan.

Yield: 2 to 3 servings per pound

Jambon au Poivre Vert
(Ham with Green Peppercorns)

1 3½-ounce jar green peppercorns in vinegar
1 1-inch-thick center slice fully cooked smoked ham
2 tablespoons butter
2 cups cooked sauerkraut, drained
1 cup dry white wine
2 teaspoons dried juniper berries, or to taste, crushed

1. Remove 6 of the green peppercorns from the jar and set aside.
2. Place remainder of the peppercorns with the liquid into an
    electric blender and chop finely, or drain the peppercorns and
    mash them in a mortar with a pestle.
3. Spread both sides of the ham with the crushed peppercorns and set
    aside for an hour or until the ham becomes impregnated with
    the taste of pepper.
4. Melt the butter in a skillet and sauté the ham slice, turning once.
    Transfer to a warm platter with as many peppercorns as you wish.
5. Meanwhile, reheat the sauerkraut with the wine, reserved
    peppercorns, and juniper berries. Simmer 5 minutes.
6. Add the sauerkraut to the ham platter.

Yield: 3 servings

Sauerkraut with Smoked Ham

3 ounces pork fat, cubed	Butter
1 small onion, chopped	1 tablespoon bread crumbs
4 cups sauerkraut	1 pound potatoes, boiled and
1 tablespoon white vinegar	sliced
Salt	8 slices cooked smoked ham
Pepper	1 cup sour cream
½ cup water or beef stock	

1. Cook the pork cubes in the fat that melts out of them until they are brown. Remove from pan.
2. Brown onion in the fat and to onion add the cubes of pork, sauerkraut, vinegar, seasonings to taste, and the water or stock. Cover and simmer slowly until kraut is tender—time may vary from 30 to 45 minutes, depending on whether bulk or canned kraut is used.
3. Preheat oven to 300 degrees.
4. Sprinkle a small greased heatproof dish with crumbs.
5. Spread in it a layer of the sauerkraut, a layer of potatoes, and a layer of ham. Repeat layers, ending with sauerkraut.
6. Pour sour cream over the dish and bake just long enough to heat through the ingredients—about 30 minutes.

Yield: 8 servings

Craig Claiborne and Virginia Lee's Spicy Fresh Pork Casserole

1 4-pound fresh uncured ham or pork butt, with bone in and skin on	2 1-inch cinnamon sticks
	1 scallion, trimmed
6 tablespoons dry sherry or shao hsing wine	½ teaspoon monosodium glutamate (optional)
	5–6 pieces star anise
5 tablespoons imported dark soy sauce	4 ¼-inch-thick round slices fresh ginger
5 tablespoons sugar	1 teaspoon peanut, vegetable, or corn oil (optional)
Salt	

1. Place the pork in a kettle and add water to cover. Bring to a boil, simmer 2 minutes, and drain. Run under cold running water.
2. Return to the kettle and add 2½ quarts cold water. Bring to a boil and add the wine, soy sauce, sugar, salt, cinnamon sticks, scallion, monosodium glutamate, star anise, and ginger. Cover and cook for 2 hours, turning the meat often in its cooking liquid.
3. Uncover and continue cooking over medium-high heat, taking care that meat does not stick. Cook 1½ to 2 hours longer, until the meat is tender.
4. Remove the meat. Strain the liquid into a wok or other open vessel, discarding the herbs and spices. Cook over high heat, stirring often, until the sauce is syrupy, 15 to 20 minutes. Glaze with 1 teaspoon oil, if desired, and pour over pork. Let stand to room temperature. Serve, sliced like a ham, in the gravy.

Yield: 8 to 10 servings

Luckskos Káposzta
(Transylvanian Cabbage Stew)

1½ pounds fatty pork stew meat or spare ribs (if spare ribs are used, have the butcher saw the piece in half)
1½ pounds brisket of beef
Salt
1 head (about 3 pounds) cabbage
¼ pound smoked bacon (optional)
3 tablespoons lard
¼ cup finely chopped red or bermuda onions

Pepper
1 tablespoon chopped fresh dill or tarragon
3 or 4 sprigs fresh or dried summer savory, tied together (optional)
2 tablespoons white vinegar
1 tablespoon flour
¼ cup sour cream, at room temperature

1. Place the pork and beef in a large pot, cover with cold water, and add 1 tablespoon salt. Slowly bring to a simmer and continue simmering until the meat is half cooked, about 1½ hours.
2. Remove the meat, saving the broth, and when it is cool enough to handle, cut it into 1- to 1½-inch cubes. (If spareribs are used, remove meat from bones and discard bones.)
3. Meanwhile, cut the cabbage into thick wedges, place them on a

rack in the sink, salt them, and pour boiling water over them.
If this is not feasible, cook the wedges for 1 or 2 minutes in boiling
salted water and drain them in a colander.

4. If you wish to use bacon, cut it into pieces 1 inch square by
¼ inch thick. In a heavy-bottomed pot large enough to hold all the
cabbage and meat, heat the lard and sauté the onions in it
until they are translucent.
5. Off the heat, place ⅓ of the cabbage in a layer on top of the
onions, salt and pepper it, and spread all the pieces of beef and
half the bacon on it. Spread half the remaining cabbage on top,
salt and pepper that layer, and sprinkle it with dill or tarragon.
6. Make another layer with the pork and the rest of the bacon pieces
and lay the bunch of summer savory in the middle. Cover with
the last wedges of cabbage. Pour on enough degreased broth from
the meats to come over the pork layer (about 6 cups; supplement
broth with water if necessary).
7. Cover and slowly bring to a simmer; simmer until the cabbage
and meat are barely done (about 30 minutes). Add the vinegar and
set the pot aside.
8. Blend the flour thoroughly into the sour cream, add a couple of
tablespoons of lukewarm sauce to it, and then slowly pour the
mixture into the stew.
9. Just before serving, let the stew simmer again for 2 or 3 minutes.
If sour cream mixture has not distributed itself downwards in the
pot, stir very gently. Take this opportunity to fish out the bunch of
savory, and serve immediately, preferably from the cooking pot.

Yield: 6 to 8 servings

Barbecued Spareribs

   3 pounds spareribs
½ cup imported soy sauce
½ cup hoisin sauce
   3 cloves garlic, crushed

1. Have butcher cut spareribs into short lengths, discarding backbone
portion.
2. Mix sauces and garlic and coat meat with mixture. Let stand
15 minutes.
3. Preheat broiler.
4. Broil on a rack about 10 minutes on first side, turn and broil 8 to 10

minutes on second side. Serve hot and crisp as an appetizer with mustard and duck sauce. As a main dish, serve rice also.

Yield: 4 servings

Sweet and Sour Pork

1 pound pork tenderloin	2 green peppers, seeded and
1½ teaspoons salt	cut into 1-inch squares
1½ teaspoons imported soy	4 slices pineapple, cut into
sauce	1-inch squares
10 tablespoons cornstarch	3 tablespoons white vinegar
1 egg yolk	4 tablespoons sugar
4 cups plus 2 tablespoons	4 tablespoons ketchup
peanut oil	2 teaspoons sesame oil

1. Pound pork with back of cleaver to tenderize. Cut into 1-inch squares.
2. Combine ½ teaspoon salt, soy sauce, 1 tablespoon cornstarch, 1 tablespoon cold water, and egg yolk in large mixing bowl. Stir well, until salt and cornstarch dissolve. Then add pork and let marinate for at least 30 minutes.
3. After pork has finished marinating, heat 4 cups oil in a wok or a skillet over high heat.
4. While oil is heating, dip pork squares in ½ cup cornstarch until thinly coated.
5. Test oil with one pork square. If it sizzles on contact with oil, put rest of pork into oil and fry until brown, which will take about 2 minutes.
6. Remove pork from oil with slotted spoon.
7. Reheat oil to same point as in Step 5, and fry pork again until crisp.
8. Remove pork from pan and discard oil.
9. Put 2 tablespoons oil in wok, then add green pepper and pineapple, stirring constantly for 5 minutes.
10. Mix vinegar, sugar, ketchup, 4 tablespoons water, remaining cornstarch, remaining salt, and sesame oil. Add mixture to green pepper and pineapple in wok, and continue stirring until sauce thickens to the consistency of molasses.
11. Turn off heat. Add the pork to mixture in wok and serve immediately.

Yield: 6 servings

Spanish Empanada Granados

2 pounds lean pork
1 pound veal
1 tablespoon chopped garlic
1 tablespoon olive oil
1 teaspoon dried rosemary
4 tablespoons stale bread
 crumbs

5 tablespoons brandy
5 tablespoons port
¼ pound walnut halves
Salt
Pastry or bread dough for
 double-crust 9-inch pie

1. Put meats through coarse grinder or chop into small pieces.
2. Brown garlic in olive oil. Add meat and rosemary and sauté until meat is brown. Strain off liquid and reserve in covered jar in refrigerator.
3. Mix together bread crumbs, brandy, and port. Add meat, walnut halves, and salt to taste. Set in the refrigerator, to marinate for 2 days.
4. Preheat oven to 400 degrees.
5. Line a 9-inch pie plate with crust or dough, add meat mixture, and cover with top crust. Bake until brown, about 30 minutes. Remove pie from oven and brush top with reserved liquid. May be served hot or cold.

Yield: 6 to 8 servings

Pennsylvania Dutch Sausages à la Jones

2–3 small hog intestines for
 casings
3 tablespoons salt
3 tablespoons sage leaves, well
 crumbled
1½ teaspoons pepper
1 tablespoon whole cloves

1 tablespoon ground
 coriander
2 pounds lean pork, and
 1 pound fatback, ground
 together
String

1. Soak casings for 1 hour in cold water.
2. Crush salt, sage leaves, pepper, cloves, and coriander together in a mortar with a pestle.
3. Mix spice mixture from Step 2 into ground meat with hands, gently.
4. Make a small cake from meat mixture, fry on both sides until

browned; taste and correct seasoning of the rest of the meat mixture.

5. Run cold water through a casing and slip over the moistened tip or horn of the sausage gun, starting from one end of the casing and pulling on more and more until all but two or three inches have been gathered on the horn.

6. Fill gun with meat mixture.

7. Brace gun vertically on counter top and push small amount of meat into the piece of casing that dangles free in order to squeeze air out of gun.

8. Tie off end of casing in a square knot with string.

9. Continue forcing meat through gun into casing. Casing will fill and slip off horn from pressure of gun. As casing fills, tie off into sausages at 3-inch intervals or longer until entire casing is used up.

10. Slip on another casing and continue as above until meat mixture is exhausted.

11. Hang sausage strings in open window overnight or for 24 hours to heighten the taste.

12. To cook, snip off desired number of sausages with scissors and fry for about 10 minutes in skillet containing ⅛ inch of water. Prick sausages with fork two or three times to allow their fat to escape and replace water as it boils away.

Yield: Approximately 2 dozen sausages

Game

Venison Steaks with Sauce Poivrade

Two tender ½-pound venison steaks, cut about ¾ inch thick, are placed in the following mixture: 1 teaspoon salt, 1 sliced onion, 4 sprigs parsley, 1 bay leaf, 1 cup dry white wine or 4 tablespoons white vinegar, 4 peppercorns, 1 sliced carrot, a little dried thyme, and 3 table-spoons salad oil.

The meat stands in this solution in a cool place for 2 to 3 days: it is turned from time to time. When ready to cook, broil steaks rare to medium as one would beefsteaks.

Serve with Poivrade sauce (see page 295).

Yield: 3 to 4 servings

Roast Venison

It is not necessary to marinate roasting joints of venison, but they should be larded, which is a reasonable precaution to take with any piece of very lean meat—hare, beefsteaks, pigeons, etc., as well as venison. Buy a piece of fat end of bacon. Chill it firm, and cut it into strips 2 inches long and just over ⅛ inch wide and thick. Push a piece into the open end of a larding needle and take a stitch in the joint as if you were sewing, leaving the fat bacon behind. Repeat until the whole joint is nicely studded with fat.

To roast the venison, tie a jacket of pork fatback (or a fatty piece of pork or bacon skin) around it and cook at 350 degrees. Venison should be slightly rare: the time required for a small roast is about 20 minutes per pound, plus 20 minutes. When roasts are larger, above 4 pounds, reduce the time per pound to 15 minutes. Should you ever have the good fortune to be presented with a haunch of venison, i.e., a leg plus half the saddle in one magnificent piece, it will require 3 to 4 hours of cooking.

Serve roast venison with Francatelli's venison sauce (see page 295).

Specialty Cuts

Sweetbreads Parmigiana

2 pairs veal sweetbreads, weighing about 1 pound each
1 teaspoon salt
4 tablespoons butter, melted (approximately)
1 cup grated parmesan cheese (approximately)
8 pieces of toast, buttered

1. Simmer sweetbreads in water to cover with salt for 15 minutes. Drain, cool under cold water, and separate the two meaty portions, removing connecting tubes and tissues. (These are tough and easy to recognize.) Peel off the thin covering membrane with the fingers. Cut each sweetbread in half. Dry portions. This step should be done on purchasing meat and sweetbreads refrigerated until cooking time.
2. Preheat oven to 425 degrees.
3. Dip sweetbreads in melted butter and then cover with cheese. Place on a shallow baking sheet and bake until lightly browned—about 20 minutes. Or brown under broiler, turning to brown both sides. Serve on toast.

Yield: 4 servings

Rassolnik

1 pound beef kidney
1 tablespoon salt
1 onion, chopped
1 stalk celery, sliced
2 tablespoons butter
2 large dill pickles, sliced
4 medium potatoes, cubed
Pickle liquid
½ large head lettuce, or 1 cup fresh sorrel, chopped
Sour cream
Parsley or fresh dill, chopped

1. Remove fat and tissues from kidney, and cut it into small pieces. Wash, cover with cold water, bring to a boil, drain, and wash again. Wash pot to remove scum from bottom and sides.
2. Return kidneys to pot. Add 1½ quarts water and salt. Cover and simmer until tender, 1 hour or longer. Cool and remove kidney.
3. Sauté onion and celery in butter until colored. Add to broth along with pickles and potatoes. Cover and cook until potatoes are almost tender, about 10 minutes. Add pickle liquid to taste and lettuce or sorrel, and cook 5 to 10 minutes longer. Add water and salt as desired.
4. Before serving, add kidney to soup and reheat. Add sour cream to taste, and sprinkle with chopped parsley or dill.

Yield: About 2 quarts

POULTRY

Chicken

Alexandre Dumaine's Coq au Vin

4 pounds chicken in pieces
3 cups dry red wine
½ cup dry white wine
¾ cup cognac
4 medium carrots, cut into thin rounds
2 medium onions, quartered
4–6 cloves garlic
2 sprigs parsley
2 bay leaves
2 sprigs fresh thyme or ½ teaspoon dried

½ cup olive oil
9 tablespoons butter
2 dozen small white onions
5 tablespoons flour
Salt
Pepper
1 cup chicken stock
2 ounces salt pork, diced and blanched
12 medium mushrooms, quartered

1. In a large bowl, combine chicken pieces with 2 cups red wine, ½ cup white wine, ½ cup cognac, carrots, onions, garlic, parsley, bay leaves, thyme, and olive oil. Marinate overnight at room temperature. Remove chicken from marinade, drain, and pat dry. Reserve the marinade.
2. Heat 4 tablespoons butter in a large heavy pot and sauté white onions until golden brown. Remove onions and reserve.
3. Cook chicken pieces in the same pot until they just begin to color. Keep pot covered. Sprinkle pieces with 2 tablespoons flour along with salt and pepper to taste, and cook 10 minutes more, still covered.
4. Heat remaining cognac until it begins to vaporize, pour over chicken, and ignite.
5. Strain marinade and reserve what remains in strainer (exception: discard garlic). Pour strained liquid over chicken along with chicken stock and all but 1 tablespoon of the remaining red wine.
6. Sauté reserved vegetables and herbs from marinade in 1 tablespoon butter and add to chicken.
7. Cook coq au vin slowly in a covered pot until done, 45 to 60 minutes.

8. Remove chicken pieces to another pot.
9. Push cooking liquid through a fine strainer into a clean saucepan. Degrease.
10. Combine 3 tablespoons butter and remaining 3 tablespoons flour to make a smooth paste. Bring degreased cooking liquid to a boil, lower heat, and whisk in the paste. Add the remaining tablespoon of red wine.
11. Correct seasoning.
12. Brown salt pork and mushrooms in remaining 1 tablespoon of butter. Add to sauce along with chicken and reserved white onions. Cook briefly until onions are done. Serve.

Yield: 6 servings

Mrs. Tiao's Anise Chicken

10 dried black Chinese mushrooms	5 dried red chilies
3 cups boiling water	1 tablespoon sugar
¼ cup dried tree ears	4 pieces star anise
4 scallions	6 tablespoons imported soy sauce
1½ pounds chicken breast	1 tablespoon sesame oil
3 tablespoons dry sherry	1 teaspoon salt
1 2-inch piece fresh ginger	(approximately)
4 tablespoons peanut oil	

1. Rinse off the mushrooms thoroughly, then put them in a bowl and pour 2 cups boiling water over them. Soak the mushrooms for about 20 minutes, or until they are soft. Cut off the hard stems and cut the larger mushrooms into 2 pieces. Reserve the water.
2. Put the tree ears in a small bowl, pour 1 cup boiling water over them, and let them soak for at least 10 minutes.
3. Cut 2 scallions into 2-inch lengths. Use both the green and white parts.
4. Pull the skin off the chicken, but leave the bones in. Chop the chicken with bones still attached into 2-inch cubes, roughly the size of a walnut.
5. Put the chicken in a shallow dish and add the cut-up scallions and 1 tablespoon of the sherry. Set it aside to marinate for 15 minutes.
6. Peel the ginger and cut it into 4 slices. When the tree

ears are soft and slightly gelatinous, rinse them thoroughly and pick over them carefully to remove any impurities, such as the tiny pieces of wood which may still be embedded in them.

7. Heat a wok or large skillet for about 15 seconds over moderate heat, then pour in the oil. It will be hot enough to cook in when small bubbles start to form and the first wisps of smoke appear.

8. Quickly throw in the ginger, red chilies, sugar, the remaining scallions tied together, and the chicken and its marinade. Stir up the ingredients while you are adding them. Continue to stir-fry for about 30 seconds.

9. Add the star anise, reduce the heat slightly, and continue to cook for about 5 more minutes until the chicken stiffens and turns white. Stir occasionally.

10. Add the remaining wine and the soy sauce, bring to a boil, and let the chicken continue to cook for 3 more minutes over a moderate flame.

11. Now add the mushrooms and the water in which they were soaked. Pour in enough additional water to barely cover the chicken. You will probably need about a cupful. Wait until the liquid boils, then lower the heat, cover the pan, and let the chicken simmer slowly for 1 hour.

12. After the chicken is very soft and the sauce reduced to almost half its original amount, add the soaked tree ears and let them cook with the chicken for about 5 more minutes.

13. Finally, add the sesame oil and stir thoroughly. Remove tied scallions and add salt to taste. Serve at room temperature.

Yield: 4 servings

Claudia Roden's Chicken Awsat

1 medium loaf bread with an attractive shape (rectangular or cottage)

1 medium chicken, boiled (reserve cooking liquid)

½ pound chicken livers Oil (originally sesame oil, but corn or nut will do well)

¼ teaspoon ground allspice

Salt

Pepper

¼ cup pistachio nuts, chopped

4 tablespoons finely chopped parsley

1 teaspoon dried crushed mint Juice of ½ lemon Sprigs of parsley and other fresh herbs

1. Cut a slice off the top of the loaf and put it aside to serve as a lid. Carefully remove the pith from the loaf, leaving the crust intact.
2. Bone and chop the cooked chicken.
3. Clean the chicken livers and sauté gently in a little oil for 3 to 4 minutes. Add about ⅓ cup of the chicken cooking liquid, and season to taste with allspice, salt, and pepper (a little brandy or sherry could be used instead of chicken stock).
4. Mash or pound liver mixture to a smooth paste, using an electric blender if you have one.
5. Mix the liver paste with the chopped chicken in a large bowl. Add pistachio nuts, parsley, mint, and lemon juice. Mix well and taste for seasoning, adding more salt and pepper if necessary. Knead the mixture vigorously until well blended, and add a little more chicken liquid if too dry.
6. Moisten the bread shell with chicken stock to make it soft and easy to cut. Fill the shell with chicken and liver mixture, packing it tightly. Cover with the lid, which has also been sprinkled with stock to soften it.
7. Chill in the refrigerator until ready to serve. Decorate with parsley and herbs. Serve cut in slices and accompanied by a light salad.

Yield: 8 to 10 slices

Poulet en Cocotte du Midi

2 tablespoons olive oil	1 clove garlic
5 slices bacon, diced	Bouquet garni (2 2-inch
12 small white onions, peeled	pieces celery, 3 sprigs
1 3½-pound chicken, cut into 8 pieces	parsley, and 1 bay leaf)
	Salt
5 carrots, halved	Pepper
4 medium tomatoes, peeled and seeded	3 cups red bordeaux wine
	2½ tablespoons cognac or
2 tablespoons tomato puree	armagnac

1. Heat the olive oil in a large, heavy stew pot and sauté together the bacon until brown and the onions until glazed.
2. Add the chicken pieces and sauté to a golden color.
3. Pour out excess oil.

4. Put into the pot (off the fire) the carrots, tomatoes, tomato puree, garlic, bouquet garni, salt and pepper to taste. Pour over these ingredients the wine and cognac. Cover tightly and cook for 1½ hours over low heat.

Yield: 4 servings

NOTE: *You can save time on the day of your dinner by doing the sautéing (through Step 3) the day before. Refrigerate the chicken overnight and just add the remaining ingredients the next day and cook.*

Chicken Cherubini

3 whole chicken breasts, boned, skinned, and halved
Brandy
Salt
White pepper
6 slices prosciutto
¼ cup grated parmesan cheese
¾ cup chopped parsley
½ cup blanched, slivered almonds
1 teaspoon finely chopped black truffles (optional)
4 tablespoons butter
½ cup dry white wine or white vermouth
⅓ cup chicken stock

1. Wash and dry the chicken thoroughly. Cut a pocket in each breast by enlarging the area under the small flap on the underside.
2. Brush the pocket with brandy. Sprinkle pocket lightly with a very small amount of salt and pepper. Line pocket with a slice of prosciutto. Repeat this step with all 6 breast halves.
3. Combine cheese, parsley, almonds, and truffles. Stuff each lined pocket with 1 to 2 tablespoons of this mixture. (Any leftover stuffing can be used as an omelet filling.)
4. Carefully seal each pocket with the back of a knife. The chicken will adhere to itself.
5. Heat the butter in a large skillet. Sauté the breasts 8 to 10 minutes per side, or until golden brown. Add white wine, bring to a boil, then reduce to a simmer, cover and cook for 10 to 15 minutes.
6. When breasts have reached desired degree of doneness, remove to serving platter. Add stock to skillet and, when hot, pour contents of skillet over the chicken. Serve with rice and sautéed mushrooms.

Yield: 4 to 6 servings

Chicken Mao Tse-tung

4 whole chicken breasts,
 halved
 Salt
¾ cup peanut oil
8 scallions, chopped
12 thin slices fresh ginger
3 cloves garlic, crushed
1 teaspoon monosodium
 glutamate (optional)
12 tablespoons imported soy
 sauce
½ cup honey
1 teaspoon brown Szechuan

peppercorns, slightly
 crushed
1½ cups hot water
¾ teaspoon crushed red
 pepper
1 tablespoon brandy
3 tablespoons cornstarch
6 drops oil of orange
 Juice of ½ lemon
1 head boston lettuce
 Peel of 1 orange, grated
1 bunch watercress

1. Put chicken breasts into boiling salted water to cover and cook
 for 15 minutes.
2. Turn off flame and let chicken breasts cool in cooking water
 for at least 20 minutes. Then remove from pot and set aside to
 cool further.
3. Combine peanut oil, scallions, ginger slices, garlic, and
 monosodium glutamate with chicken breasts in a skillet and let
 marinate for 20 minutes.
4. Sauté contents of skillet over a very low flame for 5 minutes.
 Remove from flame. Set aside chicken breasts and reserve
 cooking liquid.
5. Combine soy sauce, honey, Szechuan peppercorns, hot water,
 red pepper, brandy, cornstarch, 1 teaspoon salt, oil of orange, and
 lemon juice in a bowl and mix well. Add this mixture to cooking
 liquid in skillet and cook over low heat until it thickens to a
 light syrup.
6. Pour thickened sauce over chicken breasts and let marinate
 overnight.
7. Before serving, drain chicken breasts, reserving sauce, and
 arrange them on a bed of lettuce leaves. Garnish with grated
 orange peel and watercress.
8. At the table, pour sauce over each individual portion.

Yield: 4 servings

Chicken with Olives

4 tablespoons butter
1 2–2¼-pound chicken, cut into pieces
2 tablespoons flour
  Bouquet garni (1 bay leaf, 2 sprigs parsley, and 1 sprig fresh thyme
  or ¼ teaspoon dried)
  Salt
  Pepper
¼ cup dry sherry
5 ounces (approximately) black olives, pitted and halved (see note)

1. Melt butter over low to moderate heat until foamy.
2. Brown chicken pieces in butter.
3. Remove chicken from pan and reserve.
4. With butter remaining in pan, make a roux: Add flour over low
   heat, stirring constantly until roux turns nut brown.
5. Add bouquet garni, 2 cups water, salt and pepper to taste
   and 2 tablespoons sherry to roux. Cook 20 minutes over low heat.
   Put chicken pieces back into pan and cook until done (when
   juices from a leg piece run clear when it is pierced with a fork).
6. Remove chicken pieces, arrange on serving plate, and, if sauce
   has not reduced to desired consistency, keep chicken warm in low
   oven while you reduce sauce further. Finish sauce with the
   remaining sherry.
7. Add olives to sauce and leave on fire long enough to warm them.
   Remove bouquet garni and discard.
8. Pour sauce over chicken pieces and serve.

Yield: 3 to 4 servings

NOTE: *Olive sizes vary, but fairly small ones are most appropriate
for this recipe.*

Chicken Rosen

6 tablespoons butter
1 2–2½-pound chicken,
   quartered
   Salt
   Black pepper
¼ teaspoon dried thyme
⅛ teaspoon dried rosemary
1 bay leaf, crumbled
1 stalk celery, chopped
1 onion, diced
1 carrot, sliced

2 cups dry white wine
   (approximately)
2 cups chicken stock
   (approximately)
2 egg yolks
½ cup heavy cream
   Juice of ½ lemon
⅛ teaspoon white pepper
½ teaspoon dried tarragon
1 cup mushrooms, sliced
¼ cup chopped parsley

1. Preheat oven to 350 degrees.
2. In a skillet, in 3 tablespoons of melted butter, brown chicken
   pieces lightly.
3. Season chicken with salt, black pepper, thyme, and rosemary.
   Put in ovenproof casserole. Add bay leaf, celery, onion, and carrot.
   Cover contents of casserole with wine and stock in roughly equal
   proportions and bring mixture to a slow simmer on top of the
   stove. Cover and put in oven. Reduce heat if liquid begins to boil
   and cook for about 30 minutes or until done.
4. Remove from oven, pick out chicken pieces, drain, and set on
   a heatproof platter in a warming oven.
5. Skim surface fat off cooking liquid, strain, and reserve.
   Discard vegetables.
6. In a heavy saucepan, beat egg yolks together with cream and
   drip half cooking liquid into mixture, stirring well. Keep stirring
   over low heat until mixture coats a spoon. Add rest of cooking
   liquid, lemon juice, white pepper, and tarragon. Reduce by ¼
   and turn heat down as low as possible.
7. Sauté mushrooms in remaining butter.
8. Remove chicken from oven. Arrange on a small platter.
   Spoon sauce over chicken pieces. Decorate with mushrooms
   and parsley. Serve.

Yield: 2 to 3 servings

Fried Chicken

1½ cups flour
2 teaspoons salt
½ teaspoon pepper
1 2½-pound chicken, in pieces
2 cups buttermilk
1 teaspoon baking soda
Shortening for deep frying

1. Combine and sift flour, salt, and pepper.
2. Roll chicken in seasoned flour, then in combined buttermilk and soda, and again in flour.
3. Deep fry in shortening at 350 degrees for 15 to 20 minutes or until golden brown. Drain on absorbent paper.

Yield: 3 to 4 servings

Salem Fried Chicken

1 2½-pound chicken, in pieces
⅛ teaspoon cayenne
¼ teaspoon pepper
1 teaspoon ground ginger
½ teaspoon ground coriander (optional)
1 clove garlic, grated or mashed
Salt
Fine bread or cracker crumbs
2 eggs, beaten lightly with 3 tablespoons water
Fat for deep frying

1. Skin chicken pieces. Combine spices and grated garlic. Rub this mixture into each piece of chicken thoroughly with fingers. Sprinkle lightly with salt.
2. Place chicken in frying pan and add about ¼ cup water or enough to cover bottom of pan. Cover tightly and simmer gently about 30 minutes or until tender. Remove cover last 10 minutes to cook juices in pan down to almost nothing.

3. Roll each piece of chicken in crumbs. Dip one or two pieces at a time into egg mixture. Then drop immediately into hot deep fat (380 degrees) and dribble an extra handful of the egg mixture on top of each piece. Fry until golden brown—1 to 2 minutes. Put on paper to drain and keep warm until serving time.

Yield: 3 to 4 servings

Chicken à la Romana

1 2–2½-pound chicken, quartered	½ clove garlic, minced
Flour	1½ teaspoons salt
½ cup oil	Pepper
2 tablespoons butter	½ cup dry white wine
1½ teaspoons dried rosemary	1 teaspoon white vinegar
	½ cup chicken stock

1. Preheat oven to 350 degrees.
2. Dredge chicken with flour and sauté slowly in oil and butter until lightly browned.
3. Add rosemary, garlic, salt and pepper to taste. Continue sautéing until chicken is golden brown.
4. Add wine, vinegar, and chicken stock. Cover and bake until tender, about 20 minutes.

Yield: 3 to 4 servings

NOTE: *Chicken may be simmered on top of stove until tender.*

Kievsky Cutlet

3 large chicken breasts with wings attached
  Salt
  Pepper
½ pound unsalted butter
  Flour
2 eggs
  Fine dry bread crumbs
  Butter for frying

1. Halve each chicken breast along sides of keel bone and remove meat along with wing. Using a cleaver, chop off lower part of wing, leaving only a stump of wing bone and meat attached to the breast. Remove skin. Make tiny shallow cuts into meat but not through it and flatten out the meat. Scrape meat from wing stump onto the breast. Pound flesh with a meat mallet to make it quite thin. Sprinkle lightly with salt and pepper.
2. Make 6 rolls of butter about 2 inches long and ½ inch in diameter. Chill in ice water until hard.
3. Preheat oven to 400 degrees.
4. Place a roll of butter on each chicken breast, wrap meat around it, and skewer with picks.
5. Moisten with water, coat with flour, dip in eggs, which have been beaten until blended but not foamy and mixed with 2 tablespoons water. Roll in crumbs.
6. Fry in butter over moderate heat until golden brown, turning often, and bake for 5 minutes.

Yield: 6 servings

Breast of Chicken Versailles

4 Idaho baking potatoes
20 large mushrooms
11 tablespoons butter (approximately)
Salt
Pepper
⅔ cup sifted bread crumbs

2½ tablespoons grated parmesan cheese
2 whole chicken breasts, skinned and halved
Flour
1 egg, lightly beaten with 2 tablespoons water

1. Preheat oven to 350 degrees.
2. Cut potatoes into julienne strips. Slice mushrooms through stems.
3. Heat 3 tablespoons butter in a 9-inch skillet with heatproof handle. Add potatoes and about ⅔ of the mushrooms. Sprinkle lightly with salt and pepper and brown lightly, turning to brown second side. To do this, turn potatoes onto a plate anl then slide them back into the pan.
4. When lightly browned on both sides, transfer to oven and bake until potatoes are well browned and tender.
5. Combine bread crumbs and cheese.
6. Coat chicken breasts with flour, next with egg, and then with

crumbs. In 6 tablespoons of the remaining butter, brown chicken slowly in a second skillet.
7. Turn potato mixture out on serving plate. Put chicken on top.
8. Add remaining 2 tablespoons butter to pan and quickly brown remaining mushrooms. Pour mushrooms over chicken.

Yield: 4 servings

Pollo al Forno con Uva
(Chicken in Wine With Grapes)

2 2–2½-pound chickens, quartered, with giblets
2 tablespoons butter
2 cups dry white wine
   Salt
2 bay leaves
8 cloves
1 cup seedless white grapes, stemmed and washed
½ cup chicken stock (approximately)

1. Preheat oven to 350 degrees.
2. Dry chicken pieces and giblets thoroughly. Sauté in the butter until brown. Place in baking pan. Pour butter over chicken. Salt slightly. Add 1 cup of wine. Place bay leaves and cloves in pan.
3. Place in oven. After 30 minutes of cooking, add grapes to pan. Keep basting with remaining wine and the chicken stock. Bake another 30 minutes after introducing grapes. If wine evaporates too rapidly, lower heat and add some extra chicken stock.

Yield: 6 servings

Poulet Haitien

1 2½–3-pound chicken, in
   pieces for frying
   Flour
   Salt
   Pepper
5 tablespoons butter
1 medium onion, diced

1 green pepper, diced
½ teaspoon curry powder
   Pinch saffron
½ teaspoon paprika
¼ teaspoon sugar
   Grated meat from 1 fresh
   coconut

1. Dredge chicken in flour seasoned with salt and pepper.
2. Melt 4 tablespoons butter in a heavy skillet and, when hot, add chicken pieces. Cook and turn chicken until it is evenly browned.
3. In second skillet, melt 1 tablespoon of butter, add onion, and sauté until golden. Add green pepper, curry powder, saffron, paprika, and sugar. Add chicken, cover pan, and cook 10 minutes.
4. While chicken is cooking, heat the grated coconut in pan with 2 cups of water for 2 minutes. With a wooden spoon, press down on coconut to release the juice. Discard pressed flesh. When chicken has cooked 10 minutes, strain coconut water over it. Cover and continue cooking until chicken is tender—20 to 30 minutes.

Yield: 4 servings

Salad Olevear

4 cups diced potatoes
2 cups diced apples
1 cucumber, diced
2 cups diced celery
½ cup capers, drained
¼ cup diced and blanched green and red peppers
2 cups chopped cooked chicken or lobster meat
Fresh dill, cut into ¼-inch lengths (discard stems)

1 cup sour cream
1 cup mayonnaise
¼ cup lemon juice
Salt
Pepper
1 cup canned tiny green peas
Boston lettuce
Hard-boiled eggs, sliced or deviled

1. Cook potatoes in a small amount of boiling, salted water until just tender. Drain, wash to remove starch, and set aside in colander to dry.
2. Mix potatoes with apples, cucumber, celery, capers, peppers, chicken or lobster, and some of the dill.
3. Make a dressing by mixing together the sour cream, mayonnaise, and lemon juice. Season to taste with salt and pepper.
4. Carefully mix the salad dressing with the vegetables and chicken or lobster. Fold in peas so as not to crush them. Pile in salad bowl on leaves of boston lettuce and garnish with eggs and remaining dill.

Yield: 6 to 8 servings

Turkey

Braised Young Turkey

  1 3–5-pound turkey (ready-to-cook weight), cut into serving pieces
  1 onion, sliced
  1 stalk celery with leaves
½ carrot, sliced
    Salt
    Pepper
½ cup flour
    Shortening

1. Simmer neck, bony rib sections, heart, gizzard, and liver in water to barely cover with onion, celery, carrot, salt and pepper to taste until tender. Remove turkey and strain broth for use in gravy. Skim fat from broth.
2. If turkey breast is in one piece, cut it in half, lengthwise. Shake pieces in a paper bag in seasoned flour (½ cup flour, 2 teaspoons salt, ¼ teaspoon pepper).
3. Heat enough shortening in a large, heavy frying pan to make a layer ¼ inch deep. Or use 2 pans, so all the turkey can be browned at once. Brown the pieces over moderate heat, turning to brown all sides. This will take about 20 minutes.
4. If only 1 pan is used, remove pieces to a platter as they brown. If 2 pans are employed, place all the browned turkey in 1 pan. Strain off fat from emptied pan and return all browned particles in sieve to pan with turkey. Turn the heat low, add 1 tablespoon water and cover. If cover fits very tightly, no water will be needed. Cook until tender, about 20 minutes for small turkeys or 50 minutes for 4- to 5-pound birds.
5. Turn pieces occasionally for even cooking. Remove cover for last 10 minutes of cooking so skin will be crisp. Serve with milk gravy.

Yield: ¾ to 1 pound per person

MILK GRAVY

To make gravy, simmer drippings in pan, after turkey has been
removed, until water has evaporated. If necessary, add enough
fat to make 6 tablespoons. Add 6 tablespoons flour and
cook, stirring, until mixture is a dark golden brown, scraping
loose all browned particles in pan. Add 2½ cups reserved broth
and ½ cup milk or cream. Cook, stirring, until thickened. For
giblet gravy, add the finely chopped, sautéed liver and gizzard.

Yield: 3 cups

Juanita Kirk Lynch's Chestnut Turkey Stuffing

6 cups (about 3 pounds) chestnuts
1 tablespoon oil
4 cups chicken stock
2 tablespoons butter
2 cups cracker crumbs
  Salt
  Pepper
¾ cup heavy cream (approximately)

1. Cut gashes on the flat side of each chestnut. Heat the oil in
   a skillet and add the chestnuts. Cook over brisk heat for about
   3 minutes, stirring constantly. Remove chestnuts to paper towel.
2. When just cool enough to handle, remove the shells and inner skins.
   Place chestnuts in a saucepan with the stock, bring to a boil,
   cover, and simmer until very tender. Drain and discard broth.
3. Force chestnuts through a ricer or sieve and mix with remaining
   ingredients, using enough cream to give a moist consistency.

Yield: Enough for a 10-pound turkey

Satzive

1 large onion, minced
2 tablespoons lard or turkey fat
1½ cups (3 ounces) walnut halves
3½ tablespoons wine vinegar
¼ teaspoon salt
Pepper
2 cloves garlic, crushed
2 tablespoons chopped parsley

¼ teaspoon dried dill
⅛ teaspoon dried tarragon
2 tablespoons fresh coriander or Italian parsley (regular parsley may be substituted)
1½ cups roast turkey drippings with fat (approximately)
1½ pounds cold roast turkey, sliced or cut into serving pieces

1. Sauté onion slowly in fat until tender.
2. Grind walnuts, using fine knife or food mill.
3. Turn onion and walnuts into a wooden bowl and rub to a paste. Add all remaining ingredients except turkey, using enough water to make a smooth sauce the consistency of soft mayonnaise. Mash and mix thoroughly. Serve over turkey.

Yield: 2¾ cups sauce

Duck and Goose

Fricassee de Volaille

1 4-pound duck, cut into serving pieces	1 teaspoon tomato paste
2 heads garlic, unpeeled	2 cups chicken stock
6 tablespoons unsalted butter	3 cups veal stock (see page 291)
1½ cups wine vinegar	Fresh tarragon (optional)
¾ cup tomato sauce	

1. Brown the duck pieces, turning occasionally, with the garlic heads, in 4 tablespoons butter, until crisp. Pour off all fat.
2. Deglaze the pan with ¾ cup vinegar, without removing duck pieces. Do not allow liquid to reduce more than slightly. Degrease liquid away from heat.
3. Deglaze again with another ¾ cup vinegar, reducing slightly.
4. Add tomato sauce, tomato paste, chicken stock, and veal stock. Reduce liquid by about ¼ over moderately high heat.
5. Remove pan from heat. Drain duck pieces into an ovenproof serving platter and reserve in a low oven.
6. Working quickly so that duck pieces do not dry out, put cooking liquid through a chinois or other very fine strainer, mashing garlic heads thoroughly. If sauce is too thin, reduce further in a clean pan.
7. Add remaining butter to sauce. Pour over duck pieces, sprinkle with a little tarragon, and serve.

Yield: 4 to 6 servings

Roast Stuffed Goose

1 6–9-pound goose
  Salt
  Pepper
8 cups stuffing (see page 117)
  Goose fat
3 cups chicken or goose stock
2 tablespoons flour

1. Preheat oven to 400 degrees.
2. Remove large pieces of fat from the cavity of the goose.
   Sprinkle the cavity of the goose with salt and pepper. Fill
   loosely with the stuffing. Use skewers to close the cavity, and
   tie the wings and drumsticks close to the body with string.
3. Rub the bird with one of the pieces of fat you removed from
   the cavity.
4. Place the goose in a roasting pan. Pour ½ cup water and ½ cup of
   stock over the goose and place in the oven. After 1 hour,
   reduce oven temperature to 300 degrees. Baste about once every
   15 or 20 minutes. If necessary, add more liquid to the pan to
   keep the juices from burning. After a total of 2 hours of cooking,
   the goose should be done. Test to see if the juices in the
   drumstick run clear.
5. Remove the goose to a serving platter. Skim all but 2 tablespoons
   of the fat from the roasting pan. Discard it, or save for other
   cooking. Add the 2 tablespoons of flour to the roasting pan.
   Over medium heat on the stove top, brown and stir flour
   with the goose drippings. When the flour is browned, but not
   burned, add the remaining stock. Stir quickly with a wooden spoon
   or whisk to eliminate lumps. Cook over high heat until reduced
   to desired consistency. Taste for seasoning and correct. Strain
   into a sauceboat, and serve with the goose.

Yield: 6 servings

NOTE: *Fresh goose must usually be ordered in advance. A bird that
weighs more than 10 pounds should not be prepared in this manner.
It will be dry and tough.*

Stuffing a L'Anglaise for Goose

1 pound onions, unpeeled
Beef stock
1 pound bread crumbs, soaked in milk and pressed dry
¾ teaspoon salt
1 tablespoon dried sage
¼ teaspoon pepper
¼ teaspoon grated nutmeg

1. Preheat oven to 350 degrees.
2. Place onions in a buttered ovenproof pan and fill with beef stock to a depth of ½ inch. Bake for 1 hour or until onions can be easily penetrated by a fork.
3. Remove onions from oven, drain, and cool.
4. Peel onions. Chop finely and combine with other ingredients. Now stuff your bird.

Yield: 4 cups

NOTE: *If this stuffing is used, serve goose with applesauce on the side.*

Farce de Marrons
(Chestnut Stuffing For Goose)

1 small white onion, minced
1 tablespoon unsalted butter
½ pound pork sausage
1½ pounds chestnuts, shelled
   (if canned, use imported
   and drain)
3 tablespoons cognac

¼ teaspoon dried thyme
¼ teaspoon dried marjoram
½ teaspoon salt
¼ teaspoon pepper
½ cup bread crumbs
2 tablespoons chicken stock

1. Sauté the minced onion in the butter until lightly browned.
2. Add the sausage and cook for 5 minutes, stirring constantly. Discard the fat rendered by the sausage.
3. In a large bowl, combine the sausage and onions with the chestnuts, cognac, thyme, marjoram, salt, pepper, bread crumbs, and stock. Mix well. Try not to mash the chestnuts. They should be coarsely broken.
4. Taste for seasoning and add more salt and pepper if necessary. Now stuff your bird.

Yield: 4 cups

Pheasant

Pheasant with Sour Cream

1 3½-pound pheasant
  Salt
  Pepper
5 tablespoons butter
1 onion, quartered
½ cup sour cream, at room temperature

1. Soak the pheasant (thawed, if it has been frozen) in cold salted water for about 30 minutes. Remove and pat dry with paper towels.
2. Cut into small serving pieces and season with salt and pepper to taste.
3. Heat the butter in a heavy skillet and sauté the pheasant and onion over medium heat, until they begin to brown. Cover the skillet tightly and simmer very gently until the pheasant is tender, about 20 minutes.
4. Remove pheasant pieces to a warm platter and keep warm. Boil the juices left in the skillet until they are slightly reduced.
5. Add a little of the hot liquid to the sour cream and mix well. Return to the bulk of the cooking liquid in the skillet.
6. Return the pheasant pieces to the sour cream sauce and reheat, but do not allow to boil.

Yield: 4 servings

Pheasant à la Basquaise

½ pound slab bacon
7 tablespoons butter (approximately)
1 2–2½-pound pheasant
Salt
White pepper
1 sheet fresh pork fat or 4–5 slices blanched bacon
1 onion, finely sliced
1 carrot, finely sliced
1 bouquet garni (1 stalk celery, 1 sprig parsley, 1 bay leaf, and 1 sprig thyme or ¼ teaspoon dried)
2 cloves garlic, peeled

½ cup beef stock
1½ cups raw rice
3 cups water or chicken stock
1 tablespoon olive oil
½ cup fresh red pepper, diced (if not available, use a good brand of pimientos)
1 teaspoon crushed hot red pepper (or a good imported paprika)
4 medium tomatoes, peeled, seeded, and chopped
1½ cups thinly sliced chorizo (optional)

1. Preheat oven to 375 degrees.
2. Remove the rind, and cut the bacon into 1-inch cubes. Drop the cubes into simmering water and cook for 5 minutes and drain.
3. In a large casserole, sauté the bacon cubes in 2 tablespoons of the butter until lightly browned. Remove the bacon and reserve.
4. In the same fat, brown the pheasant, seasoned with salt and pepper, on all sides.
5. Remove the bird from the casserole and wrap in the sheet of fresh pork fat or the blanched bacon slices. If the butter in the casserole is burned, discard it and add 3 tablespoons fresh butter.
6. Sauté the sliced onion and carrot for 2 or 3 minutes.
7. Add the pheasant, bacon cubes, bouquet garni, garlic, and beef stock. Cover the casserole and place in oven. Braise the pheasant for 50 minutes or until tender.
8. While the bird is cooking, prepare the rice. Melt 2 tablespoons butter in a saucepan, add the rice and stir to cover it well with butter; add 3 cups water or chicken stock; bring to a boil, and lower the heat.
9. Simmer the rice covered for 20 to 25 minutes.
10. While the rice is cooking, heat olive oil in a skillet and add the red pepper, the crushed hot pepper, and the tomatoes. Cook mixture until it is a thick puree. Season with salt and white pepper to taste.
11. When the rice is tender, add the tomato puree together with the sliced chorizo.

12. Cover the rice and put in the oven for another 10 minutes.
13. Pour the rice onto a serving platter. Top the rice with the whole roast pheasant or carve the bird in two. Surround the pheasant with the cubed bacon.
14. Strain the cooking liquid and skim the fat. Boil sauce, uncovered, to reduce it by ⅓ and spoon over the pheasant and serve.

Yield: 4 servings

NOTE: *The chorizo can also be added to the casserole for the last 15 minutes of cooking instead of being added to the rice.*

Ed Giobbi's Fagiano al Modo Mio
(Pheasant My Way)

1 fat 3½-pound pheasant	¾ cup chopped prosciutto
½ cup (¾ ounce) dried Italian mushrooms, or 1 cup sliced mushrooms	⅔ cup dry white wine
	1 teaspoon dried rosemary
3 tablespoons olive oil	1 tablespoon chopped fresh mint or ½ teaspoon dried
3 cloves garlic	⅔ cup peeled and chopped fresh tomatoes, or drained, canned Italian plum tomatoes
2 bay leaves	
Salt	
Pepper	
½ cup finely chopped onion	

1. Soak the pheasant in cold salted water for 2 hours. Drain and pat dry. Cut into serving pieces.
2. If dried mushrooms are used, cover them with warm water and let soak 15 minutes. Drain.
3. Heat the olive oil in a heavy skillet and sauté the pheasant pieces over medium heat, stirring often. Add garlic, bay leaves, salt and pepper to taste and continue cooking and stirring occasionally until pheasant begins to brown.
4. Stir in the onion, prosciutto, and mushrooms. Cook, stirring, until the onion wilts. Add the wine, rosemary, and mint. Cover and simmer over low heat for 7 minutes.
5. Add tomatoes, cover skillet, and continue to simmer until the pheasant is tender, 20 to 30 minutes. Remove and discard the garlic cloves.

Yield: 4 to 6 servings

FISH AND SHELLFISH

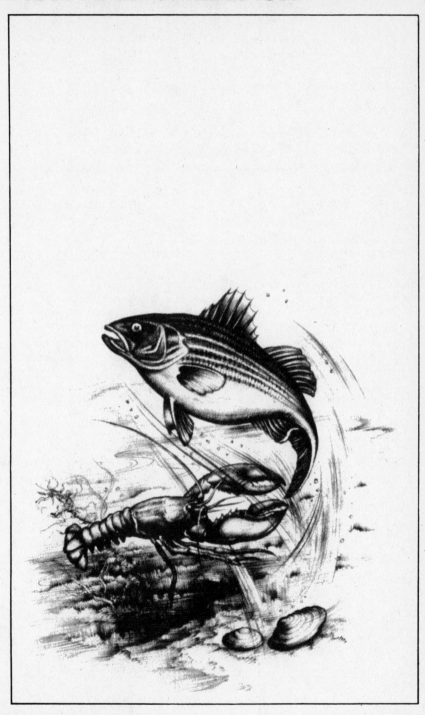

Pesci Sott'Aceto
(Marinated Fish)

2 pounds smelts, or fresh
  sardines, washed and dried, or
  2 10–12-inch mackerels, bone
  in, cleaned, quartered lengthwise, and well dried
Oil
Salt

Pepper
1 medium onion, sliced
1 stalk celery, sliced
2 cloves garlic
2 whole cloves
3 cups white vinegar
1 cup dry white wine

1. Fry the fish until golden in 1½ inches oil heated to 365 degrees. Drain on paper towels. Arrange in a deep plate and add salt and pepper to taste.
2. For the marinade: Heat ½ cup of the oil used in frying the fish in a skillet. Sauté the onion, celery, garlic, and cloves in the oil unt the onion begins to turn yellow. Add vinegar and wine and simmer, covered, for 30 minutes.
3. Pour hot marinade over the fish. Refrigerate at least 48 hours befor serving. Remove bones from mackerel.

Yield: 6 servings

Jamaican Escoveitch Fish

2 pounds any fresh fish
1 egg beaten with a little milk
  Bread crumbs to which salt and pepper have been added
  Fat for deep frying
⅔ cup white vinegar
½ teaspoon peppercorns
1½ cups thinly sliced onion

123

1. Cut fish into serving pieces, wash, and dry. Dip in the egg-milk mixture and then in crumbs. Fry in deep fat (375 degrees) until crisp and brown. Drain on absorbent paper.
2. Heat vinegar, peppercorns, and onion to boiling.
3. Place fish on a platter and cover with the onion-vinegar mixture. Serve hot or cold.

Yield: 4 servings

Escabeche

4–12 small fish (mackerel, smelts, butterfish, or whiting)	1 tablespoon chopped parsley
½ cup olive oil	1 tablespoon paprika
4 large onions	Oregano
1 green pepper, seeded and chopped	½ cup dry white wine
1 medium tomato, peeled and diced	2 tablespoons white wine vinegar
	Salt

1. Brush fish with some of the olive oil and broil, turning once, until well done. Place on a platter.
2. Slice onions, remove outer perfect rings, place in a colander, and rinse well with boiling water to remove the "bite." Arrange slices over the broiled fish. Chop remaining onion centers.
3. Sauté chopped onion and green pepper in remaining olive oil until well browned, stirring often.
4. Add tomato, parsley, paprika, oregano, wine, vinegar, and salt. Blend well and pour over sliced onions and fish. Serve hot or cold.

Yield: 4 servings

Crabmeat Mousse

2 envelopes (tablespoons)
 unflavored gelatin
½ cup mayonnaise
¼ cup lime juice
¼ cup lemon juice
2 tablespoons chopped parsley
2 tablespoons chopped chives
2 tablespoons prepared
 mustard
 Salt
 Pepper

4 cups flaked, picked over,
 and cooked backfin
 crabmeat (about 1⅓
 pounds)
1½ cups heavy cream
1 lime, thinly sliced
 Salad greens
2 ripe avocados, peeled,
 pitted, and mashed
 Lime juice
 Chopped chives

1. Soften the gelatin in 6 tablespoons cold water in a heatproof bowl.
   Heat over hot water, stirring, to dissolve the gelatin.
2. Mix the dissolved gelatin with the mayonnaise, lime juice,
   lemon juice, parsley, chives, mustard, and salt and pepper
   to taste.
3. Fold in the crabmeat and cream. Pour into a buttered 6-cup
   ring mold and chill until firm, about 3 hours.
4. Unmold onto a chilled platter and garnish edges with salad
   greens and lime slices. Mix the avocado with lime juice to taste
   and pile into the center hole. Garnish with chopped chives.

Yield: 6 servings

Crab Cakes Baltimore

1 pound fresh crabmeat
1 teaspoon salt
 Pepper
1 teaspoon dry mustard
2 teaspoons worcestershire sauce
1 egg yolk

1 tablespoon mayonnaise
1 teaspoon chopped parsley
 Flour
1 egg, lightly beaten
 Sifted bread crumbs
 Butter

1. Mix thoroughly the crabmeat, salt, pepper, mustard, worcestershire, egg yolk, mayonnaise, and parsley. Shape into 4 cakes,
   pressing hard so ingredients will adhere.
2. Coat with flour, then with egg, and finally with the crumbs.
3. Fry in hot shallow butter, turning to brown both sides.

Yield: 4 servings

Lobster Cantonese Chinese-Style

¼ cup peanut oil
¼ teaspoon chopped garlic
1 teaspoon Chinese salted
  black beans, mashed into
  a paste
¼ pound ground pork
1 1¼-pound live lobster, cut
  into serving pieces
½ teaspoon salt
½ cup chicken stock
3–4 slices fresh ginger

⅛ teaspoon monosodium
  glutamate (optional)
¼ teaspoon sesame oil
⅛ teaspoon imported dark
  soy sauce
1–2 scallions, sliced
1 teaspoon cornstarch
  dissolved in 1 tablespoon
  water
1 egg, beaten

1. Heat oil in a wok or skillet and add garlic and black beans.
   Add pork and stir-fry about 30 seconds to a minute to separate
   meat. Then add lobster and salt and stir-fry about 30 seconds.
2. Add chicken stock and ginger slices. Cover and cook for about
   4 minutes. Add monosodium glutamate, sesame oil, soy sauce,
   scallions, and dissolved cornstarch. When sauce is thickened
   and begins to bubble, add egg on top of dish on the side of the
   wok farthest from you. Do not stir. Cook 30 seconds. Tip
   onto a warm serving platter, starting from front of wok
   so that egg ends up on top of the dish when served.

Yield: 2 servings

Lobster Cantonese American-Style

¼ cup peanut oil
½ teaspoon chopped garlic
¼ pound ground pork
1 1¼-pound live lobster, cut
  into serving pieces
½ teaspoon salt
1½ cups chicken stock

⅛ teaspoon monosodium
  glutamate (optional)
Few drops sesame oil
3 teaspoons cornstarch
  dissolved in 3 tablespoons
  water
1 egg, beaten

1. Heat oil in a wok or skillet and add garlic. Add pork and
   stir-fry about 30 seconds to a minute to separate meat. Add
   lobster and salt and stir-fry about 30 seconds.
2. Add chicken stock. Cover and let cook about 4 minutes. Add
   the monosodium glutamate, sesame oil, and dissolved cornstarch.
   When the sauce is thickened and starts to bubble, add egg on top
   of dish on the side of the wok farthest from you. Do not stir.

Cook 30 seconds. Tip onto a warm serving platter, starting
from front of wok so that egg ends up on top of dish when served.

Yield: 2 servings

NOTE: *This recipe looks much like the preceding one, but isn't at all.
To my taste, the Chinese version has far more verve. Both kinds are
served in the same New York restaurant.*

Homard au Porto

2 1½–2-pound live lobsters
⅓ cup olive oil
1 very ripe medium tomato,
    peeled and diced
1 tablespoon tomato paste
3 shallots, minced
3 cloves garlic, chopped
⅓ cup dry white wine
    Salt
    Pepper
    Cayenne
8½ tablespoons unsalted butter,
    softened

1 tablespoon chopped fresh
    chervil or 1 teaspoon
    dried
1 tablespoon chopped parsley
1 tablespoon chopped fresh
    tarragon or 1 teaspoon dried
1 teaspoon cornstarch
    dissolved in 1 tablespoon
    water
⅓ cup heavy cream
⅓ cup port
3 tablespoons brandy

1. Plunge live lobsters head first into a large pot of boiling water.
   Cover, let return to a boil, and cook for 10 to 12 minutes. Remove
   from water and let cool.
2. Twist off tails. Remove sand sac near head, and discard.
   Scrape out green tomalley and reserve. Twist off claws, crack,
   and remove meat. Remove meat from tail, cut in pieces.
   Reserve tail shells. Cut out white undershell completely and
   discard.
3. Heat oil in a saucepan. Add to it tomato, tomato paste, shallots,
   and garlic. Simmer for 5 minutes. Add white wine, and salt,
   pepper, and cayenne to taste, cover and simmer for 20 minutes.
4. Cream butter with tomalley (if any), chervil, parsley, and
   tarragon. Add this paste to the sauce and simmer, covered, another
   5 minutes. Push sauce through a fine strainer. Reheat sauce and
   thicken slightly with dissolved cornstarch. Add lobster meat,
   cream, port, brandy, and simmer for 5 minutes. Spoon into tail
   shells and serve.

Yield: 4 servings

Lobster Constellation

2 1-pound rock lobster tails or
4 fresh chicken lobsters,
cooked in salted water
1½ cups chopped celery
Mayonnaise
½ cup dry white wine
12 mussels, debearded and
scrubbed

12 clams, scrubbed
1½ tablespoons flour
¼ cup chopped mushrooms
¼ teaspoon curry powder or
dash Tabasco
Lemon wedges

1. Remove lobster meat from shells and line shells with celery
   mixed with ⅓ cup mayonnaise. Cube lobster meat and pile on top of
   celery. Chill.
2. To a pint of the water in which lobster was cooked, add the
   white wine. Bring to a boil; add the mussels and clams and simmer
   until shells open. Remove meat and place on half shells. Chill.
3. Strain broth and boil until reduced to 1 cup.
4. Blend flour with a little cold water, add to broth, and cook,
   stirring until thickened. Add mushrooms and cook about 1 minute.
   Stir in 2 tablespoons mayonnaise. Flavor with curry or Tabasco.
   Chill.
5. Arrange filled lobster shells on a chilled platter, garnish with
   mayonnaise. Put mussels and clams in their half shells around
   the lobster, dressing each with the mushroom sauce. Serve
   with lemon wedges and additional mayonnaise.

Yield: 4 servings

Linguine with White Clam Sauce

36 littleneck clams, scrubbed
¼ cup dry white wine
4–6 cloves garlic, finely minced
¼ cup olive oil
½ teaspoon pepper
1 tablespoon oregano

3 tablespoons minced fresh
basil or 1 tablespoon dried
1 pound linguine
3 tablespoons minced fresh
parsley or 1 tablespoon
dried

1. Steam clams in wine until they open. Remove meat, set aside,
   and keep warm.
2. Strain cooking broth and reserve.

3. Bring 4 quarts of water to a boil for linguine.
4. In a large skillet, cook garlic in oil over low flame until golden.
5. Add pepper, oregano, and basil. Stir contents of skillet and add clam broth. Turn up heat and bring to a boil.
6. Lower flame under skillet and simmer while linguine cooks.
7. Put linguine in boiling water and cook according to package directions.
8. Five minutes before linguine is done, add clams to simmering clam broth.
9. Drain cooked linguine, empty into a large serving dish, and cover with clam sauce.
10. Toss contents of serving dish well, sprinkle lightly with minced parsley, and serve as soon as possible.

Yield: 4 servings

Shang Hop Lai Chin
(Clams in Sweet-Sour Sauce)

3 dozen clams, scrubbed	½ cup sugar
1 clove garlic, chopped	½ cup white vinegar
2 tablespoons peanut oil	3 tablespoons dry sherry
1 teaspoon salt	¼ cup cornstarch
¼ cup imported soy sauce	2 cups water

1. Steam clams until they open. While clams are steaming, fry garlic until brown in peanut oil. Discard garlic when brown.
2. Place clams, still in shells, and broth in frying pan with oil used to brown garlic.
3. Mix remaining ingredients together and add to skillet and cook for 5 minutes before serving.

Yield: 3 servings

Moules Marinière

32–36 mussels, debearded	1 sprig fresh thyme or ⅛
¾ cup dry white wine	teaspoon dried
2 shallots, finely chopped	⅛ teaspoon pepper
3 sprigs parsley	2 tablespoons butter
½ bay leaf	Chopped parsley

1. Wearing rubber gloves to protect hands, scrub outside of mussel shells with a wire brush.
2. Steam mussels in wine, shallots, parsley sprigs, bay leaf, thyme, and pepper until they open.
3. Remove mussels and set aside.
4. Strain mussel cooking liquid through cheesecloth.
5. Return liquid to pan, add butter, and boil rapidly until reduced by half.
6. Arrange mussels in hot soup plates.
7. Pour the sauce over the mussels and sprinkle with chopped parsley. Serve hot with crusty French bread.

Yield: 4 servings

Chinese Eggplant with Shrimp

 2 cups plus ½ teaspoon peanut oil
 2 medium eggplants, peeled and sliced into ½-inch-thick vertical slices
 ½ pound medium shrimp, cleaned and finely chopped
 2 cloves garlic, minced
 1 tablespoon imported soy sauce
 ½ teaspoon sugar
 1 tablespoon hoisin sauce
 Salt

1. Heat 2 cups of oil in a wok or a skillet. Put eggplant slices into hot oil and sauté until brown and tender. Mash against sides of pan with a spatula.
2. Drain eggplant in a colander and press out as much residual oil as possible with spatula.
3. Transfer eggplant to a large, clean bowl and add shrimp, garlic, soy sauce, sugar, hoisin sauce, and salt to taste. Mix thoroughly.
4. Moisten wok with oil, return eggplant mixture to wok, and simmer ingredients in it over low flame for 2 minutes.

Yield: 4 to 5 servings

Lou's Szechuan Hot Spicy Shrimp

2 cups cleaned and shelled shrimp
⅛ teaspoon salt
1 tablespoon plus 1 teaspoon cooking wine (Chinese, sake, or dry sherry)
⅛ teaspoon pepper
1 egg
½ teaspoon cornstarch
2 cups plus ½ teaspoon peanut oil
1 teaspoon chili paste with garlic

1 teaspoon minced fresh ginger
1 cup chicken stock
2 tablespoons imported soy sauce
1 tablespoon sugar
1 tablespoon monosodium glutamate (optional)
½ cup tomato sauce
2 tablespoons cornstarch dissolved in 6 tablespoons water
1 cup chopped scallions
½ teaspoon rice vinegar

1. Mix well together shrimp, salt, 1 teaspoon wine, pepper, and egg. Add undissolved cornstarch. Mix again.
2. Heat 2 cups of oil in a wok or a skillet. Add shrimp when oil is hot but not smoking and stir-fry for about 15 seconds. Drain shrimp.
3. Discard oil, clean wok, and mix in it the chili paste with garlic, ginger, chicken stock, soy sauce, sugar, remaining wine, and monosodium glutamate.
4. Put wok over high heat until mixture bubbles. Then add tomato sauce, shrimp, dissolved cornstarch, scallions, ½ teaspoon oil, and vinegar.
5. Stir-fry for a few seconds, remove from wok, and serve.

Yield: 2 to 3 servings

Shrimp in White Wine Sauce

3 pounds cleaned shrimp
2 shallots or 1 small onion, sliced
1 cup dry white wine
1 cup clam juice
Salt

4 tablespoons butter
5 tablespoons flour
1–2 tablespoons finely chopped celery leaves
1 cup light cream
Chopped parsley

1. Combine in a saucepan shrimp, shallots, wine, clam juice, and salt to taste. Simmer until shrimp are tender, 5 to 10 minutes, depending on size. Drain; reserve liquid.
2. Melt butter over direct heat in top of a 3-quart double boiler. Blend in flour and reserved liquid. Bring to a boil, stirring constantly.
3. Set over simmering water. Add finely chopped celery leaves and cream. Add shrimp after first removing any sliced shallot or onion that may have stuck to them. Taste for seasoning. Leave for at least 20 minutes over the water. Sprinkle with parsley before serving.

Yield: 8 servings

Gumbo

2 tablespoons shortening	1 6-ounce can Italian tomato paste
2 pounds okra, sliced	
½ cup finely chopped celery	1 tablespoon flour
2 cloves garlic, chopped	1½ bay leaves
1 onion, finely chopped	2 tablespoons salt
½ green pepper, finely chopped	3 pounds shrimp, shelled and deveined

1. In a heavy kettle, heat the shortening. Add the okra and sauté it until it has passed the "gummy" or "ropy" stage.
2. Add celery, garlic, onion, green pepper, tomato paste, flour, bay leaves, salt, and 2 quarts water. Cook over low heat for about 2½ hours.
3. Add shrimp and cook 5 minutes. Serve gumbo with boiled rice.

Yield: About 6 servings

Shrimp Cooked in Court Bouillon

1 cup water (may be half dry white wine)
1 tablespoon vinegar (omit if wine is used)
1 stalk celery with leaves, chopped
1 scallion or small onion, chopped
1 bay leaf
1 teaspoon salt
  Dash cayenne or Tabasco
1 pound shrimp

1. Boil together for 10 minutes water and vinegar or water and wine, celery, scallion, and seasonings. Strain.
2. While stock is cooking, peel shrimp, remove sand veins, and wash.
3. Add shrimp to stock and simmer 5 minutes. Strain shrimp from stock and use for hot or cold appetizer. Reserve stock for use in fish sauces.

Yield: 3 or 4 servings

Shrimp Creole with Rice Kiskatom Farm

2 tablespoons butter
1 tablespoon flour
2 onions, finely chopped
2 pounds cleaned, deveined raw shrimp, fresh or frozen
1¼ cups canned tomatoes or 4 medium fresh tomatoes
1 cup water
½ teaspoon dried thyme

2 teaspoons parsley
1 bay leaf
½ teaspoon garlic salt
  Salt
  Pepper
1½ cups long-grained rice
1 quart vigorously boiling water seasoned with 1 teaspoon salt

1. Melt butter in a heavy, deep pot. Gradually work in the flour, and cook to a light brown. Add onions and sauté until golden. Mix in the shrimp thoroughly.
2. Lower heat. Add remaining ingredients except rice and boiling water, and cook, stirring frequently, about 25 minutes, or until shrimp are tender.
3. While shrimp simmer, prepare rice: Wash rice and pick clean of hulls (if any). Rinse 3 times in cold water.
4. To the boiling water, slowly add the rice; stir occasionally

with a fork as the grains cook. When they begin to soften, do not stir again. Continue to boil for 20 to 25 minutes, or until grains begin to swell and feel soft if pressed between the fingers.
5. Drain rice into a colander and rinse with cold water. Put colander over boiling water and let rice steam until dry.
6. Serve with shrimp.

Yield: 6 servings

Fresh Corn and Oyster Casserole

    3 cups (4 ears) fresh corn, cut from cob
 1¼ cups soft bread crumbs
    1 cup fresh or frozen oysters, drained
    1 egg, beaten
 1¼ teaspoons salt
    1 teaspoon whole celery seed
   ⅛ teaspoon pepper
    4 tablespoons butter

1. Preheat oven to 350 degrees. Grease a 1-quart casserole.
2. Combine corn, a ¼-cup of the crumbs, oysters, egg, salt, celery seed and pepper. Break 2 tablespoons butter into small pieces and add.
3. Turn the mixture into the casserole. Melt remaining butter, mix with remaining cup of crumbs, and sprinkle over top of casserole.
4. Bake in the preheated oven for 40 minutes or until crumbs are brown and corn is tender.

Yield: 4 servings

Coquilles St. Jacques

    1 pound scallops
    1 bay leaf
      Pinch dried thyme
      Salt
      Pepper
    3 tablespoons butter
    1 cup sliced mushrooms

    2 tablespoons minced onion
    3 tablespoons flour
   ½ cup heavy cream
    2 tablespoons dry sherry
   ⅓ cup buttered fine bread crumbs
   ⅓ cup grated parmesan cheese

1. Preheat oven to 400 degrees.
2. Place scallops in a saucepan. Add ¾ cup water, bay leaf, thyme, salt and pepper to taste. Bring to a boil, lower heat, and simmer, covered, 5 minutes. Drain scallops, reserving broth. Discard bay leaf.
3. Heat butter, add mushrooms and onion, and cook over low heat about 5 minutes. Blend in flour.
4. Measure 1 cup reserved broth and add to mushrooms. Add cream and cook, stirring, until thickened. Add scallops and sherry.
5. Fill scallop shells or ramekins with creamed mixture. Mix crumbs and cheese and sprinkle over filling. Bake until crumbs are brown—about 15 minutes.

Yield: 6 servings

Seafood à la Poulet

5 tablespoons butter	½ cup dry white wine
4 tablespoons flour	¾ cup heavy cream
2 cups milk, boiling	2 egg yolks
¾ teaspoon salt	½ teaspoon lemon juice
6 peppercorns	½ teaspoon chopped parsley
1 sprig parsley	1 pound crabmeat, cooked
6–8 mushrooms, sliced	2 dozen mussels, steamed
3 teaspoons finely chopped shallots or onion	1 pound shrimp, cooked
	1½ cups lobster meat, cooked

1. Make white sauce by melting 4 tablespoons of the butter in saucepan, add flour, mix well, and cook slowly until flour just starts to turn golden. Add milk, stirring. Add salt, peppercorns, and parsley sprig. Cook slowly, stirring, until thickened. Strain through fine sieve. Set aside.
2. Melt remaining butter in saucepan, add mushrooms, and cook until just turning brown. Add shallots and wine and cook until wine is reduced to almost nothing. Add ½ cup of the cream.
3. Cook until reduced to half original quantity and add the white sauce. Bring to a boil and add additional salt, if desired.
4. Mix egg yolks with remaining ¼ cup cream, combine with sauce, and bring back to boil. Add lemon juice and chopped parsley, then crabmeat, mussels, shrimp, and lobster.

Yield: 8 servings

Louie's Whiting Stew

1 medium onion, chopped
1 tablespoon chopped parsley
¼ teaspoon dried rosemary
6 tablespoons butter
4 pounds whiting, cleaned but not boned, cut into pieces
2 cups milk
Salt
Pepper

1. Brown onion, with parsley and rosemary, in the butter.
2. Add the fish, milk, and 2 cups water. Cook 25 minutes over medium heat. Season with salt and pepper. Serve with hot toast.

Yield: 6 to 8 servings

Martinican Red Snapper Blaff

1½ pounds red snapper fillets
  Juice of 1 lemon
3 cups dry white wine
  Salt
1 medium canned hot chili pepper, chopped
3 cloves garlic, minced
3 whole cloves
  Pepper
1 small onion, sliced
1 stalk celery
1 bay leaf
2 sprigs parsley
¼ teaspoon dried thyme

1. Have the fillets cut large enough to make 1 serving each. Marinate the pieces for 1 hour in refrigerator in a shallow glass dish in lemon juice, 1 cup wine, salt to taste, hot pepper, and 1 minced garlic clove.
2. Put 2 cups of water in a large pot. Add the whole cloves, remaining garlic, pepper, onion, and the celery, bay leaf, parsley, and thyme tied together in a muslin bag. Add the remaining wine. Bring to a boil and reduce by half to about 2 cups.
3. Remove muslin bag. Add the fish and its marinade, cover, and bring to a boil. Boil for another 3 to 5 minutes or until done. Serve the fish in the liquid to which more lemon juice may be added according to taste.

Yield: 6 servings

Eel Matelote with Raisins

8 tablespoons butter
4 white onions
2 carrots, quartered
2 cloves garlic
⅓ cup flour
3 cups red burgundy wine
2 tablespoons cognac
Bouquet garni (½ stalk celery, 2 sprigs parsley, 2 sprigs fresh thyme or ½ teaspoon dried, and 1 bay leaf)
1 whole clove
Salt

Pepper
3–4 pounds live eels, heads removed, cleaned, skinned, and cut into 2-inch lengths (there should be 1½–2 pounds of pan-ready fish) (see note)
½ pound mushrooms
2 tablespoons lemon juice
Boiling water
½ cup golden raisins
6 small triangles thin white bread, crusts removed

1. Melt 3 tablespoons of the butter in a heavy saucepan. Add the onions, carrots, garlic, and flour, and cook, stirring, over medium-low heat until the vegetables are coated with a deep golden brown layer of flour. This will take about 10 minutes. Do not allow the flour to burn, or it will be bitter.
2. Stir in 1 cup of water, wine, and cognac to make a smooth sauce. Add the bouquet garni, the clove, and salt and pepper to taste. Bring mixture to a boil, cover, and simmer 45 minutes. Stir occasionally.
3. Melt 3 tablespoons of butter in a skillet. Brown the eel pieces quickly on all sides. Remove the fish and keep warm. Reserve 6 whole mushrooms for garnish; chop or slice remaining mushrooms. Add chopped and whole mushrooms to butter remaining in the skillet. Add lemon juice. Sauté mushrooms 5 minutes.
4. Pour boiling water over raisins. Let stand 3 minutes and drain.
5. Strain the sauce into a clean saucepan. Add the eel, cover the pan, and cook gently 10 to 30 minutes or until the fish is opaque through and flakes easily. The exact time will depend on the diameter of the eels.
6. Fry the bread triangles in the remaining 2 tablespoons butter. Drain on paper towels.
7. Add the chopped mushrooms and raisins to strained sauce. Arrange the pieces of eel on a platter, spoon over some of the sauce, serve the remainder separately. Garnish the platter with the whole mushrooms and fried bread triangles.

Yield: 4 servings

NOTE: *Most fish markets will prepare the eel.*

Baked Fillets of Sole with Shrimp Sauce

¼ pound cooked shrimp
1¼ cups canned cream of
mushroom soup
2 tablespoons dry sherry
Salt
Pepper
½ onion, grated
4 tablespoons butter
Juice of ½ lemon
2 pounds sole fillets

1. Halve shrimp lengthwise. Combine in saucepan with soup, sherry, salt and pepper to taste.
2. Sauté onion in butter until transparent.
3. Preheat oven to 350 degrees.
4. Add sautéed onion with butter to saucepan, along with lemon juice.
5. In a buttered, shallow baking dish, arrange sole fillets side by side and bake in preheated oven for 10 to 15 minutes.
6. Just before fish is done, mix contents of saucepan while warming over a low flame, working out any lumps in the soup.
7. Remove fish from oven, pour sauce over fillets, and serve.

Yield: About 4 servings

Braised Bass in Red Wine

6½ tablespoons butter
1 tablespoon chopped parsley
1 2½–3½-pound sea bass or striped bass, with head and tail intact, cleaned and ready for cooking
Salt
Pepper
2 cups diced carrots
2 medium onions, diced
Bouquet garni (1 stalk celery, halved, 1 bay leaf, 2 sprigs parsley, and 1 sprig fresh thyme or ¼ teaspoon dried)
2 quarts red wine fumet (see page 293)
6 cups red Graves wine
1 teaspoon anchovy paste
2 tablespoons flour

1. Preheat oven to 350 degrees.
2. Mix 2 tablespoons of the butter with the parsley and spread

over the cavity of the fish. With a sharp knife, notch the skin
on the back of the fish, making 3 or 4 shallow incisions
on each side.

3. Season fish inside and out with salt and pepper to taste.
4. Melt 3 tablespoons of the remaining butter and sauté the
   carrots and onions until the onions are translucent.
5. Butter the rack of a fish poacher and spread sautéed vegetables
   over it. Then place the fish on top of the vegetables. Place rack
   into the poacher. Add the bouquet garni.
6. Reserve ¼ cup of the fumet and then pour in equal quantities
   of the fish fumet and red wine until the liquid rises about ⅔
   the way up the fish.
7. Bring to a boil on top of the stove, cover, and place in the oven
   for 20 to 30 minutes or until fish flakes easily. The fish should
   be basted with cooking liquid at least 3 times during the
   baking.
8. Drain the fish on the rack. Transfer the fish to a heatproof
   serving platter and keep warm while making the sauce.
9. Strain the cooking liquid (discard the vegetables), and measure
   3 cups into a shallow saucepan. (See note.) Boil vigorously to
   reduce the quantity to about 2 cups. Add anchovy paste.
   Blend together the remaining 1½ tablespoons butter and the
   flour and whisk into the sauce a little at a time while cooking
   gently until the desired consistency is reached.
10. Brush the fish with some of the remaining cooking liquid and
    glaze under a preheated broiler. Serve the sauce either spooned
    over the fish or separately.

Yield: 6 to 8 servings

NOTE: *Excess cooking liquid should be reserved after straining and
can be frozen for future use in making sauce.*

Diana Kennedy's Pescado Alcaparrado
(Mexican Fish in Caper Sauce)

3–4 carrots, thinly sliced
1 medium turnip, thinly sliced
2 bay leaves
1 teaspoon salt
   (approximately)
⅔ medium onion, thinly sliced
12 peppercorns
2 tablespoons lime juice
1 3-pound striped bass or
   snook, with head and tail
   intact, cleaned and ready
   for cooking

3 ounces blanched almonds
½ cup fresh bread crumbs,
   soaked in water
1 head romaine lettuce
2 tablespoons capers, drained
1 sprig parsley
4 cloves garlic, peeled
½ cup olive oil
12 olives
½ onion, sliced into rings
1 medium tomato, thinly
   sliced

1. Put carrots, turnip, bay leaves, salt, ⅓ onion, peppercorns, lime juice, and 4 cups water in a saucepan and simmer for about 30 minutes. Strain and set aside to cool; it must be completely cool before the fish is put into it.
2. Place the fish in a fish poacher or deep ovenproof dish and just cover with court bouillon from Step 1, adding water, if necessary. Bring the liquid to the boiling point, lower flame, and let the fish simmer until it is just tender—about 30 minutes (calculate 10 minutes for each inch of fish measured at its thickest point).
3. Carefully transfer the fish to an ovenproof serving dish, and if you are using a striped bass, peel off the rather tough skin.
4. Strain and reserve cooking liquid.
5. Grind the almonds as finely as possible—in a blender or nut grinder. Three ounces of nuts should yield ½ cup.
6. In a blender, grind almonds, bread crumbs, 4 large lettuce leaves torn into pieces, capers, parsley, 2 cloves garlic, ⅓ sliced onion, and 1 cup reserved cooking liquid.
7. In a frying pan, heat oil gently, add the remaining cloves of garlic and as soon as they start to brown remove them from the oil. Let the oil cool a little, then stir into blended sauce. (Discard browned garlic cloves.) Add 1 cup reserved cooking liquid to sauce, stirring it in well, and simmer very gently for about 10 minutes. Add salt as necessary.
8. Pour the sauce over the fish and just heat it through in the oven.
9. Put the remaining lettuce leaves around the dish and garnish with remaining ingredients.

Yield: 4 servings

Shad Roe with Herb Sauce

2 tablespoons butter
1 medium pair shad roe,
   poached in acidulated (use
   lemon juice or white vinegar),
   lightly salted water for
   5 to 20 minutes, until flesh
   turns gray
   Salt

Pepper
2 teaspoons tarragon vinegar
1 teaspoon lemon juice
1 teaspoon chopped chives or
   minced onion
1 teaspoon chopped fresh dill or
   ¼ teaspoon dried

1. Heat butter in skillet until lightly browned.
2. Season roe with salt and pepper. Sauté in browned butter until
   lightly browned on both sides. Transfer to a hot platter.
3. Add remaining ingredients to fat in pan. Heat, stirring, and pour
   over roe.

Yield: 4 servings

Baked Red Snapper Lumière

2 cans flat anchovies
1 cup finely chopped
   mushrooms
8 tablespoons butter
   (approximately)
   Juice of 1 large lemon
1 tablespoon paprika
1 egg, beaten
½ teaspoon pepper
2 teaspoons finely chopped
   parsley

Salt
1 4–5-pound red snapper, with
   head and tail intact, cleaned
   and ready for cooking
6 large mushroom caps
½ pound shrimp, simmered in
   their shells until pink in
   lightly salted water
   Capers
3 cups Fernand Point's Sauce
   Lumière (see below)

1. Soak anchovies overnight to remove excess salt. Drain, pat dry
   in paper towel, and chop into a rough paste.
2. Sauté chopped mushrooms in 2 tablespoons butter and lemon
   juice. While mushrooms are cooking, preheat oven to 400 degrees.
3. In a small mixing bowl, combine anchovies, cooked mushrooms,
   paprika, egg, pepper, and parsley. Mix well together.
4. Lightly salt inside and outside of red snapper. Fill cavity with
   stuffing from Step 3; close with skewers and string.

5. Lay stuffed fish into a greased ovenproof pan lined with a buttered double layer of aluminum foil that extends out over the pan at both ends.
6. Melt 4 tablespoons of butter, brush top of fish with it, and reserve rest. Put fish in oven and bake for 30 to 40 minutes, or until flesh flakes easily with a fork. Brush with more melted butter every 10 minutes.
7. Sauté large mushroom caps in remaining 2 tablespoons butter and reserve. Begin to work on sauce (see below).
8. Remove fish from oven. Drain butter out of foil with a baster. Grasp ends of foil and remove fish from pan. Slide onto a serving platter. Remove skewers and string.
9. Shell and devein shrimp, leaving tail on and arrange them in two clusters at either end of the platter. Put mushroom caps, inverted, along the sides filled with a few capers.
10. Serve by cutting sections through the fish. Spoon a mound of sauce over each portion.

Yield: 8 servings

FERNAND POINT'S SAUCE LUMIÈRE

¾ cup wine vinegar
 2 tablespoons minced shallots
 2 egg yolks
¼ cup heavy cream
 4 egg whites
 2 tablespoons olive oil
    Pinch potato starch

1. Reduce vinegar and shallots to a glaze. Add egg yolks and cream. Cook over low heat, whisking, until sauce thickens. Strain.
2. Beat whites to soft peaks, separately, and add to them remaining ingredients. Blend and then fold carefully into mixture from Step 1. Serve with fish.

Yield: About 3 cups

VEGETABLES AND SALADS

Chinese Monk-Style Mock Abalone

4 dried red dates
6 mushroom caps, halved
8 cloud ears
4 tablespoons peanut oil
3 slices fresh ginger
6 water chestnuts, sliced
2 leaves (with stem) Chinese white cabbage (bok choy), chopped

1 10-ounce can mock abalone, drained
1 can gingko nuts, drained
½ cup bottled oyster sauce
1 tablespoon cornstarch
¼ pound snow peas

1. Boil enough water to cover dates and remove from heat. Put dates in water to soak for 2 to 3 hours. Separately, in cold water, soak mushroom caps and cloud ears until soft.
2. Put 2 tablespoons oil in a wok or a skillet. Add ginger and heat oil over medium flame. Add water chestnuts and bok choy and stir-fry until coated with oil and bok choy stems are translucent.
3. Remove mixture from wok to a plate.
4. Add remaining tablespoons of oil to wok. Heat and add mock abalone. Let mock abalone stew in oil for a minute or two. Drain and add mushrooms, cloud ears, and gingko nuts. Stir briefly. Add oyster sauce. Stir again briefly. Add drained dates. Let simmer for 2 minutes, stirring briefly after 1 minute.
5. Meanwhile, combine cornstarch with ½ cup water, mix well, and stir into mixture in wok.
6. Add snow peas, bok choy, and water chestnuts to wok. Allow them to warm up. Then remove mixture to plate. Toss all ingredients together and serve.

Yield: 6 servings

Artichoke Bottoms

8 large artichokes
2 lemons, halved
4 teaspoons flour
 Salt

1. Trim off the tough outer leaves of the artichokes. Using a sharp kitchen knife, slice off the stems of the artichokes and rub cut surfaces with lemon halves.
2. Neatly slice through the vegetables, parallel to the base, leaving intact an artichoke bottom less than 1 inch thick. Again, rub cut surfaces with lemon halves. Place bottoms in a large skillet.
3. Squeeze lemon halves and combine juice with the flour and enough water to make a smooth paste. Whisk in enough extra water to make a mixture that will cover the artichoke bottoms. Add salt to taste.
4. Bring to a boil, cover, and simmer until bottoms are tender, about 25 minutes. Drain and when cool enough to handle, remove the fuzzy choke from the center by pulling and scraping with a spoon. Reheat the bottoms in hot, salted water.

Yield: 8 artichoke bottoms

NOTE: *Serve as garnish with meat dishes; cold, with vinaigrette; or warm, as Artichokes Croisette (see recipe, p. 4).*

Italian-Style Artichokes

4 large or 8 small artichokes
2 onions, chopped
2 cloves garlic, chopped
3 tablespoons olive oil
2 tablespoons chopped parsley
1 cup minced celery
8 anchovies, chopped

4 tablespoons grated parmesan
 or romano cheese
1 cup fine soft bread crumbs
3 tablespoons capers, drained
¼ teaspoon pepper
 Salt

1. Wash artichokes well. Cut off about ¼ of tops and stems. Remove bottom leaves. Stand in 1½ inches of boiling, salted water, add stems and cook, covered, for 30 minutes. Drain. Peel and chop stems and reserve.
2. Preheat oven to 350 degrees.

3. Sauté onion and garlic in 1 tablespoon olive oil until yellow.
4. Add chopped artichoke stems, parsley, celery, anchovies, cheese, crumbs, capers, and pepper. Taste and add salt, if desired.
5. Force the leaves of the cooked artichokes apart and remove choke or thistle.
6. Fill center with stuffing and insert a little stuffing at base of large leaves. Place in a baking pan and cover bottom of dish with ¼ inch water. Pour remaining 2 tablespoons olive oil over artichokes.
7. Bake, covered, about 30 minutes or until base of leaves is very tender. Baste occasionally with drippings in pan or with additional oil.

Yield: 4 servings

Barley with Vegetables

   2 teaspoons salt
1½ cups whole hulled barley
   ¼ cup peanut oil
   2 carrots, sliced
   1 large onion, coarsely chopped
   ½ pound mushrooms, sliced
   Pepper

1. Add salt to 3 cups water and bring to a boil in a saucepan.
2. Rinse barley thoroughly and drain.
3. Add barley to boiling water. As soon as water resumes boiling, lower flame, cover, and simmer for 40 minutes or until it is tender but with a kernel in the middle.
4. Heat oil over moderate flame in a skillet after barley has cooked for 30 minutes.
5. Sauté carrots in oil for 5 minutes over moderate heat, stirring frequently.
6. Add onion to skillet and sauté until just transparent. Continue to stir.
7. Add mushroom slices to skillet and sauté until they darken slightly.
8. Drain barley and add to vegetables in skillet. Salt and pepper to taste. Stir together and serve as soon as possible.

Yield: 6 to 8 servings

Beans, South American Way

2 cups (1 pound) dried white beans
3 slices bacon, chopped
2 tablespoons olive oil or drippings
1 large onion, sliced
1 clove garlic, chopped
1 tomato, peeled and quartered
1 green pepper, seeded and chopped
1 small piece hot red pepper or pinch cayenne
1½ teaspoons salt
Pepper

1. Wash beans, add 4 cups cold water, and cook in pressure cooker at 15 pounds pressure for 2 hours. Allow pressure to drop to normal. (See note)
2. Fry bacon in olive oil until half done, remove, and reserve.
3. Add onion and garlic to fat and cook until transparent. Add tomato, green and hot red pepper and simmer 10 minutes.
4. Combine all ingredients with beans and cook at 15 pounds pressure for 30 minutes. Serve with boiled rice.

Yield: 7 servings

NOTE: *By conventional methods, the beans should be soaked in cold water overnight and simmered for 2½ hours by themselves and for another 30 minutes with other ingredients.*

Hopping John

2 cups (1 pound) dried black-eyed peas
½ pound salt pork or bacon, sliced
1 teaspoon Tabasco
½ teaspoon salt
2 tablespoons bacon fat or lard
2 medium onions, finely chopped
1 cup raw long-grain rice
1½ cups boiling water

1. Wash peas and cover with 6 cups cold water. Let soak overnight.
2. Next day, add pork, Tabasco, and salt. Cover and cook over low heat until peas are barely tender, about 20 minutes. Drain.

3. Meanwhile, heat the bacon fat and sauté the onion until tender. Add to the peas with the rice and boiling water. Cover and cook about 20 minutes longer or until rice is cooked and water is absorbed.

Yield: About 8 servings

Brussels Sprouts with Chestnuts

½ pound chestnuts
   Boiling water
1 pint brussels sprouts
2 tablespoons butter (approximately)
   Salt
   Pepper
2 tablespoons water

1. Cut a gash in the flat side of each chestnut. Cover chestnuts with boiling water and boil 20 minutes. Drain, shell as soon as you can handle them, and peel off brown skin.
2. Preheat oven to 350 degrees.
3. Trim sprouts, wash, and split stem ends. Cook, covered, in a small amount of salted water until barely tender for about 8 minutes. Drain.
4. Fill a small buttered baking dish with alternate layers of sprouts and chestnuts. Dot each layer with bits of butter and sprinkle with salt and pepper, if desired.
5. Add 2 tablespoons water to dish. Bake for about 25 minutes.

Yield: 5 to 6 servings

Cabbage with Hot Vinaigrette Sauce

1 head (1½ pounds) cabbage
1 teaspoon salt
¼ teaspoon pepper
   Dash Tabasco
1–2 tablespoons white vinegar
¼ cup olive oil
2 tablespoons chopped pimiento, green pepper, parsley, and chives, in any proportion desired (optional)

1. Cut cabbage into wedges and boil, covered, in a small amount of water, with ½ teaspoon of the salt, until just tender, 10 to 12 minutes. Drain and place on hot platter.
2. Mix remaining ingredients, heat to boiling and pour over cabbage.

Yield: 4 servings

Cabbage with Capers

1 large onion, chopped
2 cloves garlic, minced
3 tablespoons butter
1 small sprinkling of ground cloves
1 medium head Savoy or new cabbage, shredded
½ cup chopped cooked ham

2 tablespoons capers, drained
1 tablespoon white vinegar
1 cup canned tomatoes or 2 fresh tomatoes, peeled and chopped
Salt
Pepper

1. Sauté onion and garlic in butter until yellow. Add cloves.
2. Add cabbage and sauté, covered, stirring occasionally, until wilted.
3. Add remaining ingredients and cook, covered, until tender—about 15 minutes. Add water if mixture becomes too dry.

Yield: 4 to 5 servings

Cabbage Cooked in Milk

2 cups milk
½ teaspoon salt (approximately)
6 cups finely shredded cabbage (about 1½ pounds)
Pepper
2 tablespoons flour
2 tablespoons butter

1. Heat milk to simmering. Add salt and cabbage and simmer 2 minutes. Add pepper to taste. Adjust salt.
2. Cream flour and butter. Add enough milk from cabbage to give a thin mixture. Add, stirring, to cabbage and cook, stirring, 3 or 4 minutes.

Yield: 4 servings

SCALLOPED CABBAGE: *Increase flour and butter in above recipe to 3 tablespoons. Turn creamed cabbage into a casserole, top with 1 cup buttered bread cubes or crumbs and brown in a 400-degree oven.*

CABBAGE AU GRATIN: *Add ½ cup grated sharp cheddar cheese to scalloped cabbage. Turn into a casserole and top with a mixture of ½ cup each crumbs and cheese. Bake in a 400-degree oven until top has browned.*

German-Style Red Cabbage

1 small head red cabbage	Boiling water
2 tart red apples	3 tablespoons red wine vinegar
2 tablespoons bacon fat or lard	1 teaspoon sugar
Salt	1 tablespoon flour
Pepper	

1. After removing outer leaves from cabbage, quarter, core, and shred the head. Without peeling apples, core and slice them.
2. Combine cabbage, apples, bacon fat, salt and pepper to taste in a heavy aluminum or stainless steel saucepan. Add just enough boiling water to cover. Cover pan and simmer until cabbage is tender, but still somewhat crisp—about 20 minutes.
3. Drain cabbage, reserving liquid. Return cabbage to saucepan and keep hot.
4. Mix vinegar, sugar, and flour in second saucepan. Stir in reserved liquid. Cook, stirring constantly, until thickened. Stir sauce into cabbage, taste for seasoning, reheat, and serve.

Yield: 4 servings

Hungarian Kolozsvari Layered Cabbage

1½ pounds sauerkraut	2 cloves garlic, crushed
½ cup raw rice	¼ pound smoked bacon, finely diced
1 cup beef stock	
1 large onion, finely chopped	½ pound smoked sausage, sliced
2 tablespoons lard	
1 pound lean pork, ground	1 cup sour cream
1 tablespoon paprika	¼ cup milk

1. Preheat oven to 375 degrees.
2. Squeeze sauerkraut well, and wash it in cold water if it is too
   sour. Simmer sauerkraut in 1 cup water for 15 minutes.
3. In another pot, simmer rice and beef stock together for 10 minutes.
4. In a separate frying pan, fry onion in hot lard for about 5 minutes.
5. Add ground pork to frying pan, stir well, and cook for another
   15 minutes, breaking up the pork as it cooks. Remove from heat
   and mix in paprika and garlic.
6. Cook diced bacon for a few minutes. Add sliced sausage just to
   shake it together with the bacon. Remove with a slotted spoon to
   a dry bowl. Reserve fat.
7. Spread bacon fat all over the inside of a baking-serving casserole.
   Put ⅓ of the sauerkraut in the bottom.
8. On top of sauerkraut place half the ground pork, then half the
   rice, and all the sausage and bacon. Sprinkle with half the sour
   cream mixed with milk. Cover with the second third of the
   sauerkraut, remaining meat and rice, and finally the third part of
   the sauerkraut. Pour rest of sour cream and milk over the dish,
   and spread evenly on top.
9. Bake the casserole, uncovered, for 1 hour.

Yield: 6 servings

Baked Sauerkraut with Apples

  2 pounds sauerkraut
¼ cup sliced onion
  2 tablespoons butter or bacon drippings
  2 or 3 medium apples, peeled, cored, and diced
1½ cups dry white wine
½ cup beef stock
  1 teaspoon brown sugar
  1 teaspoon celery seed
    Boiling water

1. Drain kraut slightly. Sauté onion in butter or drippings until
   transparent. Add sauerkraut; stir; cook slowly.
2. Add apples, wine, and enough stock to cover sauerkraut. Cook
   slowly, uncovered, 30 minutes.
3. Preheat oven to 325 degrees.

4. Add sugar and celery seed. Cover and finish cooking in oven 30 minutes longer.

Yield: 4 to 6 servings

Browned Sauerkraut

2 tablespoons bacon fat
1 onion, chopped
2 pounds sauerkraut, drained
1 potato, grated
1 teaspoon caraway seed (optional)
  Boiling water

1. In heavy 2-quart pan, heat fat. Slowly brown onion in it. Add sauerkraut; cook 8 minutes.
2. Add potato and caraway. Cover with boiling water; simmer 1 hour or longer. Cook uncovered first 30 minutes, then cover pan for remainder of period.

Yield: 6 servings

Kraut in White Wine

1 onion, minced
2 tablespoons butter
2 pounds sauerkraut
1 tart apple, chopped
1 large potato, grated

1 teaspoon caraway seed
  Butter
1 cup beef stock or water
1 cup dry white wine

1. Preheat oven to 350 degrees.
2. Sauté onion in butter until light brown.
3. Add to sauerkraut with apple, potato, and caraway.
4. Turn into a buttered casserole. Add the stock or water and the white wine.
5. Bake, covered, for 45 minutes to 1½ hours. Use shorter time for canned kraut and the longer period for bulk kraut.

Yield: 6 servings

Cauliflower Polonaise

1 medium head cauliflower
4 tablespoons butter
2 tablespoons fine bread crumbs
1 teaspoon or less lemon juice
1–2 tablespoons minced parsley or watercress
    Salt
    Pepper
2 hard-boiled eggs, chopped

1. Simmer unbroken head of cauliflower ⅓ immersed in water in a covered saucepan. Cooking times vary according to size of head and compactness of curd. Test at the end of 12 minutes.
2. Heat butter gently until beginning to brown. Add crumbs and cook, stirring, until brown.
3. Add lemon juice, parsley, and salt and pepper to taste. Pour over cauliflower head. Sprinkle egg on top.

Yield: 5 servings

Braised Celery

4 small bunches celery
3 tablespoons butter
1 tablespoon minced onion
    Chicken stock
    Salt
    Pepper

1. Cut the bunches of celery in half lengthwise.
2. Melt 2 tablespoons of the butter. Cook the onion in it until it turns yellow. Add the halved celery bunches.
3. Add just enough stock to cover the bottom of the pan. Add salt and pepper to taste, allowing for the seasoning in the stock.
4. Cover the pan with a tight lid. Simmer the celery for about 20 minutes, or until tender.
5. Drain, swirl in remaining butter, and serve.

Yield: 4 servings

Stuffed Chayotes

Sofrito is a kind of stew, a mixture of seasoned pork that is basic in many Puerto Rican dishes. It is used here as the stuffing for chayotes, a squashlike vegetable available in Hispanic markets.

STUFFING

2 tablespoons lard
1 teaspoon annatto (red berries used for coloring)
½ pound lean fresh pork, cubed
½ pound ham, cubed
1 medium onion, chopped
1 clove garlic, minced

1 small green pepper, chopped
1 6-ounce can tomato sauce
¼ cup pitted green olives, sliced
1 teaspoon capers, drained
Salt
Pepper

1. Heat lard, add annatto, and stir until lard is red. Strain lard into a large frying pan.
2. To lard, add pork, ham, onion, garlic, and green pepper. Sauté these ingredients, stirring often, for about 10 minutes.
3. Add remaining ingredients. Simmer until meat is tender, adding water as needed. Mixture makes a thick stew.

ASSEMBLING

2 chayotes
Salt
1 egg, well beaten

1. Cut chayotes in half. Boil in lightly salted water until tender— about 20 minutes. Drain.
2. Preheat oven to 400 degrees.
3. Scoop out the inside of the chayotes, saving their shells. Mash the inside pulp.
4. To mashed pulp add the sofrito; mix well and fill the emptied shells with the mixture. Brush beaten egg across the tops.
5. Bake until tops are lightly browned—about 20 minutes.

Yield: 4 servings

Fried Eggplant

1 small eggplant
   Salt
1 beaten egg
   Fine cracker crumbs
   Shortening for deep frying

1. Cut eggplant into ½-inch slices.
2. Sprinkle with salt and let stand 15 minutes. Dry.
3. Dip dry slices in beaten egg and then in crumbs. If possible, refrigerate briefly; crumbs will adhere better.
4. Heat shortening to 375 degrees.
5. Deep fry eggplant in it for 3 to 4 minutes or until the slices are golden brown. Drain on absorbent paper.

Yield: 3 servings

NOTE: *Summer squash may be prepared in the same way as eggplant. Use yellow squash or zucchini.*

Badgerville Eggplant Spaghetti

½ cup oil
1 large eggplant, unpeeled, chopped
2 medium onions, chopped
8 cloves garlic, minced or mashed
1 green pepper, chopped
½ head cauliflower, chopped
½ cup chopped parsley
¼ pound mushrooms, sliced
2 large (35-ounce) cans tomatoes

1 15-ounce can tomato sauce
1 bay leaf
1 teaspoon dried basil
1 teaspoon oregano
1 teaspoon dried thyme
½ teaspoon dried marjoram
½ teaspoon dried rosemary
   Salt
1 cup dry red or white wine
   Green or wheat-soy spaghetti
   Grated parmesan cheese

1. Heat oil in a large sauté pan or pot that holds 3½ quarts to a gallon. Add vegetables and garlic and sauté over medium heat for 15 minutes, stirring frequently.
2. Add tomatoes, tomato sauce, and seasonings. Bring to a boil, reduce heat, and simmer for 3 to 4 hours, gradually adding wine.

3. Prepare spaghetti according to package directions. Pour sauce over spaghetti and serve with plenty of freshly grated parmesan cheese.

Yield: 10 to 12 servings

Southern Kale

1 ham bone or 3 strips bacon
2 cups boiling water
2 pounds fresh kale, coarsely chopped
1 large bay leaf
6 sprigs parsley
2–3 whole cloves
1 medium onion, grated
Salt
Pepper

1. Using a medium pot, allow the ham bone to simmer in the boiling water for 1 hour. (Bacon need simmer only 15 minutes and in only 1 cup water.)
2. Add the kale and remaining ingredients.
3. Cover and boil gently until tender, or for about 15 minutes.
4. Serve both kale and liquid in deep vegetable dish.

Yield: 4 servings

Braised Stuffed Lettuce

8 large or 16 medium romaine lettuce leaves, well washed, with about 2 inches of large center stem removed
Boiling salted water
2 tablespoons butter or oil
½ pound lean ground pork, ground beef round, or ground raw chicken breast
1 small onion, finely ground
1¼ cups bread crumbs or small diced bread cubes
¼ cup milk
1 egg, lightly beaten
Salt
Pepper
½ teaspoon dried chervil
1 cup brown sauce or canned beef gravy
½ cup buttered crumbs

1. Place the leaves in a large kettle of boiling salted water, cover, and simmer 3 minutes or until leaves are barely limp. Drain.

2. Preheat oven to 375 degrees.
3. Heat the butter or oil in a skillet and sauté the pork, beef, or chicken and onion until all pink is gone from the meat and it is lightly browned or the chicken turns opaque.
4. Combine the bread crumbs, or bread cubes, and milk; let stand 2 minutes. Squeeze out excess moisture and add to meat.
5. Add egg, salt and pepper to taste, and chervil. Mix well.
6. Spoon meat mixture onto the lettuce leaves (put 2 medium-size leaves together) and roll up, tucking in the sides to enclose the filling and make a neat ball. Set in a single layer in a shallow buttered baking dish.
7. Pour the brown sauce or gravy into the skillet and bring to a boil. Pour over the stuffed lettuce. Sprinkle with the buttered crumbs and bake 10 or 15 minutes or until bubbly hot and lightly browned.

Yield: 4 servings

Millet Soufflé

½   cup millet
1¼ teaspoons salt
    Pepper
 3 eggs, separated
⅔   cup milk
½   cup grated cheese

1. The day before, place the millet in the top of a double boiler with 1 cup of water and let soak overnight.
2. Next day, add ¾ teaspoon salt and cook over boiling water, covered, 20 minutes.
3. Preheat oven to 375 degrees.
4. Mix the cooked millet with the remaining salt, pepper to taste, egg yolks, milk, and ¼ cup cheese. Beat the egg whites until stiff, but not dry, and fold into the millet mixture.
5. Pour mixture into a 1½-quart baking dish. Sprinkle with remaining cheese and set in a pan of hot water and bake 30 minutes or until browned and set.

Yield: 4 to 5 servings

Familia

    3 cups quick-cooking oats
1½ cups raw or toasted wheat germ
    1 8-ounce package dried apricots, cut up
    1 cup chopped nuts
    3 cups rolled wheat or wheat flakes
    2 cups raisins
    1 cup natural sugar (optional)

Mix all ingredients together and store in jars in the refrigerator. Substitutions of other dried fruits or nuts can be made as can any flaked grain, such as bran or rye. Familia is eaten raw with milk and honey.

Yield: 12 to 16 servings

Creole Okra

¼ cup finely chopped green
  pepper
¼ cup finely chopped onion
1 clove garlic, finely chopped
1 tablespoon fat
1¼ cups canned tomatoes

Pinch chili powder
Small piece bay leaf
Pinch ground cloves
½ teaspoon salt
⅛ teaspoon pepper
1 pound fresh okra

1. Sauté green pepper, onion, and garlic in fat about 5 minutes or until soft but not browned.
2. Add all remaining ingredients except okra and continue cooking over low heat 40 to 50 minutes or until thick, stirring often.
3. Wash okra, cut off stems. Leave small pods whole and cut large ones in half. Cook okra, covered, in one cup salted water until just tender—15 to 20 minutes. Drain.
4. Add okra to sauce and simmer about 5 minutes.

Yield: 4 servings

Baked Okra

1 tablespoon bacon drippings
1 pound fresh okra, washed and sliced
1 large onion, chopped
1 green pepper, chopped
  Salt
  Pepper
4 strips bacon, cut in half

1. Preheat oven to 350 degrees.
2. Heat the drippings in a skillet and add the okra, onion, and green pepper. Cook over moderate to high heat, stirring constantly for 5 minutes.
3. Add salt and pepper and turn into a 9-inch pie plate or small casserole. Bake 15 minutes.
4. Arrange the bacon slices like the spokes of a wheel on top of the okra mixture and bake 15 minutes longer or until okra is tender and bacon crisp.

Yield: 4 to 6 servings

Okra Pilau Charleston

3 bacon slices, diced
1 cup sliced okra
1 cup raw rice
  Salt
  Pepper

1. Brown the bacon and remove from the fat. Reserve.
2. Cook okra in bacon fat until soft. Use low heat to keep okra from burning.
3. Add the rice and 2 cups water, cover, and cook over very low heat until rice has absorbed water and is tender.
4. Taste and correct the seasonings, adding salt and pepper.
5. Garnish with the fried diced bacon.

Yield: 4 servings

Parsnips en Casserole

1 pound parsnips
2 tablespoons butter
1 tablespoon flour
1 cup milk, heated
½ cup grated parmesan cheese
Toasted bread crumbs

1. Scrub parsnips with brush until thoroughly clean. Cook in boiling, salted water until tender, 20 to 30 minutes. Drain, peel, and cut into round slices. Arrange in bottom of buttered casserole.
2. Melt butter in small saucepan. Stir in flour and blend until smooth. Slowly add the hot milk, stirring constantly. Continue stirring and cooking until sauce is smooth and thick. Remove it from the heat and add the cheese. Pour sauce over parsnips. Top with bread crumbs and, if desired, dot with butter. Place under the broiler and heat until top is golden brown.

Yield: 4 servings

Dannan Pease Pudding

1 cup dried split peas
2 bouillon cubes
1 medium onion, chopped
1 teaspoon sugar
¼ teaspoon salt
¼ teaspoon pepper
⅛ teaspoon grated nutmeg
1 tablespoon butter

1. Soak peas overnight in lightly salted water (less than ½ teaspoon salt) to cover.
2. Drain peas and rinse them under running water.
3. Place peas in a saucepan with 2 cups water and 2 bouillon cubes. Add onion and simmer until the peas are quite soft, about 3 hours.
4. Preheat oven to 325 degrees.
5. Transfer contents of saucepan to a buttered casserole dish and add sugar, salt, pepper, and nutmeg.
6. Dot with butter and bake, uncovered, for 1 hour.

Yield: 4 servings

Dominican Parmesana de Platanos Maduros

1 ripe plantain
  Oil
¼ pound queso del país or
  mozzarella cheese
2 slices ham
1 hard-boiled egg, sliced

Butter
1 tablespoon sliced sweet
  pickles
1 egg
2 tablespoons grated parmesan
  cheese

1. Carefully peel plantain. It will be very soft. Then cut it in half and carefully slice in lengthwise strips roughly ¼ inch thick.
2. Fill a skillet to a depth of approximately ⅛ inch with any cooking oil. Heat oil over medium heat. Brown plantain strips, turning once so as to brown both sides. Drain.
3. Cut cheese in strips with an approximate cross-section of ¼ inch. Slice ham into ¼-inch strips.
4. Butter a small overproof-glass dish about 6 to 7 inches square or round. Layer the bottom with half the plantain strips. Arrange cheese strips over the plantain. Then arrange layers of hard-boiled egg and ham and pickles. Make another plantain layer with remaining strips.
5. Beat egg with a fork until yolk and white are blended together. Pour over casserole.
6. Sprinkle parmesan cheese on top of casserole.
7. Turn oven to 350 degrees (do not preheat) and bake casserole, uncovered, for 35 minutes.

Yield: 3 to 4 servings

Bavarian Potatoes

4 cups large potato cubes
1 large onion, finely chopped
2 tablespoons butter
1 tablespoon white vinegar

1. Boil potatoes in salted water, drain, and place in a covered vegetable dish.
2. Sauté onion in butter until well browned. Add vinegar and pour over potatoes.

Yield: 4 to 5 servings

French Fried Potatoes

Wash and peel old potatoes. Cut lengthwise into strips about ⅜ inch thick. Soak at least 1 hour in cold water to cover. Drain, dry.

Heat shortening to 325 degrees. Fill fry basket about ⅓ full of potatoes. Immerse in the heated shortening and let cook 4 to 6 minutes. Remove and drain. Keep at room temperature.

Just before serving reheat shortening, this time to 375 degrees. Fill fry basket, as before, ⅓ full, using the precooked potatoes. Brown potatoes 2 to 3 minutes. Drain on absorbent paper; salt and serve immediately.

The above is known as the blanch-fry method, and produces potatoes that are fluffy inside, crisp outside. Another way of French frying potatoes is to do it in one operation from raw to cooked; this does not produce the same crispness.

For the "one-shot" method, prepare potatoes as described in the first paragraph. Heat shortening to 375 degrees. Fry the sliced potatoes in it until they are crisp and brown, which will take from 6 to 9 minutes. Drain.

French Potato Salad

    4–5 medium potatoes
     1 teaspoon salt
        Pepper
    1–3 tablespoons white vinegar (use smaller amount with wine, larger with water)
    ⅓–½ cup salad oil
     ¼ cup dry white wine or water
     1 tablespoon minced onion
        Chopped fresh chives, parsley, chervil, or tarragon

1. Boil potatoes in skins until just tender. Drain, peel, and slice.
2. Mix salt, pepper, vinegar, oil, wine or water, onion, and herb. Pour over potatoes. Toss lightly with a fork to coat potatoes with dressing. Serve warm or at room temperature.

Yield: 4 servings

Ali Bab's Potato Soufflé

1½ pounds baking potatoes (3 large Idaho)
  4 tablespoons unsalted butter
    Flour
  4 eggs, separated
1½ teaspoons salt
 ¾ cup heavy cream

1. Preheat oven to 425 degrees.
2. Scrub potatoes and bake on the middle level of the oven for 40 minutes or until done. Remove from oven and let cool a bit while you butter and lightly flour a 1½-quart soufflé mold.
3. Halve the potatoes and, with a spoon, remove the flesh from the jackets and quickly put it through a potato ricer into a saucepan. Add the remaining butter to the potatoes in the saucepan, mixing vigorously with a wooden spoon over low heat. Remove from the heat. Then add the salt and the egg yolks mixed with the cream. Mix thoroughly.
4. Beat the egg whites until they are stiff, but not dry.
5. Add half the egg whites to the potatoes, folding them in with a large spatula. In the same manner, add the remaining egg whites.
6. Turn out the contents of the saucepan into the mold and put in oven. The soufflé will rise dramatically at first and then fall somewhat as it solidifies. Cook for about 30 minutes. The soufflé is done when it detaches itself slightly from the mold and feels elastic to the touch.
7. Remove the mold from the oven. Serve from the dish or wait a few minutes to facilitate unmolding. Invert and unmold onto a platter and serve immediately.

Yield: 6 servings

Finnish Rosolli

½ pound potatoes, peeled
 6 carrots, peeled
½ pound beets (weighed without tops), peeled
    Salted boiling water
½ cup diced onions

½ cup diced dill pickle
½ cup diced salt herring (optional)
¼ teaspoon salt
    White pepper
 1 clove garlic, pressed

1. Plunge potatoes and carrots in salted boiling water. Cook for about 20 minutes or until done. Drain and allow to cool before dicing.
2. Submerge beets in salted boiling water. Cook for 30 minutes or until done. Drain; reserve 2 tablespoons water. Allow to cool before dicing.
3. Mix all ingredients. Add salt, pepper, and pressed garlic. Toss. Refrigerate.

DRESSING

¾ cup heavy cream
1 tablespoon sugar
½ teaspoon salt
2 tablespoons white vinegar
1 tablespoon dry mustard
2 tablespoons beet juice for coloring

Whip heavy cream until it thickens slightly. Add remaining dressing ingredients, mix well, and serve over salad.

Yield: 6 servings

Swiss Rösti-Pragleti Hardopfel

2 pounds new waxy potatoes
  Boiling salted water
4 tablespoons butter
1 medium onion, sliced
  Salt
2–3 tablespoons beef stock

1. Scrub potatoes and cook in boiling salted water to cover until tender. Drain and cool. (This can be done the day before.)
2. Heat the butter until the foam subsides, do not burn, and pour off the clear liquid into a 9- or 10-inch skillet. Discard the sediment.
3. Sauté the onion in the butter until transparent. Peel the cold potatoes and slice on the wide cutter of a grater.
4. Add the potatoes, and salt to taste, to the skillet. Cover and cook over medium-high heat 3 minutes. Turn the potatoes with a spatula, cover and cook over medium heat 3 to 4 minutes.
5. Turn the potatoes again and then push potatoes from the sides

toward the middle to form a mound. Cover and cook 15 minutes. Carefully loosen the potatoes without breaking the crust until they slide in the pan.

6. Turn a large flat plate over potatoes, invert pan. Pan should be clean and have some fat in it. If not, clean and add more fat.
7. Slide the potatoes back into the pan, sprinkle with the beef stock, cover, and cook 10 minutes longer. Slide onto a heated platter and serve in wedges.

Yield: 6 servings

Scotch Achiltibuie Very Plain Stovies

Potatoes, peeled and sliced
Salt
Pepper
Butter

1. Put as many potato slices as you need in a pot, with very little water, just enough to cover the bottom of the pot and prevent burning.
2. Sprinkle with salt and pepper and dot with butter.
3. Cover closely and simmer over low heat gently until soft.

Radishes with Sour Cream Sauce and Chives

2 cups radishes, peeled
2 tablespoons butter
2 tablespoons flour
½ cup sour cream
1 tablespoon lemon juice
  Salt
  Pepper
2 tablespoons chopped chives

1. Cook radishes, covered, in a small amount of salted water until just tender.
2. Heat butter, blend in flour, add ⅓ cup radish broth and the sour cream. Cook, stirring, until thickened.

3. Add radishes, lemon juice, and salt and pepper to taste. Reheat and serve garnished with chives.

Yield: 4 to 5 servings

Miss Dean's Cooked Radishes

 8 tablespoons butter
½ cup chopped shallots
 3 large bunches radishes, unpeeled, washed, and trimmed at both
   ends
   Salt
   Freshly ground black pepper

1. Melt the butter in a heavy skillet and sauté the shallots until tender but not browned.
2. Add the radishes, ⅓ cup water, and salt and pepper to taste. Cover and simmer 10 to 15 minutes or until radishes are fork-tender.

Yield: 4 to 6 servings

Nut and Rice Roast

1 cup chopped mixed nuts
1 cup soft whole wheat bread
  crumbs
1 cup cooked rice
2 sprigs fresh sage, chopped, or
  ¼ teaspoon dried
2 sprigs fresh thyme, chopped,
  or ¼ teaspoon dried

1 onion, finely chopped
1 teaspoon salt
⅛ teaspoon pepper
6 tablespoons butter, melted
¼ teaspoon Maggi seasoning or
  to taste
  Cumberland sauce (see page
  300)

1. Preheat oven to 375 degrees.
2. Pass the nuts and bread crumbs through an electric blender. Mix with the rice, sage, thyme, onion, salt, pepper, 2 tablespoons butter, and Maggi. Blend well and add just enough water to make mixture stick together.
3. Shape into a loaf, place in a buttered dish, and bake 35 minutes, basting twice with remaining melted butter. Serve with the sauce.

Yield: 4 servings

Brown Rice

1 cup brown rice
1½ cups water
¼ teaspoon salt

1. Rinse rice thoroughly 3 times in cold water. Drain.
2. Place ingredients in a pressure cooker. When pressure comes up full, lower heat and cook 40 to 45 minutes.
3. Turn off heat and allow pressure to return to normal. Let stand for 10 to 20 minutes. Remove cover and mix rice thoroughly before serving.

Yield: 2 servings

NOTE: *For larger amounts, decrease liquid slightly.*

Spinach au Gratin with Chicken Livers and Chestnuts

4–6 ounces chestnuts
1 pound spinach
Salt
2 tablespoons unsalted butter
6–8 chicken livers, sliced

Grated nutmeg, to taste
Pepper
2 cups béchamel sauce (see page 296)
Grated parmesan cheese

1. Boil chestnuts for 12 to 15 minutes, remove shells and inner skins. Slice. You should end up with ¾ to 1 cup of slices roughly ⅛ inch thick.
2. Remove long stems from spinach and wash leaves thoroughly.
3. Cook cleaned spinach for 1 to 2 minutes in ½ cup lightly salted boiling water. Drain well.
4. Sauté liver slices in butter for about 2 minutes on each side or until firm outside and pink inside.
5. Divide spinach in half. Arrange one half in a low, ovenproof, 8-inch serving dish, lightly buttered. Sprinkle lightly with nutmeg and salt and pepper, to taste.
6. Arrange sliced chestnuts in a layer over spinach.
7. Arrange chicken liver slices over chestnuts. Cover with rest of spinach, and sprinkle with more nutmeg.
8. Prepare béchamel and pour over spinach. Sprinkle with parmesan cheese.
9. Place dish 5 or 6 inches under broiler until heated through and lightly browned.

Yield: 8 to 10 servings

Spinach Soufflé with Poached Eggs

8 eggs
1 10-ounce package spinach or
   about 1 pound fresh spinach
   on stalks
2 tablespoons butter
2 tablespoons flour

2 tablespoons grated parmesan
   cheese
½ cup milk
   Salt
   Pepper
   Grated nutmeg

1. Preheat oven to 425 degrees. Butter a 6-cup soufflé dish.
2. Poach 4 eggs (see page 5) just long enough so that you can lift them from the simmering water with a slotted spoon, about 2 to 3 minutes. Poach only 1 or 2 at a time. Drain and transfer the eggs to 2 or more saucers to cool. (Do not use metal cups for poaching, since it would be difficult to turn the barely cooked eggs out of the cups.)
3. Trim off large stalks and wash the spinach. Shake off as much water as possible. Blanch spinach over medium-high heat in an uncovered saucepan, stirring frequently. Do not overcook. Chop finely. Measure out ¾ cup and squeeze out remaining moisture.
4. Melt butter in a saucepan. Add the flour and 1 tablespoon of the cheese. Cook briefly. Add the milk and stir until smooth and thickened. Add the spinach to this sauce.
5. Separate 4 eggs, adding the yolks to the hot, but not boiling, sauce. Stir in the yolks, and season the sauce with 1 teaspoon salt, pepper, and nutmeg. Transfer sauce to a good-sized bowl.
6. Beat egg whites with a pinch of salt until very stiff. Stir a small amount of the egg whites into the sauce to lighten it. Gently fold in the remaining egg whites.
7. Cover the bottom of the soufflé dish with several spoonsful of the soufflé mixture. Cook for 4 minutes in preheated oven.
8. Gently transfer the drained poached eggs onto the partially cooked layer of soufflé. Make a mark on the outside or bottom of the dish to indicate the location of the eggs so that you can avoid breaking as you serve the soufflé. Spoon the rest of the soufflé mixture onto the eggs. Sprinkle on the remaining cheese.
9. Bake the soufflé 12 to 15 minutes. It will have a good crust and be slightly runny in the center. The poached eggs should be cooked, with the yolks still runny.

Yield: 4 servings

Sweet Potato Pudding

1 cup light brown sugar	½ teaspoon salt
2½ cups mashed baked sweet potatoes	2 tablespoons butter, melted
1 tablespoon dark molasses	3 eggs, well beaten
1 teaspoon ground cinnamon	Peel of ½ tangerine, finely shredded
1 teaspoon ground ginger	1½ cups milk

1. Preheat oven to 350 degrees.
2. Mix sugar and sweet potatoes together and beat until smooth; add molasses, spices, salt, butter, eggs, and finely shredded peel. Mix thoroughly.
3. Add milk and when thoroughly blended turn into a buttered baking dish. Bake about 1 hour, or until firm. Remove from oven and let stand 15 minutes. Serve with heavy cream.

Yield: 6 servings

Creamed Spring Greens, French-Style

1½ pounds spinach, dandelion, turnip, or other tender leafy greens	2 tablespoons flour
1 teaspoon salt	¾ cup chicken stock
2 tablespoons butter	¼ cup light cream
1 tablespoon minced onion	Pinch dried thyme
	Pinch grated nutmeg
	Pinch cayenne

1. Remove roots and any tough stems from spinach or other greens and wash thoroughly. Cook, covered, in water that clings to the leaves, until tender, 5 minutes or longer, adding ½ teaspoon salt when greens are half-done. Drain well and chop or force through a food mill or coarse sieve.
2. Heat butter, add onion, and cook, stirring, until lightly browned. Blend in flour. Add stock, cream, remaining salt, thyme, nutmeg, and cayenne, and cook until thickened.
3. Add chopped greens to the sauce and boil, stirring until well blended.

Yield: 4 servings

Vegetable Charlotte

12 slices bread (approximately), cut into ½-inch-wide pieces
 4 tablespoons butter, melted
 1 cup pureed carrots
 1 cup pureed turnips
 1 cup pureed Brussels sprouts
1½ cups tomato sauce (see page 298)

1. Preheat oven to 425 degrees.
2. Line a 1- to 1½-quart baking dish with the strips of bread that have been dipped in the butter.
3. Mix the pureed vegetables together and spoon into the lined dish. Cover with more bread strips dipped in butter. Bake 20 minutes or until browned and heated through. Serve with tomato sauce.

Yield: 4 servings

Salat Shkolnyi
(Russian School Salad)

4 carrots
1 apple
2 tablespoons sugar
½ cup sour cream
½ teaspoon lemon juice
½ teaspoon minced fresh dill

1. Cut the carrots into julienne strips. Peel, core, and finely chop the apple.
2. Combine and mix carrot, apple, sugar, about ⅔ of the sour cream, and lemon juice.
3. Just before serving, add rest of sour cream on top of salad, sprinkle with dill, and serve.

Yield: 2 servings

Russian Salat Vesna

½ small head lettuce, sliced into thin strips

2 hard-boiled eggs, cut into small pieces

½ cup coarsely sliced radishes

2 cucumbers, peeled and diced

1 carrot, cooked and diced

2–3 potatoes, boiled and diced

2 tomatoes, cut in eighths

¼ cup chopped scallions

⅔ cup sour cream

1 tablespoon white vinegar

½ teaspoon confectioners sugar

½ teaspoon salt

1. Pile lettuce strips in a mound in the center of the serving dish. Arrange the egg pieces in the center of the mound.
2. Arrange vegetables around the mound.
3. Blend sour cream, vinegar, and sugar. If mixture is too thick to pour, add a small amount of water. Just before serving, sprinkle the salad with salt and pour sour cream mixture over it.

Yield: 2 to 3 servings

BREADS

Dark Whole Wheat Bread

  2 packages dry-active yeast
  2 cups lukewarm water (approximately)
2½ cups lukewarm coffee
  ½ cup yellow cornmeal
 10 cups whole wheat flour (approximately)
 1½ tablespoons salt
      Oil
      Milk

1. Dissolve yeast in ½ cup of the water, which should be lukewarm, around 110 degrees.
2. Combine yeast mixture with coffee.
3. Put cornmeal, 9 cups of flour, and salt in a large, warm bowl. Add yeast-coffee mixture and enough lukewarm water to make a dough that cleans the sides of the bowl.
4. Let dough rest 10 minutes.
5. Turn out dough onto a surface floured with some of the remaining whole wheat flour. Knead for 10 minutes, adding more flour gradually until dough has almost lost its stickiness.
6. Put dough in a clean, lightly oiled bowl. Cover with a dish towel dampened in hot water and leave to rise in a warm place or in a shallow pan of warm water.
7. When dough has doubled in bulk, which may take as long as 1½ hours, turn out on a surface lightly floured with whole wheat flour and knead briefly.
8. Let rise as before until doubled in bulk again. This time rising should occur more rapidly.
9. Turn out again on barely floured surface. Form carefully into a ball. Cut ball in half with a sharp knife and roll halves gently into cylinders or rounds.
10. Arrange loaves on a baking sheet lightly sprinkled with cornmeal. Brush tops of loaves with water. Leave them to rise for about 20 minutes and preheat the oven to 375 degrees.
11. Brush tops of loaves with milk and put in oven. Bake for 1 hour.

Yield: 2 small loaves

Carrot Bread

1 pound carrots
(approximately)
1 6-ounce can crushed
pineapple, drained
4 ounces crystallized ginger,
diced
2 tablespoons lemon juice
2 cups sugar
1 cup plus 2 tablespoons oil
(approximately)
3 eggs, lightly beaten
3 tablespoons grated orange
peel

3 cups flour
2 teaspoons baking soda
2 teaspoons baking powder
½ teaspoon salt
2 teaspoons ground cinnamon
½ teaspoon grated nutmeg
½ teaspoon ground allspice
1 teaspoon vanilla extract
1 cup regular (non-instant)
oats
½ cup chopped pecans

1. Peel and grate carrots to produce roughly 1½ cups finely grated carrots and 1½ cups more coarsely grated carrots.
2. Preheat oven to 350 degrees.
3. Combine carrots, pineapple, ginger, and lemon juice in a bowl and let rest while you beat together sugar and oil until creamy.
   To the oil-sugar mixture, add the 3 eggs and the grated orange peel.
4. Combine carrot mixture with orange peel mixture. Mix well.
5. Sift together flour, baking soda, baking powder, salt, cinnamon, nutmeg, and allspice. To this mixture, add vanilla.
6. Beat together carrot mixture with flour mixture. To this add oats and pecans. Stir until well mixed and spoon into 2 8½-by-4½-by-2½-inch oiled loaf pans.
7. Bake for 45 to 55 minutes. The loaves are done when a testing needle comes away clean. Cool in pans on racks.

Yield: 2 8-inch loaves

Piper Laurie's Dill Bread

1 cup creamed cottage cheese
3 tablespoons butter
¼ cup plus 1 teaspoon dried,
minced onions
3 tablespoons sugar (or 6
tablespoons raw sugar)
  2 tablespoons dill seed

2 teaspoons salt
1 egg
Oil
2–2¼ cups unbleached white
flour, sifted and warmed
1 package dry-active yeast

1. Mix cottage cheese, butter, onion, sugar, dill seed, salt, and ¼ cup water in a medium saucepan. Add egg.
2. Heat contents of saucepan to lukewarm, between 105 and 115 degrees.
3. Oil insides of a mixing bowl and warm in oven.
4. Oil a 1½- or 2-quart casserole generously.
5. Mix contents of saucepan in the mixing bowl of an electric mixer together with 1 cup of flour and the yeast. Beat with electric beater at medium speed for 2 minutes.
6. Add 1 more cup of flour and beat at high speed or knead on a board for 2 minutes.
7. Work in the rest of flour vigorously and gradually with hands, dough hook of an electric mixer, or a heavy rubber spatula. Continue beating or kneading until very difficult to beat and then beat for 1 minute more.
8. Transfer contents of mixing bowl to the clean, oiled, warm bowl.
9. Cover bowl with a plastic bag and set to rise in warm place.
10. When dough has doubled in bulk (which may take as much as 1½ hours), stir down with spatula and transfer to pre-warmed casserole.
11. Cover and let rise in a warm place until it doubles in bulk and, without preheating oven, bake on bottom level at 350 degrees for 40 to 50 minutes.

Yield: 1 loaf

Mary Pat Bread

```
      1 cup lukewarm water
      1 package dry-active yeast
      1 cup milk
     ¼ cup sugar
      1 teaspoon salt
      2 tablespoons honey
      1 cup boiling water
7–7½ cups unbleached white flour
```

1. Into a small bowl, pour the cup of lukewarm (110 degrees) water. Sprinkle the yeast over the top and let stand 5 minutes.
2. Into a large bowl, pour the milk, sugar, salt, honey, and boiling water. Stir to dissolve. Combine the two mixtures.

3. Add 3 cups of flour and mix well. Beat in 2 more cups of flour. Batter will become quite heavy. Add the sixth cup of flour and mix well to incorporate it evenly. Sprinkle the seventh cup of flour on any spots in the batter that still appear wet. The remaining ½-cup of flour will be added during the kneading process.
4. Flour a board. Turn out the dough onto the board and cover with the bowl for 10 minutes. Knead the dough for 3 or 4 minutes on the board, working in the last ½ cup of flour as you knead. Divide the dough in half and knead each half until the dough becomes rubbery and resistant to additional folding. Form each half into a ball and cover for at least 25 minutes and up to 1½ hours with a damp towel. Dough should be protected from cold and drafts.
5. Knead each half again for 3 or 4 minutes and spread the dough in 2 buttered and floured 8½-by-4½-by-2½-inch loaf pans. Return to the draft-free place (a cold oven will do, even if it has a modest pilot light), covered with the damp towels, for ¾ to 1 hour, or until dough has risen 1½ inches above the rims of the pans. The pilot light may hasten the second rising.
6. Meanwhile, preheat the oven to 400 degrees, then reduce to 350 degrees when loaves are put in. Bake the loaves in the middle of the oven for 45 to 50 minutes, or until browned. Cool on a rack, laying each loaf on its side. Do not slice for at least 40 minutes.

Yield: 2 8-inch loaves

⅔ Time Bread
(For Younger Bakers)

1 package dry-active yeast
1 cup lukewarm water (about 110 degrees)
  Olive or peanut oil
1 tablespoon sugar or honey
1 teaspoon salt
4 cups all-purpose white flour (approximately)

1. Put the yeast into a large bowl. Pour water in and stir briefly.
2. Add 1 tablespoon oil, honey, and salt; stir until smooth. Let rest for 5 minutes.
3. Gradually add flour to mixing bowl, stirring until a soft dough is formed.
4. Knead dough on floured surface until it is smooth and elastic.

5. Let dough rest on the kneading surface while you wash and oil mixing bowl.
6. Turn the dough into the bowl and cover with a damp dish towel.
7. Put bowl in a warm, draft-free place and leave for about 1 hour while dough rises to double its original bulk.
8. Remove dough from bowl, punch down, shape like a small loaf and put into a 9-by-5-by-3-inch oiled loaf pan.
9. Put loaf in warm, draft-free place to rise for about 45 minutes or until it doubles in bulk.
10. Preheat oven to 350 degrees during second rising.
11. Put loaf pan in preheated oven and bake for 50 minutes to 1 hour or until you like the color.
12. Remove loaf pan from oven and loaf from pan. Cool on a rack.

Yield: 1 9-inch loaf

Welsh Bara Brith Bread

1½ cups milk (approximately)
2 packages dry-active yeast or or 2 ounces compressed yeast
½ cup sugar
10 tablespoons butter
6 tablespoons lard
8 cups sifted all-purpose flour (approximately)
1 teaspoon salt

1 teaspoon ground cinnamon
½ teaspoon grated nutmeg
½ teaspoon ground allspice
¼ teaspoon ground cloves
6 ounces raisins or sultanas
6 ounces currants
4 ounces candied citron peel, diced
2 eggs, at room temperature
Oil

1. Warm ½ cup milk and combine with yeast and 1 teaspoon of the sugar. Let stand.
2. Meanwhile, cut butter and lard into chunks (lard can be measured against a graduated butter wrapper).
3. Cut butter and lard chunks into flour in a mixing bowl, working with the fingertips until the resulting lumps of flour and butter or lard are no larger than peas.
4. Mix salt, remaining sugar, and spices into flour. Then stir in raisins or sultanas, currants, and citron peel bits (if you start with whole peel, cut it up with a scissors).
5. Add 1 tablespoon of flour to the yeast mixture and stir in.
6. Beat the eggs together until well blended and add them to the yeast mixture, stirring in lightly. Warm remaining milk.

7. Make a well in the flour and pour yeast mixture into it. Stir lightly, then begin adding warm milk to dough by ¼ cups until dough holds together and becomes soft and manageable.
8. Work dough with a wooden spoon for a minute or two, then turn out onto a lightly floured board and knead for 10 to 15 minutes, until it has become very elastic and palpably lightened.
9. Cover and set dough to rise in a warm bowl in a warm, draft-free place until it doubles in bulk.
10. Preheat oven to 375 degrees. Oil the insides of 2 8½-by-4½-by-2½-inch loaf pans or 2 8-inch (2-quart) ovenproof-glass circular dishes.
11. Punch down risen dough, divide in half, and reform each half into a smooth roll the length of a loaf pan or size of dishes.
12. Put loaves in loaf pans or dishes, cover, and let rest at room temperature for 30 minutes, and bake for 50 minutes (45 minutes, if glass is used).
13. If a shiny surface is desired, brush loaf tops with milk 5 minutes before baking is done.
14. Let finished loaves cool on a rack for at least an hour.

Yield: 2 8-inch loaves

Hoe Cakes

1 cup white cornmeal
½ teaspoon salt
1 cup rapidly boiling water
1 tablespoon shortening

1. Mix cornmeal and salt. Add the water, stirring.
2. Mix well. By tablespoonsful shape into balls and flatten with the hand.
3. Brown on both sides in the shortening, which should be hot but not smoking. Serve hot.

Yield: 14 small cakes

NOTE: *In the South, where hoe cakes date back to colonial times, white cornmeal is traditional. But yellow may be substituted.*

Spoon Bread

1 cup yellow cornmeal
¾ teaspoon salt
1 teaspoon sugar (optional)
1½ cups boiling water
3 tablespoons butter
3 eggs, separated
1¼ cups milk

1. Preheat oven to 350 degrees.
2. Mix cornmeal, salt, and sugar. Add boiling water and butter and mix well.
3. Beat egg yolks, add milk, and add to cornmeal mixture.
4. Fold in stiffly beaten egg whites.
5. Turn into a greased casserole and bake 40 to 45 minutes, or until browned.

Yield: 6 servings

Bacon Muffins

Butter
6 strips bacon
2 cups sifted flour
2 teaspoons combination baking powder

2 tablespoons sugar
¾ teaspoon salt
1 egg, beaten
1 cup milk
2 tablespoons melted fat or oil

1. Butter 12 to 15 2½-inch muffin cups. Preheat oven to 400 degrees.
2. Sauté bacon till crisp; then chop.
3. Sift together flour, baking powder, sugar, and salt.
4. Mix egg, milk, and fat. Add to dry ingredients along with bacon and stir only until flour is dampened. Mixture will look somewhat lumpy, but do not beat.
5. Fill the muffin cups ⅔ full. Bake about 25 minutes.

Yield: 12 to 15 muffins

Batter Bread

1 cup white cornmeal (water-ground, if possible)
1¼ cups boiling water
½ teaspoon salt
1 tablespoon butter (approximately)
2 eggs, well beaten
1 cup buttermilk
½ teaspoon baking soda

1. Preheat oven to 450 degrees.
2. Pour meal in a bowl without sifting. Pour boiling water slowly over it, beating all the while to prevent lumps from forming. (If lumpy, strain mixture.) Add salt and butter and let butter melt.
3. Mix well and set aside to cool slightly. Then add eggs beaten with buttermilk and soda. Beat well. Pour into a buttered, 8½-by-4½-by-2½-inch shallow baking dish—the batter bread is served in the same dish in which it is baked.
4. Bake from 30 to 40 minutes, or until mixture just sets and no longer shakes in the middle. Do not overcook. If properly baked, this is light and airy. Serve at once.

Yield: 1 8-inch loaf

Doughnuts

Buttermilk Doughnuts

3 cups sifted flour
½ teaspoon baking soda
1 teaspoon baking powder
½ teaspoon salt
¼–½ teaspoon grated nutmeg
2 eggs
¾ cup sugar
1 tablespoon butter, melted
⅔ cup buttermilk
Shortening or oil for deep frying
Powdered sugar (optional)

1. Sift together flour, soda, baking powder, salt, and nutmeg.
2. Beat eggs, add sugar gradually, and then butter. Mix well. Add buttermilk.
3. Blend liquid and dry ingredients and chill well.
4. Roll dough on a floured board or pastry cloth to ¼-inch thickness and cut with a floured cutter. Let stand while heating fat.
5. Drop doughnuts carefully into deep hot fat (370 degrees) and fry until brown on one side. Turn and brown second side. Drain on absorbent paper and then dust with sugar if desired.

Yield: About 2 dozen.

Clarita Garcia's Churros
(Spanish Doughnuts)

2 cups water
½ teaspoon salt
1 tablespoon butter
2 cups flour
4 eggs
Fat or oil for deep frying with a basket
Confectioners sugar

1. Place the water, salt, and butter in a saucepan and bring to a boil. Stir to melt the butter.
2. Add the flour all at once and continue to cook while stirring vigorously until mixture leaves the sides of the pan clean. Remove from the heat and cool.
3. Beat in the eggs one at a time very well. Spoon the mixture into a pastry bag fitted with a ½-inch plain tube.
4. Heat the fat or oil to 370 degrees. Heat the basket in the oil. Pipe 3-inch circles into the bottom of the basket, immerse in the hot fat immediately and cook until golden, turning once.
5. Drain on paper towel and sprinkle with confectioners sugar. Serve warm.

Yield: 18 to 24 churros

Pancakes

Blintzes

BATTER

  3 eggs
  ½ teaspoon salt
  ¾ cup matzoh meal
1½ cups water

1. Beat eggs and salt together. Beat in matzoh meal and water alternately to make a smooth batter.
2. Heat an 8-inch skillet until a drop of water sputters when dropped on surface. Grease pan lightly.
3. Pour about ¼ cup of batter onto center of skillet, tipping pan in all directions so that batter forms a thin pancake. Cook about 2 minutes or until edges of pancake start to pull away from sides of pan.
4. Turn out, cooked side up, on clean dish towel. Repeat until all the batter is used.

FILLING

  1 pound cottage cheese
  1 egg
  ½ teaspoon salt
  ½ teaspoon ground cinnamon
  3 tablespoons sugar
  2 tablespoons honey

Place cottage cheese in bowl, stir in egg, salt, cinnamon, sugar, and honey; blend well.

ASSEMBLING

2 tablespoons shortening

1. Preheat oven to 350 degrees.
2. Place about 2 tablespoons of filling in center of browned side of each pancake. Roll up pancake over filling and place in well-greased baking pan.
3. Dot blintzes with shortening. Bake 30 minutes. Slip under broiler and broil until lightly browned.

Yield: 8 blintzes

Mrs. Pinciaro's Pizzelle

8 tablespoons butter, softened at room temperature
¾ cup sugar
3 large eggs, at room temperature
Grated peel of 1 lemon
3 tablespoons fresh orange juice
¼ cup milk
2 teaspoons anise extract or any anise liqueur
3 cups sifted all-purpose flour
2 teaspoons baking powder

1. Cream butter and sugar together. Add eggs, one at a time, beating after each addition.
2. Add lemon peel, juice, milk, and anise.
3. Add flour with baking powder until all is absorbed, making a sticky dough.
4. Grease and heat a pizzelle iron (see note) or electric pizelle iron (you can make two at a time with the electric one). Add 2 heaping teaspoons across the center of the iron and cook 1 minute or until golden in color. Turn and cook the other side for nonelectric iron.

Yield: About 36 pizzelle

NOTE: *The yield will vary with the size of the iron. Pizzelle irons (large, manual Italian waffle irons) can be bought in New York at E. Rossie & Co., 1919 Grand Street.*

For her 7½-pound pizzelle iron Mrs. Pinciaro makes a less sticky dough by adding another cup of flour. Her favorite flavorings are liqueur extracts Goccia d'Oro (drop of gold) and cannella (cinnamon). These extracts were used to make homemade liqueurs.

Buttermilk Waffles

    2 cups sifted flour
    1 teaspoon baking powder
    ½ teaspoon baking soda
    1 teaspoon salt
    2 tablespoons sugar
    2 eggs, separated
1½ cups buttermilk
    ⅓ cup shortening, melted and cooled

1. Sift together flour, baking powder, baking soda, salt, and sugar.
2. Beat egg yolks; add buttermilk and shortening.
3. Add to dry ingredients and stir only until flour is moistened. Batter will be somewhat lumpy.
4. Fold in stiffly beaten egg whites.
5. Bake in a moderately hot waffle iron 4 to 5 minutes.

Yield: 6 waffles

Sweet Cream Waffles

1½ cups cake flour
    1 tablespoon double-acting baking powder
    ½ teaspoon salt
    1 teaspoon sugar
    3 eggs, separated
    1 cup heavy cream
    4 tablespoons butter, melted

1. In a small bowl, combine the flour, baking powder, salt, and sugar. Stir with a fork.
2. In a medium bowl, place the egg yolks, cream, and butter, and whisk together until well mixed.
3. Sift the dry ingredients into the cream mixture. Whisk until well mixed and smooth.
4. Heat a waffle iron to medium heat. Brush lightly with butter if the iron does not have a nonstick surface.
5. Beat the egg whites until stiff, but not dry, and fold gently into the batter. Spoon about ⅓ cup of batter into each of 4 depressions,

spread slightly, but not all the way to the edge. Close the iron and cook until waffles are golden, about 5 minutes.

6. Remove waffles to warm plates and serve with desired topping. Repeat cooking with remaining batter.

Yield: 4 servings

Crêpes
(Breton Pancakes)

1	cup unsifted flour
1½–2	tablespoons sugar
1	egg
2	egg yolks
1	teaspoon vanilla extract
1¼–1½	cups milk
¼	cup heavy cream
8	tablespoons butter in 16 equal slices

1. While batter is being mixed, let a well-seasoned, 12-inch griddle heat thoroughly. It is the right temperature when water dropped on it sizzles and evaporates immediately.
2. Using fingers, mix flour, sugar, egg, egg yolks, and vanilla. Add about ½ cup milk gradually, while hand-mixing. When smooth, add enough additional milk to make a thin batter, about ¾ cup. Add cream and blend.
3. Grease hot griddle lightly. For each pancake pour about ⅓ cup batter on griddle. Spread batter evenly and thinly over entire griddle. Let brown until deep golden color and turn, using a long spatula. Brown very lightly on second side. Remove from griddle.
4. Turn pancake over (light-colored side is up) and rub with 2 squares of butter until butter has melted. Fold in thirds to make a long strip. Fold again in thirds to make a square. This gives 9 layers of pancake. To eat, fold in half and eat with fingers.

Yield: 8 pancakes (1 is a serving)

NOTE: *If batter becomes too thick, add a bit more milk as needed.*

George Lang's Hungarian Pancakes

3 eggs
1¼ cups flour
1 cup milk
1 teaspoon sugar
⅛ teaspoon salt
1 cup carbonated water
4 teaspoons clarified unsalted butter (approximately)

1. Mix eggs, flour, milk, sugar, and salt to make a smooth pancake dough. Let the dough rest for 1 to 2 hours.
2. Heat an 8-inch frying pan. When the pan is hot, add ¼ teaspoon of the butter. Let the butter melt and cover the bottom of the pan.
3. Stir in the carbonated water at the last moment, just before cooking the pancakes.
4. Pour a ladle of the batter into the pan, and gently tip and twist the pan so that the batter covers the entire pan. When the top of the batter bubbles, turn the pancake over and cook for 4 or 5 seconds longer. Remove the cooked pancake.
5. Continue until the batter is all cooked; add butter before each pancake.

Yield: 12 to 14 pancakes

NOTES: *If you are very skillful in twirling the pan so that a small amount of batter covers the surface of the pan, you may be able to make 14 to 16 pancakes.*

Palacsinta Teszta
(Pancakes)

2 cups milk (approximately)
4 eggs, separated
1 tablespoon sugar
2 cups flour
Soft butter
1 12-ounce jar apricot preserves

1½ cups sliced almonds
2 cups sour cream
Confectioners sugar (optional)

1. Beat together 2 cups milk, egg yolks, sugar, and flour until well blended.
2. Beat the egg whites until stiff but not dry and fold into the batter.
3. Heat a heavy, 7-to-8-inch skillet, grease lightly with butter. Ladle about ⅓ cup of the batter into the hot pan while tilting the pan to distribute evenly. If the batter is too thick to spread easily, stir in a small quantity of extra milk.
4. Cook until lightly browned on the bottom, turn and brown the other side. Continue making pancakes (the thinner they are the better they taste) until all the batter is used.
5. Set pancakes on a towel, or a wooden board, spread with preserves, sprinkle with almonds, and roll. Place in a buttered baking dish.
6. Preheat oven to 325 degrees.
7. Spoon the sour cream over the rolled pancakes and sprinkle with remaining almonds. Bake 10 to 15 minutes or until heated through. Serve sprinkled with confectioners sugar, if desired.

Yield: 12 to 15 pancakes

Latkes
(Potato Pancakes)

6 medium potatoes	Pepper
1 medium Spanish onion	2 eggs, separated
3 tablespoons bread crumbs	Peanut oil
5 tablespoons matzoh meal	Applesauce
Salt	

1. Peel and grate potatoes and onion. Add bread crumbs, matzoh meal, and salt and pepper to taste.
2. Add egg yolks to potato-crumb mixture. Beat egg whites until stiff and add.
3. Heat peanut oil in frying pan until hot. Oil should be about ¾ of an inch deep in the skillet.
4. Drop mixture by spoonsful into hot fat and fry until crisp and golden brown. Lift out and drain on absorbent paper. Serve with applesauce.

Yield: 4 to 6 servings

Mrs. Fishburne's Corn Pancakes

1 cup boiling water	1 teaspoon salt
1 cup yellow cornmeal	1 teaspoon baking powder
2 tablespoons bacon fat	1¾ cup milk
1 tablespoon sugar	1 egg, beaten
½ cup flour	Honey

1. Pour boiling water over cornmeal. Add bacon fat and sugar and stir until blended.
2. Sift together flour, salt, and baking powder.
3. Mix dry ingredients and milk alternately into cornmeal mixture. Add egg.
4. Drop by dessertspoonsful on hot greased griddle, making the pancakes small. Turn to brown second side. Serve with honey.

Yield: About 2 dozen small pancakes or 4 to 6 servings

Timbale

CRÊPES

5 large eggs
¼ teaspoon salt
1 cup all-purpose flour
1 teaspoon oil

1. Beat eggs, add 1 cup cold water from tap, and salt. Add flour a bit at a time until all is used. Add oil.
2. Lightly grease a 6-inch frying pan and place over moderately high heat.
3. Remove pan from heat. Place small amount of batter (3 to 4 tablespoons) in the center of the pan and quickly spread it over the bottom. Return to heat until the edges of the crêpe rise slightly away from the pan. Do not brown. Turn crêpe over for a second and remove to a dish.
4. Continue until all batter is used.

Yield: About 20 to 22 crêpes

SAUCE

¼ cup olive oil
1 whole chicken breast, bone included
½ small onion, chopped
Salt
Pepper
¼ cup dry white wine

1 can (2 pounds, 3 ounces) Italian plum tomatoes with paste, sieved through a mill or put in a blender
1 teaspoon sugar
3 leaves fresh basil or ½ teaspoon dried

1. Heat oil in a saucepan. Add chicken and sauté until brown.
2. Add onion and cook until soft, but not brown. Salt and pepper the chicken. Add the wine and cook until wine evaporates.
3. Add the remaining ingredients and salt to taste and simmer for 1½ hours. Remove chicken, cut into cubes, and set aside.

MEAT BALLS

½ pound chopped beef
2 tablespoons grated parmesan cheese
Pinch garlic salt
Pepper
Pinch salt

1 egg
1 slice white bread, softened in water and squeezed to dry
3 sprigs parsley, chopped
¼ cup olive oil

1. Mix all the ingredients except oil together until well mixed. Form into meat balls the size of chick peas.
2. Fry in oil. Remove with a slotted spoon when brown. Add to the tomato sauce and simmer for 30 minutes longer.

FILLING

½ pound ricotta cheese
1 egg
¼ pound mozzarella cheese, cut into small cubes
2 tablespoons chopped parsley
½ cup grated parmesan cheese

1. Beat ricotta and egg with electric beater until smooth.
2. Add mozzarella, parsley, and parmesan cheese to the ricotta mixture.

ASSEMBLING

2 slices prociutto, diced (optional)

1. Preheat oven to 350 degrees.
2. Spread a shallow 2-quart casserole with a thin layer of sauce.
    Line the pan with crêpes, leaving an overhang.
3. Place half the chicken pieces on the crêpes, cover with a thin
    layer of sauce and meat balls. Cover with 2½ crêpes.
4. Spread with half the cheese filling and spoon over more sauce and
    meatballs. Cover again with 2½ crêpes. Spread with prosciutto,
    if used, and sauce.
5. Cover with 2½ crêpes. Use remaining chicken and sauce,
    more crêpes, remaining cheese filling, ending with 3 crêpes to
    cover all. Turn the overhang into casserole and spread with any
    leftover sauce.
6. Bake 30 minutes.

Yield: 6 to 8 servings

Pasta

Wein Lokschen
(Wine Noodles)

2 cups fine noodles
1 cup dry white wine
3 tablespoons plus 1 teaspoon sugar
3 tablespoons shortening
3 eggs, separated
1 tablespoon grated lemon peel
 Juice of ½ lemon

1. Boil noodles in salted water until tender, drain, and rinse with hot, then cold water.
2. Preheat oven to 350 degrees.
3. Heat wine with the teaspoon of sugar and mix with the noodles. Cool.
4. Cream shortening, the 3 tablespoons of sugar, egg yolks, lemon peel, and juice until smooth.
5. Add to noodle mixture. Fold in stiffly beaten egg whites.
6. Pour mixture into well-greased baking dish. Bake for about 15 to 20 minutes.

Yield: 4 to 6 servings

Gnocchi Piemontese

1½ pounds potatoes
2¼ cups sifted flour (approximately)
 Salt
 Grated nutmeg

1. Boil potatoes in skins, peel, and mash while hot.
2. Add remaining ingredients. Blend and work with fork or fingers to produce a compact dough.

3. Roll a small ball of dough on a floured board into a sheet about ¼ inch thick. Cut into ¾-inch squares. Press each lightly onto tines of fork and roll off the back of the fork, making a hollow cylinder. Spread well apart on trays or towels and let stand 6 hours, so dough will dry. Proceed with remaining dough in same manner.
4. Boil in a large quantity of salted water until gnocchi come to the surface. Drain and serve with a meat-tomato sauce or with melted butter, and parmesan cheese.

Yield: 4 servings

Baked Lasagne

SAUCE

3 small onions, diced	3 leaves fresh basil or ½
1 clove garlic, chopped	teaspoon dried
¼ cup olive oil	1 6-ounce can tomato paste
1 No. 2½-can Italian tomatoes	Salt
1 tablespoon chopped parsley	Pepper

1. Brown onion and garlic lightly in oil in saucepan.
2. Add remaining ingredients and simmer 15 minutes.

MEATBALLS

½ pound ground round steak	3 tablespoons grated parmesan
¼ cup bread crumbs	cheese
2 tablespoons chopped parsley	Salt
2 tablespoons milk	Pepper
1 egg, beaten	Olive oil

1. Mix ingredients thoroughly and shape into tiny meatballs.
2. Brown in frying pan with a small amount of olive oil and then add to sauce in saucepan.
3. Simmer 30 minutes, while preparing lasagne, below.

LASAGNE

1 pound lasagne
3 tablespoons salt
1 tablespoon oil

Cook lasagne by adding slowly to 6 quarts rapidly boiling water to which 3 tablespoons salt and 1 tablespoon oil have been added. Cooking time is about 25 minutes. Drain well.

ASSEMBLING

½ pound mozzarella cheese
1 pound ricotta cheese
1 cup grated parmesan cheese

1. Preheat oven to 350 degrees.
2. Place several spoonsful of sauce in bottom of casserole, then a layer of lasagne, and several slices of mozzarella. On top of this, place 4 or 5 tablespoons ricotta and sprinkle with some of the grated cheese; spread over ¼ of the sauce and meatballs.
3. Repeat layers, ending with grated cheese. Bake 20 minutes.

Yield: 6 servings

Pizza Casalinga

PIZZA DOUGH

1¼ cups flour
  ½ teaspoon salt
  1 teaspoon sugar
  1 tablespoon butter

½ cup hot water
½ package (1½ teaspoons) dry-active yeast
Olive oil

1. Combine flour, salt, and sugar in a medium bowl. Mix well with a wooden spoon.
2. In a separate small bowl, stir butter in hot water. When water has cooled to lukewarm (90 to 115 degrees), add yeast and let it develop for 5 minutes.
3. Add yeast mixture to flour mixture. Mix until a dough forms that leaves the sides of the bowl. It will still be somewhat sticky. This process may take several minutes of vigorous mixing.
4. Make a ball of the dough with hands dusted lightly in flour and transfer to a very lightly oiled, clean bowl. Let rise for about 45 minutes or until doubled in bulk, in a draft-free place that is between 80 and 90 degrees.

PIZZA SAUCE

1 tablespoon olive oil	1 teaspoon oregano
1 medium onion, finely chopped	1 teaspoon finely chopped fresh basil or ½ teaspoon dried
1 clove garlic, finely chopped	
1⅓ cups peeled Italian tomatoes, coarsley chopped but not drained	½ bay leaf
	½ teaspoon sugar
	½ teaspoon salt
2 tablespoons tomato paste	Pepper

1. Heat olive oil in skillet or medium saucepan.
2. Sauté onion in oil until transparent but not brown.
3. Add garlic to pan. Sauté for 1 minute with onion, stirring.
4. Stir into same pan the remaining ingredients.
5. Simmer sauce at very low heat, uncovered, for 1 hour or until thick. Stir from time to time to prevent burning.
6. Remove bay leaf.

Yield: About 1 cup

ASSEMBLING

½ pound mozzarella cheese, grated
1 cup grated parmesan cheese
15 slices pepperoni or chorizo; or 10 anchovies, washed, dried, and cut into ½-inch segments; or 1 cup mushrooms, sliced and sautéed; (See note.)

1. Turn ball of dough onto floured, flat surface. Punch down.
2. Preheat oven to 450 degrees.
3. Pulling at edges with fingers and rolling, shape dough as nearly as possible into a circle 1 foot in diameter.
4. Transfer dough to buttered cookie sheet. Readjust shape into a circle, if necessary.
5. Pour sauce evenly over dough, leaving roughly ½ inch at the perimeter uncoated.
6. Sprinkle mozzarella and parmesan over sauce as evenly as possible.
7. Distribute pieces of topping over coated surface of pizza.
8. Place in oven and bake for 20 to 25 minutes.
9. Score pizza like a pie and serve hot.

Yield: 4 servings

NOTE: *This selection of toppings is meant only as a suggestion. Almost any kind of prepared meat, seafood, or vegetable will do.*

Theresa Laudo's Pizza Rustica

2 pounds ricotta cheese	½ cup grated Parmesan cheese
4 eggs	¼ pound prosciutto, diced
½ pound sweet Italian sausage, fried, cooled, and chopped	½ pound mozzarella, cut into cubes
½ pound fresh fillet of pork cut into small cubes, fried and cooled	¼ cup finely chopped Italian parsley
	Pepper

1. Preheat oven to 400 degrees.
2. Beat ricotta with eggs by hand or mixer until smooth.
3. Add the remaining ingredients and mix well.

PASTA FROLLA

2 cups sifted all-purpose flour	¼ pound butter
¼ cup sugar	2 large eggs
2 teaspoons baking powder	1 egg yolk (optional)

1. Combine flour, sugar, and baking powder in a bowl.
2. With fingers break butter into flour until the flour is mealy.
3. Make a well, break the eggs in it, and beat with a fork. Blend into the flour mixture, knead quickly, and gather into a ball.
4. Let rest 10 minutes under a bowl.
5. The dough is soft and quite sticky. Therefore, it must be lightly floured on both sides as it is rolled out.

ASSEMBLING

1. Using about two-thirds of the dough, roll out to fit a 9-by-9-by-2-inch pan, with a half- inch overhang.
2. Pour mixture into the pastry-lined pan.
3. Roll out the remaining dough and cover the top.
4. Trim the overhang and press with the tines of a fork. With a fork, prick the top crust to allow steam to escape.
5. Brush the top with one beaten egg yolk (optional).
6. Place in oven for 15 minutes, then reduce oven heat to 325 and cook 45 to 55 minutes longer. Turn off the heat and let cool in the oven.
7. Cut into two-inch squares and serve as a warm or cold hors d'oeuvre. The flavor is best when cold. The pizza can be frozen.

Yield: 12 two-inch squares -

DESSERTS

Cakes

Genoise

6 eggs, at room temperature or warmer
1 cup superfine sugar
1 teaspoon vanilla extract
   Butter
1 cup sifted cake flour
5 tablespoons butter

1. Beat the eggs with the sugar and vanilla at the highest speed in an
   electric mixer until the mixture is so thick that it stands in stiff
   peaks when the beater is withdrawn. This should take from
   20 to 30 minutes. It is important not to underbeat the mixture.
   From time to time, scrape the sides of the bowl with a
   rubber spatula so the ingredients will be well blended.
2. In the meantime, butter 2 9-inch or 3 8-inch cake pans that are
   1½ inches deep. Line the pans with wax paper and butter
   the paper. Sift and measure flour. Melt 4 tablespoons butter and
   cool.
3. Preheat oven to 350 degrees and place oven rack in the lower third
   of the oven.
4. Remove bowl from mixer and remove beaters. Sift flour over
   egg mixture roughly 2 tablespoons at a time, using a rubber
   spatula to fold each addition in gently.
5. Add melted butter about 1 teaspoon at a time and fold it in gently
   but completely.
6. Turn batter into prepared pans and bake 35 to 40 minutes in
   preheated oven. When done, cake will rebound to the touch when
   pressed gently in the center.
7. Loosen cake around sides of pan and turn out on cooling rack.
   Remove paper and let cool before icing (see page 287).

Yield: 2 9-inch or 3 8-inch layers.

Chef Spry's Wedding Cake

GENOISE

Butter (for greasing layer pans)
Flour (for layer pans)
8 eggs, at room temperature
1 cup superfine sugar
¼ teaspoon salt
1 teaspoon vanilla extract

1 tablespoon Grand Marnier
Grated rind of 2 oranges (optional)
1½ cups flour, sifted into measuring cup
½ pound unsalted butter, melted and cooled

1. For wedding cake, this recipe will be made three times. The first and third batches will each go into a layer pan 10 inches in diameter and 2 inches high. The second batch will fill 2 7-by-2-inch pans and 1 5-by-2-inch pan. Pans should be generously buttered. Flour and shake off excess.
2. Preheat oven to 375 degrees.
3. Beat eggs in electric mixer at medium speed until mixed together. Add sugar and salt gradually at same mixer speed. Turn speed to high and continue beating until mixture forms a stiff ribbon. At same speed, beat in vanilla, Grand Marnier, and grated orange rind. Turn off mixer.
4. Pour about ¼ of the sifted flour back into the sifter and sift onto mixture from Step 3. With a wooden spoon or spatula, fold flour into mixture. Then pour about ⅓ of the melted butter onto mixture and fold in. Continue alternating similar amounts of flour and butter and folding, until flour and butter are used up. You will end with the last ¼ measure of flour.
5. Fill pans to about ⅘ their depth. Bake 10-inch pan for 35 to 40 minutes or until cake starts to separate from sides of mold. Bake 2 7-inch pans and 5-inch pan for 20 to 25 minutes.
6. Remove pans from oven as they are done. Unmold on racks and let cool and settle for at least 3 hours, preferably overnight.

ASSEMBLING

Cardboard
2 10-inch genoise layers
2 7-inch genoise layers
1 5-inch genoise layer
3 pounds bitter orange marmalade
4 tablespoons Grand Marnier
Cornstarch
3 pounds marzipan

1. Cut 3 circles out of cardboard with the following diameters: 9½ inches, 6½ inches, 4½ inches.
2. Using a serrated knife, slice all 5 layers in half horizontally.
3. Heat marmalade with Grand Marnier until it flows like syrup and push through a large strainer with a wooden spoon or a wire whisk.
4. With a pastry brush, coat surfaces of cake layers with marmalade mixture where cut was made in Step 2. Reassemble layers. Then coat sides and tops of reassembled genoise with marmalade.
5. Take 1 reassembled 10-inch genoise and set it on top of the other. Then mount double genoise on 9½-inch cardboard circle. Proceed similarly with 2 7-inch layers and 6½-inch circle. Mount 5-inch layer on 4½-inch cardboard circle.
6. Sprinkle a work surface generously with cornstarch. Knead 1¼ pounds of marzipan (which is sold in 1-pound cylinders) until smooth and pliable (add a small amount of water if too dry). Then roll into an 18-inch tube with hands. Flatten with rolling pin and roll out into a band 36 inches long and 3½ inches wide. Square off ends and sides with a sharp knife. Roll up band like a bandage. Then unroll onto side of 10-inch double layer, pressing against layer. Roll out ¼ pound marzipan into a circle and place on top of 10-inch layer. Press marzipan seams so that layer is sealed in marzipan.
7. Knead rest of marzipan and roll into a band 42 inches long and 3½ inches wide. Proceed as before, covering sides of both smaller (7-inch and 5-inch) layers. Roll excess marzipan into 2 circles and cover layer tops. Seal and let stand overnight unrefrigerated.

ICING AND DECORATION

1½ pounds unsalted butter
1½ pounds shortening
  4 pounds confectioners sugar
  4 tablespoons vanilla extract
    or Grand Marnier
  1 cup (about 8) egg whites
  1 yard ¼-inch wood dowel

1. Blend butter and shortening together.
2. Sift sugar and combine gradually with butter and shortening, beating at high speed.
3. Add vanilla or Grand Marnier.
4. Continuing to beat at high speed, add egg whites until butter cream is thoroughly blended, thick, and smooth.

5. Chill.
6. With a large, flat metal spatula, ice the sides and top of each cake layer smoothly with butter cream.
7. Cut dowel into 4 pieces the height of the 10-inch double layer and 4 pieces the height of the 7-inch double layer. Insert dowels into appropriate layers so that they are distributed straight up and down along an imaginary circle 2 inches less in diameter than the layer. The tops of the dowel should just reach the top of the layer. They support the cake during cutting.
8. Fill a pastry bag with butter cream and decorate sides of each layer. Use a No. 10 tube for grape design and a No. 44 ribbon tube for lovers' knots. Alternate 2 designs around sides (see pictures).
9. Assemble layers on top of each other, centering them.
10. Use a No. 30 star tube to make a circle of ripples around the top edge of each layer. If colored decoration is desired, add food coloring by the drop to a half cup or so of butter cream, mix, and put in clean pastry bag. Leaves, for example, can be added to grape design with green butter cream and a No. 65 tube.

Yield: 40 to 50 servings

Jane Brown's Carrot Cake

1 teaspoon butter	2 teaspoons baking soda
1½ cups salad oil	3 cups finely grated carrots
2 cups sugar	(about 1½ pounds)
4 eggs	1 cup blanched and finely
1 teaspoon salt	chopped almonds (or
1 teaspoon ground cinnamon	walnuts)
2 cups flour	

1. Grease a 10-inch tube cake pan with the butter.
2. Preheat oven to 325 degrees.
3. Blend the oil and sugar together in a large bowl with a wooden spoon. Add the eggs, one at a time, beating well after each addition.
4. In another bowl, sift together the salt, cinnamon, flour, and baking soda. Add the sifted ingredients to the egg mixture, and stir until they are thoroughly incorporated.
5. Next, beat in the carrots and almonds and mix them to blend thoroughly.

6. Pour the batter into the prepared cake pan and bake for 1¼ hours, or until a knife inserted in the center of the cake comes out clean.
7. Let cake cool, remove from pan, bottom side up, onto a serving dish. Smooth icing (see below) over top, sides, and center hole.

Yield: 1 10-inch cake

CREAM CHEESE ICING

8 ounces cream cheese, softened
4 tablespoons butter, melted
2 tablespoons vanilla extract
1 pound confectioners sugar

1. With an electric mixer, beat the cream cheese until it is light and fluffy.
2. Gradually add the melted butter, beating until it is completely absorbed. Add the vanilla and the sugar, beating well after each addition so that the icing is smooth.

Molasses Spice Cake

2 cups sifted flour
1 teaspoon salt
¾ teaspoon baking soda
1 teaspoon baking powder
¼ teaspoon grated nutmeg
⅛ teaspoon ground cloves
½ teaspoon ground cinnamon
½ cup shortening
¾ cup sugar
½ cup molasses
1 egg
¾ cup buttermilk

1. Preheat oven to 375 degrees.
2. Sift together all dry ingredients except sugar.
3. Cream together shortening and sugar. Gradually blend in molasses; stir in ¼ cup dry ingredients. Beat in egg.
4. Alternately add remaining dry ingredients and buttermilk. Beat for 30 seconds.
5. Pour into 2 well-greased and lightly floured round 8-inch cake pans. Bake 25 minutes.
6. Cool. Ice with molasses seven-minute frosting.

Yield: 2 8-inch layers

MOLASSES SEVEN-MINUTE FROSTING

- 1 egg white
- ¼ cup water
- 1 cup sugar
- 2 tablespoons molasses
- ⅛ teaspoon salt
- ½ teaspoon lemon extract

1. Mix first 5 ingredients in top of double boiler. Beat over rapidly boiling water with rotary or electric beater until frosting stands in high peaks.
2. Remove from heat. Add lemon extract; beat until spreading consistency.

Yield: Frosting for tops of 2 8-inch layer cakes

Ciastka Miodowe
(Polish Honey Cakes)

- ½ cup honey
- ½ cup sugar
- 1 whole egg plus 2 egg yolks
- 4 cups flour
- 1 teaspoon baking soda
- ½ teaspoon ground cinnamon
- ½ teaspoon grated nutmeg
- ¼ teaspoon ground cloves
- ¼ teaspoon ground ginger
- Blanced almonds, halved
- Butter

1. Warm the honey slightly and combine with the sugar.
2. Add eggs, reserving a small amount of egg white, and beat well.
3. Sift the flour with the soda and spices and stir thoroughly into the honey mixture. Let the dough rest overnight.
4. Preheat oven to 375 degrees.
5. Roll dough to a ¼-inch thickness; cut out with a cookie cutter.
6. Brush with the reserved egg white, which has been beaten slightly. Press half a blanched almond into each cookie and bake for about 15 minutes on a buttered cookie sheet.

Yield: About 2 dozen, depending on size of cutter(s).

Colonial Peach Cake

CAKE

2 cups flour
½ teaspoon salt
½ teaspoon baking powder
2 teaspoons sugar
14 tablespoons butter
2 egg yolks
½ cup bread crumbs

1. Sift togther flour, salt, baking powder, and sugar. Cut in 11 tablespoons butter and when thoroughly mixed make a well in the center and add egg yolks and ⅓ cup cold water. Mix well.
2. Turn out onto a floured board and knead for a few minutes. Place in refrigerator to chill for 1 hour before using.
3. Roll dough into a thin sheet and cover bottom of a jelly-roll pan. Sprinkle with bread crumbs and dot generously with remaining butter.
4. Preheat oven to 350 degrees.

FILLING

2 pounds fresh ripe peaches, peeled and sliced
1 cup plus 2 tablespoons sugar
2 egg yolks
2 tablespoons heavy cream

1. Place the peach slices in rows on top of the bread crumbs and sprinkle with 1 cup of the sugar.
2. Beat the egg yolks, add remaining 2 tablespoons of sugar, and the cream. Pour over peaches.
3. Bake for 45 minutes. Cool.

Yield: 6 servings

Cheese-Filled Spongecake

1 envelope (tablespoon) unflavored gelatin	½ cup heavy cream, whipped
1¼ cups unsweetened canned pineapple juice or fresh orange juice	½ cup mixed candied or dried fruits (cherries, orange rind, citron, prunes, etc.), finely chopped or thinly sliced
2 tablespoons lemon juice	
½ cup sugar	1 9-inch spongecake about 4 inches high, chilled cherries or other fruit
½ pound creamed cottage cheese	

1. Soften gelatin in ¼ cup cold fruit juice and dissolve in 1 cup of juice which has been heated.
2. Add lemon juice and sugar and stir until sugar is dissolved. Chill until syrupy.
3. Whip until smooth and fold in cheese, cream, and candied or dried fruit. Chill until beginning to set.
4. Cut top off cake in a round about an inch thick. Remove center of cake, leaving a 1-inch rim and base.
5. Fill with the gelatin mixture and replace top. Frost with cream cheese frosting (see below) and chill until firm. Garnish with cherries or other fruit.

Yield: 12 servings

CREAM CHEESE ICING

2 ounces (¼ cup) cream cheese
1 teaspoon grated lemon or orange peel
2 tablespoons lemon juice
Salt
1½ cups confectioners sugar sifted (approximately)
Yellow food coloring (optional)

1. Cream the cheese with fruit peel, lemon juice, and salt.
2. Add enough of the sugar to give a good spreading consistency. Beat until very creamy. Color, if desired.

Yield: Frosting for 1 9-inch cake

Tipsy Cake

4 egg yolks
4 tablespoons sugar
½ teaspoon salt
2 cups milk, scalded
½ teaspoon vanilla extract
¼ teaspoon almond extract

1 8- or 9-inch spongecake sliced into 2 layers
1 cup whiskey or apple brandy
1½ cups almonds, split and toasted

1. Blend egg yolks, sugar, and salt in the top of a double broiler.
2. Add milk, stirring, and cook over simmering water, stirring constantly, until mixture coats spoon. Chill.
3. Flavor with vanilla and almond extracts.
4. Place one layer of cake on a serving dish. Pour over it half the whiskey and let it stand until absorbed. Top with half the custard. Cover with second layer of cake, soak with remaining whiskey, and top with remaining custard.
5. Garnish generously with toasted almonds.

Yield: 10 servings

Pineapple Chiffon Cake

2¼ cups sifted self-rising flour
1½ cups sugar
½ cup oil
5 egg yolks
¾ cup unsweetened pineapple juice
1 cup (about 8) egg whites, beaten stiff with ½ teaspoon cream of tartar

1. Preheat oven to 325 degrees.
2. Mix flour with sugar.
3. Add oil, egg yolks, and pineapple juice, beating until smooth.
4. Fold batter gradually into egg whites.
5. Pour batter into 10-inch ungreased tube pan and bake for about 45 minutes.
6. Cool cake on a rack and frost with pineapple frosting (see below).

Yield: 10 servings

PINEAPPLE ICING

½ cup crushed pineapple
8 tablespoons butter
1 pound confectioners sugar, sifted
¼ teaspoon salt

Blend ingredients until smooth.

Yield: Frosting for 1 10-by 2½-inch cake

Ted's Passover Spongecake

Shortening
8 eggs, separated
1½ cups sugar
Juice and finely grated peel of 1 lemon
1 cup, less 1 tablespoon, matzoh cake meal, sifted 3 times

1. Lightly grease the bottom of a 9-inch tube pan with shortening. Line with wax paper. Dampen paper with a little cold water.
2. Preheat oven to 350 degrees.
3. Beat egg whites until very stiff. Gradually add the sugar, beating after each addition.
4. Beat the yolks well and add to the whites along with the lemon juice and peel. Mix with a spoon.
5. Fold in the cake meal, a spoonful at a time. Turn into the prepared pan and bake for 40 to 50 minutes.

Yield: 8 servings

NOTE: *For nut cake, add ¼ cup of finely chopped nuts to the above recipe, when the lemon juice and peel are being added.*

Molasses Spongecake

1 cup sifted cake flour
½ teaspoon salt
5 eggs, separated
½ cup sugar
½ cup unsulphured molasses
1 tablespoon grated orange peel
1½ teaspoons grated lemon peel
2 teaspoons lemon juice

1. Preheat oven to 325 degrees.
2. Sift together flour and salt.
3. Beat egg yolks with rotary or electric beater until thick and lemon-colored. Gradually beat in sugar and molasses. Then beat with rotary or electric beater at low speed for an additional 3 minutes.
4. Stir in orange peel, lemon peel, and juice. Add flour mixture ⅓ at a time, mixing after each addition until smooth. When all flour has been added, beat until light and fluffy, about 30 seconds.
5. Beat egg whites until stiff enough to stand in peaks, but not dry; fold by hand into batter.
6. Bake 45 minutes in an ungreased, 9-inch tube pan. Turn cake pan upside down on wire rack. If cake has not dropped out of pan when cool, loosen from sides with spatula.

Yield: 12 servings

Festival Squash Cake

2 cups sifted cake flour
1 cup sugar
1 teaspoon salt
2 teaspoons double-acting baking powder
¼ teaspoon baking soda
½ teaspoon ground cloves
¾ teaspoon each ground

nutmeg, ginger, and cinnamon
½ cup shortening
½ cup unsulphured molasses
¾ cup dry mashed squash
2 eggs
2 tablespoons milk

1. Preheat oven to 375 degrees.
2. Sift together all dry ingredients except squash.
3. Add shortening, molasses, and squash. Mix just enough to dampen dry ingredients. Beat 2 minutes by hand or with electric beater at low speed.
4. Add eggs and milk. Beat 2 minutes.
5. Bake 25 minutes or until done in 2 well-greased, lightly floured, 8-inch layer pans. Cool cake on a rack and frost with squash butter frosting (see below).

Yield: 12 servings

SQUASH BUTTER ICING

  4 tablespoons butter
  2 tablespoons unsulphured molasses
¼ cup mashed squash
  3 cups sifted confectioners sugar

Brown butter in saucepan. Blend molasses and squash alternately with sugar in roughly equal amounts. Spread between layers and on exterior of cake.

Currant Upside-down Cake

  4 tablespoons butter
  2 cups sugar
1½ cups currants, washed and stemmed
  3 eggs, separated
⅓ cup currant juice or water (see note)
  1 cup sifted cake flour
  1 teaspoon baking powder

1. Preheat oven to 350 degrees.
2. Melt butter in an 11-by-7-by-1½-inch baking pan. Add 1 cup of the sugar and stir until melted. Spread the currants over this mixture.
3. Beat the egg yolks until thick and lemon-colored.
4. Gradually add the second cup of sugar to the egg yolks; add the currant juice or water.
5. Sift the flour and baking powder together and cut and fold into the egg yolk mixture.

6. Beat the egg whites until stiff peaks are formed. Fold the whites into the mixture.
7. Pour this batter over the butter, sugar, and currants.
8. Bake for 50 to 60 minutes. Invert cake on platter for serving.

Yield: 6 to 8 servings

NOTE: *To make ⅓ cup currant juice, slightly crush 1⅓ cups currants. Heat with 2 tablespoons water until soft. Strain through cloth.*

June Platt's Raisin Gingerbread

⅔ cup sugar
⅔ cup unsulphured molasses
⅔ cup boiling water
2 tablespoons butter
1 teaspoon baking soda
½ cup raisins, washed and
  dried

½ cup chopped walnuts or
  pecans
1 egg, well beaten
1½ cups flour
1 teaspoon ground cinnamon
1 teaspoon ground ginger
¼ teaspoon ground cloves

1. Preheat the oven to 350 degrees.
2. In a large bowl, mix together the sugar, molasses, boiling water, and butter. While the mixture is still hot, stir in the baking soda. Cool to room temperature.
3. Add the raisins, nuts, and egg.
4. Sift together the flour, cinnamon, ginger, and cloves. Stir into the molasses mixture.
5. Pour the batter into a well-buttered, 9-inch square cake pan and bake 35 to 40 minutes or until it tests done.
6. Frost with butter cream and decorate (see below).

Yield: 6 servings

NOTE: The recipe may be doubled and baked in a very well buttered 9-by-13-by-2½-inch cake pan for about 1 hour and 15 minutes.

BUTTER CREAM ICING AND DECORATION

8 tablespoons butter
4 cups sifted confectioners sugar
¼ cup light cream
½ teaspoon vanilla extract

1. Whip butter with electric beater at high speed until fluffy. Gradually add 2 cups sugar. Turn beater to low speed and add cream, vanilla, and rest of sugar. Blend well.
2. Sketch out a picture in color. Then test for color by working a very small amount of food coloring into a dab of icing and comparing with sketch. When you are ready, work with 1 color at a time and prepare roughly the amount of colored icing you think you will need for your design.

Noi Szeszely
(Lady's Whim)

3 cups flour	9 egg whites
¼ teaspoon salt	1½ cups confectioners sugar
1½ teaspoons baking powder	1½ cups (6 ounces) coarsely
½ pound unsalted butter	ground walnuts or hazelnuts
1 cup vanilla sugar (see note)	(use a Mouli grater or nut
6 egg yolks	grinder instead of a blender,
1 cup (12-ounce jar)	if possible)
raspberry jam	

1. Preheat oven to 350 degrees.
2. Sift together the flour, salt, and baking powder. Cut the butter into small pieces and work them into the flour, using your hands or a pastry blender.
3. Work in the vanilla sugar and the egg yolks, and squeeze the dough together into a mound.
4. Pat it into an unbuttered jelly-roll pan (5½ by 10½ by 1 inch), place it in the preheated oven, and bake for 10 minutes or until surface starts to brown. Let the cake cool for 10 minutes, then spread the jam evenly over the entire surface. Turn the oven down to 300 degrees and beat the egg whites until frothy. Add the confectioners sugar ¼ cup at a time, and continue beating until very stiff.
5. Fold in the ground nuts and spread the mixture evenly over the jam. Bake in the 300-degree oven for 20 minutes or more, until the meringue is lightly browned (not dried out, but sticky).
6. Remove from oven, cool in pan, and cut into neat squares. Do not cover the cake.

Yield: 18 to 24 servings

NOTE: *Vanilla sugar, which is used in many other recipes, can be prepared in quantity by bending a vanilla bean in two places and putting it in a jar filled with sugar. Keep the jar sealed and replace sugar as you use it. If you have no time to wait while the bean's flavor pervades the sugar, you can flavor sugar with a few drops of vanilla extract.*

Trudy Solin's Pecan Roll
(In the style of Michael Field)

Butter	pecans (use a Mouli or nut
7 eggs, separated	grinder, not a blender)
1 cup sugar	2 cups heavy cream
1 teaspoon baking powder	Confectioners sugar
¼ teaspoon almond extract	1 teaspoon vanilla extract
1½ cups (4 ounces) ground	

1. Butter bottom and sides of an 11½-by-17½-inch jelly-roll pan. Cover pan with a sheet of wax paper long enough so that the paper extends 4 inches or so beyond both ends of the pan. Push the paper down tightly against the bottom and sides of the pan. Butter the top of the paper.
2. Preheat oven to 350 degrees.
3. Beat yolks together and then gradually beat sugar into them. Continue beating until mixture is smooth and turns almost white.
4. Next beat in baking powder, almond extract, and, finally, the ground pecans.
5. In another bowl, beat the whites until they form stiff peaks. Stir a little of the whites into the yolk mixture to lighten it. Then pour the yolk mixture into the whites. Fold in until the whites no longer show.
6. Pour batter into prepared pan. Tilt the pan back and forth until the batter is spread uniformly over the surface.
7. Bake in preheated oven for 18 to 20 minutes, until the top of a knife stuck into the center comes out clean.
8. Remove from oven, cover with wax paper, and then with a dry kitchen towel. Let cool completely.
9. Whip heavy cream. Flavor with confectioners sugar to taste (2 to 3 tablespoons should do it) and the vanilla.
10. Gently remove towel and wax paper from top of pecan roll.

Sprinkle roll with confectioners sugar and turn out (invert) onto a triple layer of wax paper.

11. Set the serving dish you intend to use at one end of the triple wax paper, ready to receive the finished roll.

12. Trim off crusty edges of roll. Spoon whipped cream over top of roll.

13. To roll up: Grasp the corners of the near end of the wax paper and use them like handles to start rolling the pecan roll away from you into the serving dish. Speed is not of the essence. Roughly 2½ turns should completely roll up the roll and leave it sitting pretty on the dish, seam down. After the first turn, the roll will have slid away from the end of wax paper you are holding. Advance your hands along the sides of the paper and grasp the paper just behind the partly rolled roll. Raise paper slowly until the roll rolls forward one more turn. Repeat, but this time the process should be completed and the rolling action should carry the roll into the dish.

14. Sprinkle with confectioners sugar. Serve immediately or refrigerate.

Yield: 8 servings

Naomi Rubinstein's Marjolaine à la Point

CAKE BATTER

½ pound almonds, blanched and peeled
5 ounces shelled hazelnuts
1 cup sugar
¼ cup flour
8 large egg whites, about 1 cup

1. Preheat oven to 350 degrees.
2. Toast almonds and hazelnuts in a pan, stirring once or twice, for about 10 minutes, until lightly browned.
3. Rub away hazelnut skins; then grind nuts together in a nut grinder. Lower oven heat to 300 degrees.
4. Combine ground nuts with sugar and flour.

5. Beat egg whites to stiff peaks. Fold into nut mixture.
6. Spread batter evenly in a greased 10-by-15-inch jelly-roll pan and bake for 40 to 45 minutes. The batter should solidify and dry out but not brown very much. Hence, take a peek after 30 minutes.
7. Let cool and cut into 4 rectangles along the length of the tin, to make 10-by-3¾-inch pieces. Chill.

CREAM FILLINGS

4 cups heavy cream, at room temperature	¼ cup slivered almonds
4 teaspoons buttermilk, at room temperature	¼ cup sugar
	1 tablespoon water
8 tablespoons butter, softened	Oil
1½ pounds semisweet chocolate	Confectioners sugar

1. Combine cream and buttermilk in a jar a day ahead and let sit, sealed with plastic wrap, at room temperature (80 degrees is optimum) for several hours or overnight, until thickened but not strongly soured. Chill.
2. Beat butter into half the crème fraîche (thickened cream). Chill well.
3. Melt chocolate and combine with remaining crème fraîche. Chill until stiff but spreadable.
4. Toast almonds as in previous section. Boil sugar and water in a small, heavy saucepan until sugar caramelizes. Add almonds immediately and bring to a boil once more. Remove from heat and pour onto an oiled marble or baking sheet. Let cool and then pulverize in a blender to make praline.
5. On an appropriate serving dish, lay first of 4 cake layers. Ice top with ½ of chocolate cream.
6. Place second cake layer on chocolate cream and cover it with half of butter-cream mixture.
7. Add third layer. Combine remaining butter-cream with ¼ cup praline or to taste and ice third layer.
8. Add fourth layer. Ice completed cake with remaining chocolate cream. Chill. Sprinkle top with confectioners sugar before serving.

Yield: 8 to 10 servings

Schnee Torte
(Snow Torte)

CAKE

12 egg whites
 2 teaspoons vanilla extract
¾ cup sifted cornstarch
 3 cups sifted confectioners sugar
 1 cup sifted pastry flour
12 tablespoons butter, melted and lukewarm
    Dry bread crumbs

1. Preheat oven to 350 degrees.
2. Beat egg whites until stiff, but not dry, with a rotary beater or an electric beater at low speed. Add vanilla.
3. Sift together cornstarch, sugar, and flour, and add to the beaten egg whites. Stir in the lukewarm butter and when ingredients are well mixed, pour into a well-greased 9-inch spring mold that has been dusted with dry bread crumbs.
4. Bake for 1 hour. After the cake has cooled, ice with rum frosting.

FROSTING

1 cup confectioners sugar
2 tablespoons dark rum
   Candied fruits

Sift 1 cup confectioners sugar into a pan. Add 1 tablespoon water and place over medium heat. Stir constantly until sugar is completely dissolved. Continue to stir, adding rum drop by drop until mixture coats the spoon. After cake is frosted, garnish with candied fruits.

Yield: 8 to 10 servings

Croquembouche

CREAM PUFFS

 1 cup water
 8 tablespoons butter
 1 cup flour
¼ teaspoon salt
 4 eggs

1. Preheat oven to 400 degrees.
2. For the cream puffs, place the water and butter in a saucepan and bring to a boil, stirring to melt the butter.
3. Add the flour and salt all at once and continue cooking, while stirring, until mixture leaves the sides of the pan clean.
4. Remove pan from heat and beat in the eggs, one at a time, very well. Mixture should be smooth and shiny.
5. Drop the mixture by rounded teaspoons 1 inch apart on an ungreased baking sheet. Bake 25 to 30 minutes or until well puffed and golden. Cool on a wire rack.

FILLING I: WHIPPED CREAM

  1 cup heavy cream
  2 tablespoons confectioners sugar
  3 tablespoons Grand Marnier

OR FILLING II: PASTRY CREAM

  ⅔ cup sugar
  6 tablespoons flour
  ½ teaspoon salt
2½ cups milk, scalded
  3 egg yolks, lightly beaten
1½ teaspoons vanilla extract

1. To make the whipped cream filling, whip the heavy cream until it starts to form peaks. Beat in the confectioners sugar. Fold in the Grand Marnier.
2. To make the alternate pastry cream filling, place the sugar, flour, and salt in a saucepan and mix well. Stir in the milk.
3. Bring mixture to a boil, stirring, and cook over low heat, still stirring, 3 minutes.
4. Add a little of the hot mixture to the yolks and mix well.
5. Return yolk mixture to bulk of mixture in the saucepan and cook, stirring, until mixture thickens further.
6. Cool mixture. Stir in the vanilla and chill.

SYRUP AND ASSEMBLING

  ¾ cup cold water
  1 cup sugar
  ¼ teaspoon cream of tartar
    Hot water

1. To make the syrup and assemble the dessert, place the cold water, sugar, and cream of tartar in a small heavy skillet. Bring to a boil, stirring until sugar has dissolved. Boil, stirring occasionally, until mixture turns a light amber color; do not allow to overburn.
2. Remove from heat and place skillet over pan of hot water.
3. Make a small hole in the base of each puff. Place either the whipped cream or the pastry cream in a pastry bag fitted with a plain tube. Insert the tube in the hole and fill each puff.
4. Test the syrup by dipping one puff in the warm syrup and letting it set until cool. If the syrup hardens, stir ¼ cup hot water into the warm syrup and test again.
5. The syrup should remain glossy and very slightly sticky on the puffs when cooled to room temperature.
6. Dip the filled puffs in the syrup and arrange around the outside edge of an 8-inch plate or compote.
7. Fill in the center with dipped puffs. Build up a cone shape with dipped puffs. Those forming the outer ring of each layer should have tops facing out. Continue making successively smaller layers until all are used. Top with 1 cream puff.
8. Extra syrup can be drizzled over the croquembouche, if desired. The dessert should be stored in the refrigerator. Start serving the puffs, three or four per person, from the top.

Yield: About 3 dozen puffs or 9 servings

Savarin

¼ cup milk
1 package dry-active yeast
3¼ cups flour (approximately)
4 eggs
14 tablespoons unsalted butter, clarified

¼ cup confectioners sugar
1 teaspoon salt
3½ cups rum syrup (see below)
Apricot glaze (see below)
Glacéed fruits

1. Heat milk until lukewarm and dissolve yeast in it. Add about ½ cup of the flour to milk-yeast mixture. Stir vigorously until a dough forms. Shape dough into a ball. Put in a bowl, cover with cloth moistened with hot water and set to rise in a warm place.
2. When dough has doubled in bulk, after 45 minutes to 1 hour, beat

eggs in a double boiler over hot water until they are lukewarm and foamy.

3. In a large mixing bowl, combine risen dough with 2 cups of remaining flour, half the clarified butter, and half the beaten eggs, the sugar, and salt.

4. Mix well with a spoon and knead for 10 to 15 minutes. Then add remaining egg and butter to the dough. Mix in with a spoon or the hands. Sift in additional flour gradually until mixture is smooth and shows no signs of butter oozing out. Use as little flour as possible.

5. Knead dough, which will be quite slippery, until smooth and well blended.

6. Place the dough in a clean bowl, cover with a moist cloth, and set in a warm place until it shows signs of rising, about 10 minutes.

7. Preheat oven to 375 degrees.

8. Butter a 6-cup savarin mold. Fill a little more than half full with dough. Try to pat the dough into as smooth a ring as possible. Cover mold with damp cloth and set to rise as before until dough has almost filled mold, about 20 minutes.

9. Bake in preheated oven for 30 minutes or until a trussing needle stuck into savarin comes out clean.

10. Remove from oven, let cool completely, and unmold on a cake rack. While cake is cooling prepare rum syrup.

11. Pour cooled rum syrup into a 2-inch-high skillet of greater diameter than the savarin. Gash the bottom crust of the savarin (the surface that was exposed in the oven) in several places or simply slice it off and discard. Put savarin gently, bottom down, into the pan with the rum syrup. Leave the savarin in the syrup for 30 minutes while it soaks up the syrup through the cuts in the bottom crust. Spoon remaining syrup over top of savarin.

12. Tilt pan to pour off any excess syrup. Reserve syrup for future use. Invert pan, steadying savarin with your hand, and lay to rest, bottom up, on cake rack. Remove pan.

13. With hand on savarin bottom, invert rack, and place savarin right side up on a serving platter.

14. Make glaze (see recipe below) and paint on savarin with a pastry brush while hot.

15. Decorate with pieces of glacéed fruit.

Yield: About 10 servings

RUM SYRUP

1 cup sugar
2 cups plus 2 tablespoons water
2 pieces star anise
½ cinnamon stick
12 coriander seeds
⅛ teaspoon mace
7 tablespoons dark rum

1. Melt sugar in water over moderate flame.
2. Add star anise, cinnamon, coriander, and mace. Bring mixture to a boil. Add rum. Remove from heat. Strain into pan described in Step 11 of savarin recipe (see page 221).

Yield: About 3½ cups

APRICOT GLAZE

1½ cups apricot preserves
6 tablespoons sugar

1. Push apricot preserves through a fine sieve into a saucepan.
2. Add sugar and heat, stirring to dissolve sugar. Remove from heat and apply immediately.

Hartford Election Day Cake

1 cake fresh or 1 package dry-active yeast
½ cup lukewarm water
2 cups milk, scalded
1 teaspoon salt
6 cups sifted flour
2 cups chopped raisins
½ cup sliced citron

11 tablespoons butter, at room temperature
2 cups brown sugar
1 teaspoon ground cinnamon
½ teaspoon grated nutmeg
3 large eggs or 4 medium eggs
Molasses

1. Sprinkle yeast on lukewarm water.
2. Cool milk to lukewarm and add salt and softened yeast.
3. Add ⅓ cup of the flour to the chopped raisins and sliced citron. Mix well.

4. Add yeast mixture to remaining flour and beat with a wooden spoon until well blended. Set in a warm place (80 to 90 degrees) to rise until double in bulk. Setting the pan of dough in water of 90 to 100 degrees in temperature helps to give rapid rising— 45 to 60 minutes.
5. While dough is rising, cream butter, add sugar gradually, and cream until fluffy. Add cinnamon and nutmeg.
6. Add eggs one at a time and mix thoroughly.
7. Add creamed mixture to dough and beat until no spots of white dough show. Add raisins and citron and mix.
8. Let dough rise until double in bulk, 30 to 40 minutes.
9. Cut down dough and stir until smooth.
10. Turn into 3 well-greased 1-quart round pans or casseroles and let rise until dough reaches tops of pans, 45 to 60 minutes.
11. Preheat oven to 350 degrees.
12. Bake on lower shelf of oven for 30 minutes; lower temperature to 325 degrees and continue baking 30 to 35 minutes longer. If tops brown too fast, cover after first 30 minutes with aluminum foil. Glaze when done with molasses; return to oven for 5 minutes to set glaze.

Yield: 24 servings

Brownstone Front Cake

8 tablespoons butter
2 cups sugar
2 eggs, separated
2 cups flour, sifted twice
1 teaspoon baking soda dissolved in ½ cup warm water
½ teaspoon vanilla extract

⅛ teaspoon salt
1 egg yolk
½ cup water
4 ounces unsweetened chocolate, melted
2 cups chocolate icing (see page 287)

1. Preheat oven to 350 degrees.
2. Cream butter and 1 cup sugar with a wooden spoon or mixer until sugar is thoroughly dissolved.
3. Beat in 2 egg yolks one by one.
4. Gradually stir in flour, alternately with dissolved baking soda. Add vanilla and salt.
5. Mix remaining sugar, egg yolk, water, and melted chocolate

together in a saucepan. Bring to a boil and continue boiling, stirring occasionally, for 3 minutes, and add to cake batter. Beat egg whites until stiff but not dry and fold into the batter.

6. Pour batter into 2 8-inch layer cake pans greased with butter and sprinkled with flour. Bake approximately 45 minutes or until tester comes out clean. Cool on rack. When cool, fill and frost with icing.

Yield: 8 servings

Susan's Blueberry Cottage Cheese Cake

1 tablespoon butter
4 cups blueberries
2 envelopes (tablespoons) unflavored gelatin
¾ cup sugar
¼ teaspoon salt
1 egg, separated
¾ cup milk
1 teaspoon grated lemon peel

3 cups cottage cheese (mashed, sieved, or blended)
2 tablespoons fresh lemon juice
1 teaspoon vanilla extract or kirsch
¾ cup heavy cream

1. Butter a shallow, 1⅓-quart dish. Arrange 3½ cups blueberries in dish to form a shell.
2. Off heat, in top of double boiler, mix together gelatin, sugar, and salt. Separately, beat together egg yolk and milk and add to top of double boiler. Cook over simmering water, stirring for 6 minutes. Add lemon peel and cool.
3. When mixture has cooled, stir in cottage cheese, lemon juice, and vanilla or kirsch. Chill until slightly thickened.
4. While cottage cheese mixture is chilling, combine egg white and heavy cream in a chilled mixing bowl, beat until stiff and fold into chilled cottage cheese mixture. Pour filling into shell. Arrange remaining blueberries on top. Chill.

Yield: 6 to 8 servings

Chestnut Almond Torte

4 egg yolks
¾ cup sugar
2¼ heaping cups (roughly ½ pound) unshelled chestnuts, peeled and put through food mill
2 tablespoons dark rum
1 cup whole, shelled almonds, blanched, peeled, and put through food mill

5 egg whites
Unsalted butter
Flour
1 recipe chocolate whipped cream filling (see page 285)
1 apricot glaze (see page 284)
1 recipe chocolate icing (see page 286)

1. Preheat oven to 350 degrees.
2. Beat yolks and sugar until very light and fluffy. This will take several minutes even with an electric beater. The end product should have an off-white color.
3. Add chestnuts and rum to yolk-sugar mixture. Blend together and add half the almonds.
4. Beat egg whites to stiff peaks and fold into mixture in Step 3. Fold in rest of almonds and pour mixture into a buttered, floured 10-by-2½-inch spring mold.
5. Place filled mold in oven. After 10 minutes, reduce heat to 325 degrees and bake for 35 to 50 minutes more, until cake has pulled away slightly from sides of mold.
6. Remove from oven, let cool, unmold, and cut into 2 layers of equal thickness, leaving spring mold bottom attached to bottom of 1 layer.
7. Apply chocolate whipped cream to top of bottom layer, and arrange the other layer on top of that.
8. Several hours before serving, glaze top of top layer with hot apricot glaze.
9. When glaze has set, prepare icing. Balance cake in one hand, with hand under spring mold bottom, and dribble icing over top of cake. Tilt cake back and forth to coat evenly. Put cake on a rack and finish icing sides with a table knife or spatula.
10. Refrigerate until icing sets.

Yield: 10 to 12 servings

Pies

Mrs. Foster's Frosty Lime Pie

GRAHAM CRACKER CRUST

1¼ cups graham cracker crumbs
¼ cup superfine sugar
4 tablespoons butter, at room temperature

1. Preheat oven to 350 degrees.
2. Place the graham cracker crumbs and sugar in a bowl. Add the butter and work with a wooden spoon, or the fingers, to blend well.
3. Press the mixture evenly into a 9-inch pie plate using the fingertips or an 8-inch pie plate to press down into the mixture.
4. Bake 10 minutes. Cool to room temperature.

FILLING

5 eggs, separated
¾ cup superfine sugar
⅔ cup freshly squeezed, strained lime juice
2 teaspoons grated lime peel
1 pinch salt

1. Beat the yolks in the top of a double boiler until very stiff. Gradually beat in ½ cup sugar until mixture is very pale and stiff and forms a rope when dropped from the beaters.
2. Stir in the juice and the rind and heat over simmering water, stirring, until mixture coats the back of the spoon. Do not allow to boil.
3. Turn into a large bowl to cool to room temperature.
4. When the yolk mixture is room temperature, beat the egg whites with the salt until soft peaks form. Gradually beat in the remaining sugar until mixture is stiff and shiny.
5. Stir ⅓ of the meringue mixture into the cooled yolk mixture. Fold in remaining egg whites until evenly distributed.

6. Turn into cooled graham cracker pie shell and bake 15 minutes or until lightly tinged with brown. Cool. Chill and freeze. Once frozen, cover with plastic wrap and keep frozen until just before serving.

TOPPING

1½ cups heavy cream, whipped
Thin slices lime or fresh strawberries
Sugar

Remove from the freezer 10 minutes before serving. Cover with the whipped cream and garnish with lime slices dipped in sugar or fresh strawberries.

Yield: 8 servings

NOTE: *Pie will keep frozen 2 or 3 weeks. If a sweeter pie is desired, cut down the lime juice to ½ cup. Extra pie can be refrozen. If desired, pie can be well chilled and served without freezing.*

Apple Tart

PASTRY

2 cups flour
4 tablespoons sugar (approximately)
1 teaspoon salt
½ pound butter
2 egg yolks
Bread crumbs

1. Mix flour with sugar and salt. Cut in butter with a pastry blender or 2 forks until the flour-coated pieces are reduced to about the size of peas.
2. Beat yolks lightly and mix into flour well.
3. Pat crust into a 10-by-2-inch fluted metal pan with a removable bottom. Sprinkle with bread crumbs and a small amount of sugar. Refrigerate.

FILLING

12 medium apples, peeled, cored, and sliced
 5 tablespoons flour
½ teaspoon ground allspice
½ teaspoon grated nutmeg
¼ teaspoon ground cinnamon
 1 cup sugar
 3 tablespoons butter, melted
⅓ cup dark corn syrup

Combine all ingredients and mix well. Put in a large skillet (or 2 skillets, if necessary) and cook over low heat, uncovered, for 20 minutes or until apples are barely tender.

CRUMB TOPPING

½ cup brown sugar
½ cup sifted flour
 4 tablespoons butter

Mix sugar and flour well. Cut in butter with pastry blender until well blended.

ASSEMBLING

1. Preheat oven to 400 degrees.
2. Pour apple mixture into pastry shell.
3. Distribute crumb topping evenly over the top of filling.
4. Bake for about 30 minutes, until crust is lightly browned.
5. Let cool completely before removing rim of pan. To do this, set pan on top of a can whose diameter is less than the circular opening in the bottom of the rim.
6. Pull the rim gently downwards until it is completely detached. Set it down and move the tart to a serving platter.

Yield: 8 servings

Apple Tart

7 medium apples
⅓ cup sugar
1 unbaked pâte brisée shell baked in a 9-inch tart tin with fluted
   edge and removable bottom or a 10-by-1-inch flan ring
   (see page 263)
2 tablespoons apricot preserves
1 tablespoon kirsch or water

1. Peel and core apples. Cut 4 apples into chunks and 3 into thin
   slices.
2. Combine the apple chunks (reserve slices) with sugar and cook
   over low heat until a thick puree is formed. Let cool.
3. Fill pâte brisée shell, whose bottom has been pricked all over with
   a fork, with puree.
4. Preheat oven to 425 degrees.
5. Lay an overlapping circle of apple slices around the outer
   perimeter of the filling with the ends of the slices pointed toward
   the center of the tart.
6. Cover the rest of the filling with concentric circles of overlapping
   slices, with these slices roughly perpendicular to the slices
   in the circle made in Step 5, so as to form a rose pattern.
   Eventually, a small uncovered hole at the center will be left, which
   should be filled with 2 or 3 small pieces of apple cut from any
   remaining slices.
7. Bake tart 20 minutes. Remove side of tart tin or flan ring and bake
   15 to 20 minutes more or until golden.
8. Bring the apricot preserves and kirsch or water to boil. Strain and
   brush lightly on outside crust and apples.

Yield: 6 to 8 servings

Apple Pie

PASTRY

2 cups flour
1 teaspoon salt
⅔ cup shortening

1. Place the flour and salt in a bowl. Remove ⅓ cup of the flour mixture to a small bowl and stir ¼ cup water in to make a paste. Set aside.
2. Add the shortening to the remaining 1⅔ cups flour in the bowl and, with 2 knives or a pastry blender, cut it in until the pieces are the size of small peas.
3. Add the paste to the shortening mixture and mix to a dough with the fingers.
4. Roll half the dough out to ⅛-inch thickness on a lightly floured board. Line a 9-inch pie plate with the pastry.

FILLING

2 ¼-inch-thick slices fat salt pork, diced (about 1 cup)
6 large tart apples, peeled
1 cup sugar
⅛ teaspoon ground cinnamon
⅛ teaspoon grated nutmeg

1. Preheat oven to 450 degrees.
2. Render the salt pork pieces in a skillet until they are crisp. Set pieces and accumulated fat aside.
3. Core and slice the apples into the lined pie plate. Mix together the sugar, cinnamon, and nutmeg, and sprinkle over the apples.
4. Pour the pork pieces and the fat over the apples. Roll out the remaining pastry to ⅛-inch thickness and cover the pie.
5. Seal and decorate the edges. Make steam holes and bake 10 minutes. Reduce the oven heat to 350 degrees and bake 30 to 40 minutes longer or until pastry is cooked and apples tender.

Yield: 6 servings

Banana Cream Pie

½ cup sugar
5 tablespoons flour
¼ teaspoon salt
2 cups milk
2 egg yolks, lightly beaten

1 tablespoon butter
½ teaspoon vanilla extract
3 ripe bananas
1 baked 9-inch pastry shell
Whipped cream

1. Combine sugar, flour, and salt in top of double boiler. Add milk slowly, mixing thoroughly. Cook over rapidly boiling water until well thickened, stirring constantly.
2. Cook 10 minutes longer, stirring occasionally.
3. Stir small amount of the hot mixture into egg yolks; then pour back into remaining hot mixture while beating vigorously. Cook 1 minute longer.
4. Remove from heat and add butter and vanilla. Cool.
5. Peel and slice bananas into pie shell and cover immediately with filling. Top with whipped cream.

Yield: 8 servings

Rhubarb and Strawberry Bavarian Pie

1 cup sugar
1 pound rhubarb, cut into 1-inch pieces
1 baked 9-inch pastry shell of cookie dough (see page 264)
2 envelopes (tablespoons) unflavored gelatin
1 cup mashed strawberries
1 cup heavy cream, whipped
2 egg whites, stiffly beaten
Whole strawberries

1. Sprinkle ¾ cup sugar over rhubarb and let stand to extract juice while making pie shell.
2. Soften gelatin in ¼ cup cold water.
3. Heat rhubarb to boiling, lower heat, and simmer until just tender —5 minutes or longer. Stir gently or shake pan to prevent sticking.
4. Add softened gelatin and stir gently until dissolved. If desired, remove the most perfect pieces of rhubarb for garnishing, and put a spoonful of syrup over them. Set them aside, but do not chill.
5. Add strawberries to rhubarb mixture and more sugar, if desired. Cool and then chill until beginning to set.
6. Fold in half the whipped cream and the meringue made by beating remaining sugar into beaten egg whites. Turn into pie shell and chill until set.
7. At serving time, garnish with reserved whipped cream, reserved pieces of rhubarb, and additional whole strawberries.

Yield: 6 to 8 servings

NOTE: *This rhubarb and strawberry bavarian may be served as a gelatin mold rather than as a pie filling. Simply turn the mixture—Step 6—into a 1-quart mold and chill until set.*

Mrs. Dill's Bucket

- 2 cups sifted flour
- 2 teaspoons baking powder
- ½ teaspoon salt
- 1½ tablespoons butter (approximately)
- 1½ tablespoons shortening
- 2 eggs, lightly beaten
- ⅔ cup milk
- 1 quart sweetened fresh berries or 2½–3 cups any canned fruit, chopped, if necessary

1. Sift together flour, baking powder, and salt.
2. Chop in butter and shortening until particles of fat are the size of coarse cornmeal.
3. Add eggs and milk and stir until all flour is dampened.
4. Turn into a buttered 3-pound shortening can or 2-quart mold and spread dough over bottom and sides.
5. Place fruit in center, using enough to fill can not over ⅔ full. Cover with lid of can or several thicknesses of wax paper.
6. Place can on a rack in a deep pot. Add enough boiling water to reach ⅔ up the outside of the can. Cover pot and steam 3 hours. Unmold and serve hot.

Yield: 8 servings

Maple Chiffon Pie

- 1 envelope (tablespoon) unflavored gelatin
- ½ cup milk
- ½ cup maple syrup
- Pinch salt
- 2 eggs, separated
- ¾ cup heavy cream
- 1 teaspoon vanilla extract
- ¼–½ cup broken nut meats (optional)
- 1 baked 9-inch pastry shell

1. Soften gelatin in 2 tablespoons cold water.
2. In the top of a double boiler, scald milk, syrup, and salt.
3. Beat egg yolks and add syrup mixture gradually while stirring. Return to double boiler and cook over simmering water, stirring constantly, until thickened. Remove from heat, add softened gelatin and stir until dissolved. Chill until mixture begins to thicken.
4. Whip cream, add vanilla, and fold into maple custard.
5. Beat egg whites until stiff and fold into mixture. Fold in nuts, if used.
6. Turn into pastry shell and chill until firm. Garnish with additional whipped cream and nuts, if desired.

Yield: 8 servings

Currant Chiffon Pie

CRUST

16 graham crackers, finely crushed
 1 teaspoon flour
 8 tablespoons butter, softened
½ cup sugar
 1 teaspoon cinnamon

1. Preheat oven to 375 degrees.
2. Blend all ingredients thoroughly. Press evenly and firmly over bottom and sides of a 9-inch pie plate. Bake 10 minutes.
3. Cool and chill.

FILLING

 1 envelope (tablespoon) unflavored gelatin
 3 eggs, separated
⅓ cup sugar
 1 cup sweetened currant juice (See note)
 1 tablespoon lemon juice
¼ teaspoon salt
 1 cup heavy cream, whipped

1. Soften gelatin in ¼ cup cold water. Beat egg yolks and half the sugar. Add currant juice, lemon juice, and salt.
2. Cook, stirring constantly, over very low heat until mixture coats a spoon. Add softened gelatin and stir until dissolved. Cool and then chill until mixture begins to thicken. Whip until fluffy.
3. Beat egg whites, adding remaining sugar gradually, until mixture holds up in peaks. Fold into gelatin.
4. Turn into chilled pie shell and chill until firm.
5. At serving time, whip cream until stiff and spread over pie or garnish pie with cream, using a pastry tube.

Yield: 6 to 8 servings

NOTE: *To make 1 cup currant juice, wash 1 quart of fresh berries, crush slightly, and heat with a small amount of water until softened. Strain through cloth, squeezing. Sweeten with 2 tablespoons sugar.*

Transparent Pie

```
8 ounces currant jelly
1 9-inch pastry shell, baked but not browned
½ pound butter, softened
1 cup granulated sugar
3 eggs, well beaten
```

1. Preheat oven to 450 degrees.
2. Spread the jelly evenly over the bottom of the pastry shell. Cream butter with sugar, using an electric beater. Add eggs and continue to beat until mixture is light and spongy. Spread evenly over jelly.
3. Bake pie 5 minutes at 450 degrees. Reduce heat to 375 degrees and bake until top mixture sets, about 20 to 25 minutes. When the center of the filling is almost firm (ascertained by slightly shaking the pan), remove from oven. Be careful not to overcook. Serve warm or cold, but never hot.

Yield: 10 servings

NOTE: *This dessert is extraordinarily rich and should be cut in small wedges.*

Cherry Cobbler

> 1 pound sour cherries, pitted (about 3 cups on the stem or 2½ cups if pitted)
> 1 tablespoon butter
> 1 cup plus 1 tablespoon sugar
> 1 cup plus 1 tablespoon sifted flour
> 1½ teaspoons double-acting baking powder or 2 teaspoons any other type
> ½ teaspoon salt
> 2½ tablespoons shortening
> ⅜ cup milk (approximately)

1. Preheat oven to 425 degrees.
2. Heat together to boiling the cherries, butter, and ¼ cup water. Mix 1 cup sugar and 1 tablespoon flour. Add to cherries and heat, stirring, to boiling. Turn into a casserole.
3. Sift together remaining cup flour, remaining tablespoon sugar, baking powder, and salt. Cut in shortening until mixture resembles coarse cornmeal. Add enough milk to make a thick batter. Drop by spoonsful on cherries in casserole.
4. Bake about 30 minutes. Serve, if desired, with hard sauce.

Yield: 4 to 5 servings

Spanische Windtorte Mit Obersschaum
(Meringue Torte with Whipped Cream)

> 8 egg whites
> 1¾ cups confectioners sugar
> 1 teaspoon white vinegar
> 2 teaspoons vanilla extract
> 1 cup heavy cream, whipped
> 1 tablespoon sugar

1. Using an 8-inch cake pan as a guide, draw circles on 4 sheets of wax paper.
2. Preheat oven to 225 to 275 degrees.
3. Beat egg whites until foamy. Add sugar, 2 tablespoons at a time, and continue beating. When the mixture begins to form peaks, add vinegar, 1½ teaspoons vanilla, and the rest of the sugar, if any is left.

4. Put this mixture in a pastry bag. Pipe out 4 ½-inch thick circles of meringue on the 4 pattern circles. Fill 1 circle with concentric circles of meringue. Pipe a lattice of crisscrossing lines of meringue across another of the circles.
5. Transfer the wax paper sheets, with the meringues, to the bottoms of 4 inverted 8-inch cake pans. Bake for about 1½ hours, or until firm. Remove from paper. Let cool on a rack.
6. Just before serving the dessert, set the filled-in circle of meringue on a cake plate, to form the base of the torte. Put the 2 rings on top of it. Fill with whipped cream, flavored with ½ teaspoon vanilla and sweetened with sugar. Put the lattice on top.

Yield: 8 servings

NOTE: *Instead of sweetened vanilla-flavored whipped cream, torte can be filled with whipped cream into which cut-up brandied fruits have been mixed, or with ice cream, or any other dessert mixture desired.*

Maple Syrup Pie

1 cup plus 1 tablespoon maple syrup
¼ teaspoon salt
1 tablespoon butter
2 tablespoons cornstarch
2 eggs, separated
1 baked 8-inch pastry shell

1. Preheat oven to 350 degrees.
2. Place 1 cup each syrup and water in saucepan and heat to boiling point. Add salt and butter.
3. Mix cornstarch with 1 tablespoon cold water and add to egg yolks. Beat well.
4. Add hot syrup gradually to egg mixture and cook over low heat, stirring constantly until thick. Cool slightly. Strain into pastry shell.
5. Beat egg whites until stiff. Slowly add remaining tablespoon maple syrup. Spoon over pie. Form into peaks with back of spoon.
6. Bake 12 to 15 minutes, or until golden brown. Serve warm or cool, never hot.

Yield: 8 servings

Grasshopper Pie

1 8½-ounce package
  chocolate wafers
⅔ cup sugar
4 tablespoons butter, at room
  temperature
1 envelope (tablespoon)
  unflavored gelatin
¼ teaspoon salt
3 eggs, separated
3½ tablespoons green crème
  de menthe

4½ tablespoons white crème
  de cacao
6–8 drops green food coloring
1 egg white
⅛ teaspoon cream of tartar
2 cups heavy cream
3 tablespoons vanilla extract
3 tablespoons confectioners
  sugar
Chocolate shavings

1. Preheat oven to 375 degrees.
2. Crush chocolate wafers, combine with 1 teaspoon sugar and cream with butter, using an electric beater. Line a 10-inch pie plate with mixture and bake in preheated oven for about 12 minutes.
3. While crust is cooling, sprinkle gelatin into ½ cup cold water in a saucepan or the top of a double boiler. Add ⅓ cup sugar, ⅛ teaspoon salt, and egg yolks. Stir until well mixed and heat gently, stirring constantly until gelatin has dissolved and mixture has thickened. Thickening will take place well below the boiling point.
4. Remove mixture from heat and stir into it the green crème de menthe and white crème de cacao. Stir in the green food coloring. Refrigerate for about 15 minutes or until mixture starts to gel slightly and is the consistency of unbeaten egg white.
5. Beat the 4 egg whites with cream of tartar and remaining salt to stiff peaks. Gradually beat in remaining sugar and fold into liqueur-flavored mixture.
6. Combine 1 cup heavy cream with 1½ tablespoons vanilla and 1½ tablespoons confectioners sugar and whip. Fold whipped cream into liqueur-flavored mixture and then turn mixture into pie crust.
7. Chill pie for several hours or overnight. Top with remaining cream, whipped and flavored with remaining vanilla and confectioners sugar. Garnish with chocolate shavings.

Yield: 8 to 10 servings

Sweet Potato Custard Pie

PASTRY

1½ cups flour
 ½ cup plus 2 tablespoons shortening
 ¼ teaspoon salt
    Ice water

1. Place the flour, shortening, and salt in a bowl. Blend in the shortening until the mixture resembles coarse cornmeal. Stirring with a fork, add just enough ice water to make the dough cling together.
2. Roll out the dough on a lightly floured board and line a 9- to 10-inch pie plate. Fold under the extra pastry at the edge and decorate. Chill.

FILLING

3 large sweet potatoes, scrubbed
  Boiling water
2 tablespoons butter
1 cup sugar
1 teaspoon grated orange peel
⅓ cup orange juice

3 eggs, separated
1 cup milk
2 tablespoons cognac (optional)
2 tablespoons confectioners sugar

1. Preheat oven to 450 degrees.
2. Place the potatoes in a saucepan with boiling water to cover. Cover and simmer until tender, about 30 minutes.
3. Drain, peel, and pass the potatoes through a ricer or sieve. Add the butter, sugar, orange peel, and juice. Beat the egg yolks lightly and combine with the milk. Stir into the potato mixture.
4. Stir in the cognac.
5. Bake the chilled crust 7 to 8 minutes or until just set, but not browned. Pour in the potato filling, reduce oven heat to 375 degrees, and bake 40 minutes or until set.
6. Beat the egg whites until frothy. Add the confectioners sugar gradually while beating and continue to beat until mixture is thick and glossy. Pile on top of the pie so that meringue touches pastry at all points. Bake 5 minutes longer or until lightly browned.

Yield: 6 to 8 servings

Raspberry Tart

2 cups flour
1 cup sugar
2 tablespoons vanilla extract
1 hard-boiled egg yolk
2 fresh egg yolks
¾ pound butter, at room temperature
1 pound raspberry jam
2 cups Grand Marnier Sauce (see page 302)

1. Mix together flour, ½ cup sugar, vanilla extract, hard-boiled egg yolk, fresh yolks, and ½ pound (2 sticks) of butter; form into a ball.
2. Refrigerate dough for 30 minutes.
3. Preheat oven to 450 degrees.
4. Butter bottom and sides of a shallow, preferably fluted, 10-inch pie plate. Then pour sugar liberally over buttered surface. Shake off excess sugar and reserve.
5. Remove dough from refrigerator. Cut slices about ⅛ inch thick from ball of dough. Arrange slices so as to completely cover bottom and sides of pan. Press the joints together and fill any cracks with small pieces of dough.
6. Spread jam evenly over bottom of dough.
7. Cut out strips from remaining dough (again cutting them quite thin) and lay across the top of the jam in a crisscross or other pattern.
8. Dust decorative strips carefully with sugar.
9. Bake for 10 to 15 minutes, until crust has browned slightly.
10. Lower oven heat to 375 degrees and continue baking for another 15 minutes.
11. Remove pie from oven and let cool. Serve cold with generous amounts of Grand Marnier Sauce.

Yield: 8 to 10 servings

Tarte aux Pêches

4–6 medium peaches
1¼ cups sugar
  1 tablespoon vanilla extract
  ½ cup raspberry jam
  1 unbaked 10-inch pâte sucrée shell (see page 263)
  2 cups crème frangipane (see page 285)

1. Halve and pit peaches. Bring enough water to cover them to a boil with 1 cup sugar and vanilla. Plunge peaches into boiling syrup and lower heat so that syrup is just below a simmer. Poach for 10 minutes. Turn off heat and let peaches cool in syrup for 15 minutes. Peel immediately. Drain.
2. Push raspberry jam through a fine sieve. Heat with remaining sugar until mixture is smooth and has slightly thickened. Brush onto inside of sucrée shell, which has been placed on a serving dish. Let set for 15 minutes. Reserve excess glaze.
3. Fill shell with frangipane cream. Arrange peach halves on top of frangipane. Reheat glaze until it liquefies; pour and brush it over top of peaches and frangipane. Let set and refrigerate until ready to serve.

Yield: 8 servings

Dolce al Burro

  ½ pound lightly salted butter
  5 egg yolks
  1 cup confectioners sugar (approximately)
  ⅓ cup anisette
  ⅓ cup very strong, drip, Italian-roast coffee, chilled
 36 ladyfingers (approximately)

1. Soften the butter with a spoon or electric mixer. When creamy, add yolks one at a time. With each yolk add a tablespoon of sugar. Blend well after each addition of yolk and sugar. When all yolks and accompanying 5 tablespoons sugar have been blended in, add remaining sugar.
2. Pour in anisette and coffee slowly, continuing to mix as you pour.

If mixture starts to curdle, beat in a small quantity of confectioners sugar.

3. Line an 8-inch springform pan with parchment paper cut in 2 pieces: a circle slightly greater in diameter than the bottom of the pan and a band to cover the inside wall. Put the circular paper over the bottom of the pan, folding the excess up the sides. (It will be necessary to cut small wedges into the circle so that the fold will fit smoothly against the wall of the mold.) Then put in the band.

4. Cut off curved ends of ladyfingers and reserve. Begin arranging ladyfingers vertically around the wall of the pan, sugar side toward the pan. Spread a ¼-inch layer of butter cream on the exposed sides of the ladyfingers as you put them in.

5. Then arrange a layer of ladyfingers along the bottom, sugar side down. It will take some ingenuity with cutting the ladyfingers and using the reserved tips as filler to create a flush layer. Coat finished layer with butter cream ¼ inch thick. Continue to add alternating layers of ladyfingers and butter cream, pressing down lightly on the horizontal layers from time to time. When a horizontal layer of ladyfingers can be laid in level with the tops of the vertical ladyfingers, stop.

6. Cover cake with a circle of parchment and a circle of cardboard. Put a weight (approximately 2 pounds) on top of the cardboard. Refrigerate overnight.

7. To serve, remove weight, cardboard, and paper. Invert cake on a serving platter and unmold, removing paper liners very carefully. Sprinkle with confectioners sugar and serve.

Yield: 6 to 8 servings

Cranberry Charlotte

2¼ cups sugar
1 pound cranberries
2 envelopes (tablespoons) unflavored gelatin
1 tablespoon lemon juice
1 tablespoon rum

¼ teaspoon salt
18 ladyfingers (approximately), split in half
3 egg whites
2 cups heavy cream

1. Boil 2 cups sugar and 2 cups water for 5 minutes. Add cranberries; cook until all skins burst.

2. Turn a cup of above mixture into a hot, sterilized, heatproof glass jar, top with melted paraffin, and use as a side dish at a later meal. Force remaining mixture through food mill or puree in a blender.

3. Soften gelatin in ½ cup cold water. Add 1 cup puree; heat, stirring, until gelatin has dissolved. Add to remaining puree. Add juice, rum, salt. Chill until mixture starts to set.

4. Meanwhile, line 2 5-cup molds with the ladyfingers.

5. Whip egg whites, gradually adding remaining sugar. Beat until stiff. Whip cream and chilled gelatin mixture separately.

6. Fold cream into gelatin mixture; fold in egg whites. Turn into lined molds. Chill; unmold.

Yield: 6 to 8 servings per mold

Soufflés

Michael Field's Praline Soufflé Fifi

PRALINE

½ cup sugar
½ cup shelled pecans

1. Place the sugar and ¼ cup cold water in a small, heavy, porcelainized saucepan. Heat, stirring, until sugar dissolves. Continue to heat without stirring until the mixture turns a pale caramel color.
2. Stir in the pecans and pour immediately onto an oiled cookie sheet. Let cool completely.
3. Break up the cooled praline into rough pieces and blend in an electric blender, a few pieces at a time, until it is reduced to a powder. There will be about 1¼ cups. Set aside.

SOUFFLÉ

 1 cup (about 8) egg whites, at room temperature
10 tablespoons superfine sugar

1. Preheat oven to 350 degrees.
2. Beat the egg whites until frothy. Gradually beat in the sugar until the mixture forms unwavering peaks and does not slip in the bowl. It will be stiff and glossy. Do not overbeat.
3. Fold in ½ cup of the praline powder, using a rubber spatula. The remaining praline powder can be used for other desserts.
4. Spoon the meringue mixture into a buttered and sugared 2-quart soufflé dish. Set the dish in a deep roasting pan and set on a shelf in the middle of the oven. Pour boiling water into the roasting pan until it comes halfway up the sides of the soufflé dish. Bake 40 minutes or until a cake tester thrust into the middle comes out clean.
5. Remove the dish from the water bath, set on a rack, and run a

spatula carefully around the soufflé to loosen the outside edge. The soufflé will sink as it cools.

6. When the soufflé has reached room temperature, turn a serving plate upside down over the soufflé dish and invert so that the soufflé is transferred to the plate.

SAUCE

2 10-ounce packages frozen raspberries
 Superfine sugar to taste (optional)
2 tablespoons kirsch
 Whipped cream (optional)
 Fresh raspberries for garnish (optional)

1. Set the raspberries in a sieve over a bowl and allow to thaw completely.
2. Discard the liquid or use for another dessert or beverage mixture. Blend the raspberries in an electric blender until smooth. Force the mixture through a very fine sieve, so that none of the seeds go through. Chill the mixture.
3. Add sugar to taste to the chilled sauce if desired. Stir in the kirsch and spoon over the soufflé. Decorate with whipped cream if desired.

Yield: 6 servings

Chocolate Soufflé

4 ounces sweet chocolate
4 eggs, separated and at room temperature
4 tablespoons unsalted butter
 Confectioners sugar

1. Cover chocolate in saucepan with hot tap water and let soften.
2. When point of knife will penetrate chocolate easily, pour off water and add yolks to chocolate. Whisk chocolate and yolks together thoroughly.
3. Preheat oven to 475 degrees.
4. Add butter to chocolate and egg yolk mixture. Stir mixture over low heat until butter melts, being careful not to cook yolks.
5. Pour chocolate mixture into mixing bowl.

6. Beat egg whites with large whisk until they hold stiff peaks.
7. Knock off egg whites on whisk into chocolate mixture. Stir in whites with small whisk until smooth.
8. Scrape rest of whites into chocolate mixture with rubber spatula and fold in with wooden spatula.
9. For mousse, scrape mixture into glass bowl and refrigerate overnight.
10. For soufflé, scrape into buttered, sugar-dusted 1-quart soufflé mold and put in oven so that bottom of mold is slightly below center level.
11. As soon as top of soufflé has set and there has been visible rising —after 2 minutes or so—reduce heat to 425 degrees.
12. Cook for aproximately 6 more minutes, until the outer surface is firm and center is still soft.
13. Dust with confectioners sugar and serve with 2 dessert spoons, using soft inside of soufflé as a sauce for the firmer outer portions.

Yield: 6 servings

Grand Marnier Soufflé

4 tablespoons butter
3 tablespoons flour
1 cup light cream
4 egg yolks
4 tablespoons sugar
½ teaspoon salt
7 tablespoons Grand Marnier (approximately)

6 egg whites, stiffly beaten
6 ladyfingers
⅓ cup chopped candied fruits (optional)
Berries or other fruit, sweetened

1. Heat butter, blend in flour, add cream, and cook, stirring, until thickened.
2. Preheat oven to 325 degrees.
3. Beat egg yolks with sugar and salt. Add to sauce and cook over very low heat until thickened.
4. Flavor with 4 tablespoons Grand Marnier. Fold in stiffly beaten egg whites. Pour half the mixture into a buttered and sugared 3-quart casserole.
5. Moisten ladyfingers with 2 tablespoons Grand Marnier and arrange in a layer over soufflé mixture in the casserole. If desired, add fruits which have been soaked in 1 tablespoon Grand Marnier. Cover with remaining soufflé mixture.

6. Bake 45 minutes or longer. Serve immediately with a fruit sauce made of crushed or sliced sweetened fruit which has been flavored with Grand Marnier.

Yield: 6 servings

NOTE: *Other liqueurs may be substituted for Grand Marnier.*

Simone Beck's Soufflé Meringué à la Liqueur

Butter
Confectioners sugar
5 egg yolks
1⅓ cups granulated sugar
½ teaspoon vanilla extract
¼ cup orange liqueur or Benedictine
8 egg whites
Pinch of salt

1. Put a collar of buttered aluminum foil around a 2-quart soufflé dish. Butter the insides of the dish and collar and sprinkle with confectioners sugar.
2. Beat the egg yolks with half the sugar until the mixture is smooth and a pale creamy yellow. Beat in the vanilla and the liqueur.
3. Whip the egg whites with a pinch of salt until they are white and frothy; gradually pour in the remaining sugar and continue to beat to make a meringuelike mixture, very white, shiny, and firm.
4. Stir ¼ of the egg whites into the egg yolk mixture to lighten it; then fold back lightly and evenly into the remaining egg whites.
5. Fill the prepared soufflé dish. The recipe can be made up to 2 to 3 hours in advance to this point if the egg whites have been properly beaten and folded.
6. Preheat oven to 375 degrees.
7. Bake the soufflé in the oven for 25 to 30 minutes. Sprinkle it with confectioners sugar just before serving.

Yield: 8 servings

Individual Orange Soufflés

  8 oranges with thick skins
  3 eggs, separated
1¼ cups sifted confectioners sugar
  2 tablespoons cornstarch
  1 tablespoon Grand Marnier, Cointreau, or Triple Sec

1. Cut a wide slice off the top of each orange. Then make sure the oranges will sit steadily on a flat surface. If not, cut a thin slice off the bottom to make them balance. Do not cut through skin.
2. With a grapefruit spoon, scrape out the flesh and juice of the oranges, being careful not to pierce the skins. Collect the contents of 6 oranges in 1 bowl. Reserve the remaining flesh and juice separately; it will not be used in this recipe, but can be used for juice.
3. Preheat oven to 450 degrees.
4. Put the flesh and juice from 6 oranges through a juicerator or strain twice, once through an ordinary strainer, once through a fine mesh strainer, preferably a chinois. Push vigorously with a wooden spoon on the flesh until all juice has been extracted. Reserve.
5. Blend egg yolks together with sugar and cornstarch in a heavy-bottomed saucepan with a wooden spoon until the mixture turns a whitish color. Pour in orange juice and blend well.
6. Heat orange juice mixture over low heat, stirring constantly. At the first sign of boiling—the mixture will have noticeably thickened—remove from heat. Add liqueur, and cool.
7. Beat egg whites to stiff peaks and fold into orange juice custard.
8. Without delay, pour soufflé mixture into orange peels, which have been arranged securely on an ovenproof baking dish. Depending on the original size of the oranges you will be able to fill from 6 to 8 oranges.
9. Reduce oven to 400 degrees and bake for 20 minutes.
10. Serve immediately. Use a large serving spoon to transport individual oranges from baking dish to plates.

Yield: 6 to 8 soufflés

Custards, Mousses, Puddings, Ice Cream

Oeufs à la Neige
(Floating Island)

MERINGUE BALLS

1¾ cup sugar (approximately)
  8 egg whites

1. Fill a big shallow pan with water to a depth of 2 inches or slightly less. Place on the stove. The size of the pan is not crucial, but the greater the surface area it permits, the greater the number of balls of beaten egg white you will be able to poach at once, an important consideration when you actually get down to producing this dessert.
2. Dissolve ¾ cup sugar in the water. This amount is calculated on 3 quarts of water in the pan, or ¼ cup sugar per 1 quart of water.
3. Bring the poaching liquid to a slow boil, reduce heat so that a steady temperature just below boiling is maintained.
4. With a whisk, beat the egg whites until stiff. Then gradually beat in the remaining sugar until mixture is smooth and no longer granular.
5. With an ice cream scoop (the kind with a scoop-expelling mechanism), plop a ball of the egg white-sugar mixture (meringue) into the poaching liquid.
6. Continue putting balls of meringue into the poaching liquid until the meringue is exhausted. You will probably not have enough room to poach them all in one batch. Keep dipping the ice cream scoop into cold water as you work.
7. Make sure the water does not boil. Poach meringue balls for 8 to 10 minutes. About halfway through, pick them up and turn them over with a slotted spoon. When they are done, remove from water with a slotted spoon and drain them on paper toweling.
8. Drained balls should be arranged on a serving platter and

allowed to cool. Just before serving, spin a light tracery of spun sugar over them and pour crème anglaise on top (see recipes below).

CRÈME ANGLAISE

2 cups milk
½ vanilla bean
5 egg yolks, at room temperature
½ cup sugar

1. Combine milk and vanilla in a saucepan. Bring to a boil, remove from heat.
2. Mix well together yolks and sugar. Combine with milk and cook until liquid thickens and coats a wooden spoon. Contrary to received opinion in some quarters, this process can be done over direct heat. Thickening will occur very quickly; therefore, you should stir constantly to remain in touch with your custard. At the first sign of thickening—or the appearance of a piece of scrambled yolk on the bottom—remove to a bowl of ice and keep stirring.
3. Pour through a fine strainer, preferably a chinois, and reserve.

SPUN SUGAR

1 cup sugar
1 tablespoon corn syrup

Combine sugar and corn syrup. Heat until the mixture caramelizes, that is, until it turns golden brown, just above 310 degrees on a candy thermometer. Remove from heat, as mixture will turn black and dreadful at about 350 degrees.

ASSEMBLING

1. Cover work area with newspaper. Put sugar-syrup mixture near platter of oeufs à la neige. While sugar is still very hot and pliable, take 2 forks in 1 hand so that tines are lined up side by side, and spread apart. Dip tines in sugar, let excess drip off, and swing rapidly back and forth over oeufs à la neige, coating them with a web of spun sugar. It is a good idea to practice this maneuver a few times, until you get it, before spinning sugar over the actual dish.
2. Pour crème anglaise over meringue balls as you serve them.

Yield: 6 to 8 servings

Basic Custard

     4 eggs or 6–8 egg yolks
 4–6 tablespoons sugar
   ½ teaspoon salt
     3 cups milk, scalded
     1 teaspoon vanilla extract
       Nutmeg (optional)

1. Beat eggs slightly. Add sugar and salt.
2. Add scalded milk gradually while stirring.
3. Strain to remove any portions of egg white and add vanilla.

BAKED CUSTARD: *Turn into 6 custard cups or a 1½-quart casserole. Sprinkle with nutmeg, if desired. Set in a pan of hot water, with the water as high as the level of the custard. Bake in a moderate oven (350 degrees) until a knife inserted in the center comes out clean. Custard should be baked in about 30 minutes for cups or 50 minutes for casserole. Cool quickly.*

Yield: 6 to 7 servings

SOFT CUSTARD: *Add vanilla only after custard has cooled. Cook mixture in the top of a double boiler over hot, not boiling, water until mixture thickens and coats a metal spoon—about 5 minutes. Cool quickly, stirring occasionally. Add vanilla.*

Yield: About 4 cups

French Wine Custard

   6 eggs, separated
 ⅔ cup sugar
 ¾ cup sweet sherry
 ¼ teaspoon salt

1. Mix egg yolks and sugar in the top of a 1½-quart double boiler. Set over simmering water and beat with a rotary beater until fluffy.
2. Add sherry gradually and continue beating until mixture resembles whipped cream. Cool and chill.

3. Before serving, beat egg whites with salt until stiff. Fold into chilled custard. Turn into a glass serving dish. Serve plain, or garnished with strawberries or cherries.

Yield: About 8 servings

Madeleine Kamman's Apple Mousse

3 pounds McIntosh apples (about 6–8 large)	½-inch piece cinnamon stick
½ cup sugar	3–4 tablespoons Calvados
Grated peel of ½ lemon	1 cup heavy cream
⅛ teaspoon salt	3 glacéed orange slices, halved
2 tablespoons butter	

1. Peel, core, and slice the apples into a heavy saucepan. Add ½ cup water, sugar, lemon peel, and salt. Cover tightly and cook until apples are soft, stirring once or twice to prevent sticking.
2. Add the butter and cinnamon stick and cook uncovered, stirring occasionally, until mixture is very thick and measures about 2 cups. Cool and chill at least 4 hours. Remove cinnamon stick.
3. Stir in the Calvados. Whip the cream until it is thick, but not quite stiff enough to form peaks. Fold into the chilled applesauce and chill again. Decorate with glacéed orange slices.

Yield: 4 to 6 servings

Rote Grütze

1 10-ounce package frozen raspberries, thawed
⅔ cup currant jelly
½ cup quick-cooking tapioca

1. In a saucepan, bring raspberries, 1½ cups water, and jelly to a boil.
2. Add tapioca to ½ cup water, stirring to mix, then add gradually to boiling fruit in saucepan. Cook 1 minute, stirring constantly. Pour pudding into bowl. Stir every few minutes until pudding cools. Refrigerate. Serve chilled.

Yield: 4 to 6 servings

Rum and Fruit Bavarian

2 tablespoons rum	1 cup scalded milk
½ cup chopped mixed candied fruits	¾ cup sugar
	½ teaspoon salt
1 envelope (tablespoon) unflavored gelatin	¾ cup heavy cream
	¼ cup chopped pecans
¼ cup cold milk	Whole maraschino cherries
3 eggs, separated	Angelica

1. Pour rum over fruits and let stand, covered, until ready to use.
2. Soften gelatin in cold milk.
3. In top of a double boiler, beat egg yolks; add scalded milk, ½ cup sugar, and salt. Cook over hot water, stirring constantly, until mixture coats spoon.
4. Add gelatin, stir until dissolved, and chill until mixture begins to thicken.
5. Beat egg whites stiff. Gradually add remaining ¼ cup sugar, beating constantly; fold into custard mixture.
6. Beat ¼ cup cream until slightly stiff; fold into custard.
7. Add rum-soaked fruits and nuts.
8. Pour into 2-quart ring mold that has been rinsed in cold water. Chill until firm.
9. Unmold. Garnish with cherries and angelica. Whip remaining cream and place in center of mold.

Yield: 8 to 10 servings

Strawberry Bavarian

   1 quart strawberries, hulled
   1 cup sugar
   1 envelope (tablespoon) unflavored gelatin
   3 tablespoons boiling water
   1 tablespoon lemon juice
2½ cups heavy cream, whipped

1. Crush the berries and add the sugar. Let stand for 30 minutes at room temperature.
2. Soak the gelatin in 3 tablespoons cold water until soft. Dissolve it in the boiling water. Stir the gelatin into the strawberries. Add the lemon juice.

3. Chill the mixture and, when it is about to set, fold in 2 cups whipped cream.
4. Pour the mixture into a cold wet 2-quart mold. Chill until it is firm. Unmold, garnish with remaining whipped cream and strawberries.

Yield: 8 servings

Spiced Rhubarb Pudding

   1 recipe spiced baked rhubarb (see page 309)
   1 cup biscuit mix
   1 tablespoon sugar
   1 egg, beaten
3–4 tablespoons milk

1. Preheat oven to 400 degrees.
2. Place rhubarb mixture in casserole.
3. Mix biscuit mix and sugar. Blend egg and 3 tablespoons milk, and add, stirring only enough to blend. Add more milk, if necessary, to give a drop-biscuit dough.
4. Pour over top of rhubarb, and bake until dumplings are brown— about 20 minutes.

Yield: 6 servings

Spring Rhubarb Pudding

   8 slices toasted bread, crusts trimmed off
1½ cups milk, scalded
   4 tablespoons butter
   5 eggs, lightly beaten
   1 cup honey or 1½ cups sugar

½ teaspoon ground cinnamon
¼ teaspoon salt
 2 cups diced rhubarb
¾ cup wheat germ
  Half-and-half

1. Cut the toast into ½-inch cubes and place in a buttered casserole.
2. Combine the milk and butter and stir to melt the butter. Pour over the toast cubes and let stand 15 minutes.
3. Preheat oven to 325 degrees.

4. Mix together the eggs, honey or sugar, cinnamon, salt, and rhubarb. Stir into the bread mixture.
5. Sprinkle with the wheat germ and bake 45 minutes. Serve warm with half-and-half.

Yield: 8 to 10 servings

Rhubarb Cream

1 pound rhubarb, cut into small pieces
  Grated peel and juice of 1 lemon
3 whole cloves
1 small cinnamon stick
1½ cups sugar
1 cup heavy cream, whipped and sweetened

1. Combine rhubarb, lemon peel and juice, cloves, cinnamon, and sugar. Let stand 2 hours.
2. Cook slowly until mixture has consistency of marmalade. Remove the spices. Cool.
3. Before serving, fold in whipped cream. Serve in sherbet glasses or on thin pieces of cake.

Yield: 6 servings

Maple Parfait

4 egg yolks
½ cup maple syrup
¼ teaspoon salt
½ teaspoon vanilla extract
1½ cups heavy cream, whipped
¼ cup chopped nuts or ⅓ cup crushed nut brittle (optional)

1. Beat egg yolks in the top of a 1½-quart double boiler. Add maple syrup and salt, and cook over simmering water, beating with a rotary beater until mixture is thick and fluffy.
2. Add vanilla, set in a pan of ice water, and continue beating until cold.
3. Fold in whipped cream and nuts or brittle, if used.
4. Turn into a 1-quart mold or freezer tray and freeze as quickly as

possible (with temperature control set at coldest point). Serve plain or with maple syrup and nuts.

Yield: 4 to 6 servings

Maple Crème Brûlée

2 cups heavy cream
   1-inch piece vanilla bean
4 egg yolks, well beaten
3 tablespoons granulated sugar
   Maple sugar (or light brown sugar)

1. Scald cream with vanilla bean in top of double boiler.
2. Mix egg yolks and granulated sugar. Add cream gradually while stirring.
3. Return to double boiler, stirring constantly until custard coats a spoon. Cool slightly and remove vanilla bean.
4. Turn into a glass serving dish and chill. This much may be done a day ahead if desired.
5. When ready to serve, cover the cream custard with ¼- to ⅓-inch layer of maple sugar. Set the dish in a pan of ice and broil until sugar caramelizes, watching it carefully to prevent scorching. Serve immediately or chill again.

Yield: 5 to 6 servings

Crème Brûlée with Peaches

1 cup milk
1 cup light cream
4 egg yolks, lightly beaten
¼ cup granulated sugar
⅛ teaspoon salt
1 teaspoon vanilla extract
¾ cup brown sugar
12 peach halves

1. Heat milk and cream in top of double boiler to scalding.
2. Combine egg yolks, granulated sugar, and salt, and gradually stir into hot mixture.

3. Cook in double boiler until mixture coats spoon, stirring constantly. Add vanilla and cool.
4. Pour into a shallow glass baking dish and chill.
5. At serving time, place in a larger pan and surround with ice. Sprinkle with brown sugar to cover. Broil until sugar is bubbly and melted. Watch carefully so that sugar does not burn. Serve over chilled peach halves.

Yield: 6 servings

Cabinet Pudding Ring

3 cups cake crumbs
3 tablespoons butter (approximately)
4 cups basic custard (see page 250)

1. Add crumbs and butter to milk before scalding for basic custard.
2. Proceed as for baked custard (see page 250).
3. Preheat oven to 350 degrees.
4. Turn into a buttered 9-inch ring mold, set in pan of hot water, and bake until a knife inserted in the center comes out clean— about 35 minutes.
5. Cool quickly and then chill thoroughly.
6. To turn out of ring, loosen around edges of mold and invert on a cold plate. Fill center with whipped cream or fruit.

Yield: About 8 servings

Pfitzauf

2 cups flour
1½ cups milk
5 eggs
2 tablespoons butter, melted
Sugar

1. Combine flour and milk. Beat until mixture is very smooth.
2. In another bowl, beat eggs until foamy, then stir into the milk-flour batter. Add melted butter. Beat well. Let stand 30 to 40 minutes.

3. Preheat oven to 350 degrees.
4. Fill 16 large or 24 small well-greased muffin tins about ¾ full and bake for 45 minutes. Serve hot, sprinkled heavily with sugar and with stewed fruits or dessert sauces on the side.

Yield: 8 to 10 servings

Bettelmann
(Beggar)

    4 cups fresh or canned applesauce
1½ cups bread crumbs, ready-made, or grated stale bread, preferably dark rye
    ¾ cup raisins plumped in water for 1 hour
    ½ cup chopped nuts (walnuts, hazelnuts, almonds, or peanuts)
    4 eggs, beaten

1. Preheat oven to 350 degrees.
2. Combine applesauce, bread crumbs, raisins, and chopped nuts. Put in a well-greased, ovenproof dish.
3. Pour beaten eggs over above combination and bake for 30 to 40 minutes.

Yield: 8 servings

German Bread Pudding

    8 ounces pumpernickel bread
1–1½ cups rum
    3 cups heavy cream
    1 cup sugar
    1 teaspoon vanilla extract
    8 ounces semisweet chocolate, grated
    ½ cup strawberry jam

1. Spread pumpernickel slices on baking sheet and dry in a 325-degree oven. Bread should be thoroughly dried.
2. Pour rum over dried bread. With a fork, break soaked bread into small pieces.
3. Whip cream, adding sugar gradually; then add vanilla.

4. In a deep serving dish, spread a layer of whipped cream. Sprinkle with grated chocolate. Top with a layer of the pumpernickel mixture and dot with strawberry jam. Continue the layers until all ingredients are used. Refrigerate overnight or at least 8 hours before serving.

Yield: 8 servings

Wellington Pudding

4 ounces suet, finely chopped
1 cup sifted flour
4 cups soft bread crumbs, toasted and lightly packed
1 cup raisins
2 tablespoons finely chopped candied orange peel
½ cup sugar

3 eggs, beaten
½ cup milk
½ teaspoon ground cinnamon
½ teaspoon grated nutmeg
¼ cup cream sherry or marsala
Butter
Chestnut puree (see below)

1. Mix suet, flour, crumbs, raisins, orange peel, and sugar. Use fingers to separate pieces of fruit. Add remaining ingredients except butter; mix.
2. Turn into a buttered 8½-inch ring mold. Cover top with foil by pressing it against outer and inner rims of ring. Leave center hole uncovered. Steam for 2 hours on rack in pot containing an inch of boiling water. Turn out; fill with chestnut puree.

CHESTNUT PUREE

Cook and shell a pound of chestnuts (see page 168). Force through a sieve. Thin with heavy cream, sweeten to taste, and flavor with vanilla. Heat. Pile in hot pudding ring.

Yield: 10 servings

Fig Pudding

8 ounces dried figs
6 ounces suet
½ cup soft white bread crumbs
1 cup sifted flour
2 eggs

1 cup milk
Pinch salt
Pinch nutmeg
Butter
Eggnog sauce (see page 303)

1. Grind together figs and suet, using medium blade of food chopper. Mix in crumbs and flour.
2. Beat eggs; combine with milk, salt, and nutmeg. Stir thoroughly into fig mixture. Turn into 6 to 8 buttered custard cups. Cover with foil. Steam on rack in pot containing an inch of boiling water about 45 minutes. Turn out; serve with eggnog sauce.

Yield: 6 to 8 servings

Macrobiotic Coffee Pudding

1 cup whole wheat flour
1 teaspoon peanut oil
¼ teaspoon salt
2 tablespoons Ohsawa coffee (fine ground)
1 teaspoon ground cinnamon
3 tablespoons chopped mixed hazelnuts, almonds, and walnuts

1. Sauté the flour in oil over very low heat until it is slightly browned and imparts a nutlike fragrance.
2. Cool flour.
3. Add 3 cups water, salt, and coffee to flour and cook until thickened.
4. Add cinnamon and nuts.
5. Serve hot or pour into a casserole which has been rinsed in cold water and refrigerate.
6. Unmold and serve.

Yield: 6 servings

Philadelphia Vanilla

6 cups light cream
1¼ cups sugar
2 3-inch vanilla beans, split
⅛ teaspoon salt

1. In top of double boiler, combine 3 cups cream, sugar, vanilla beans, and salt. Cook, stirring constantly for 10 minutes. Remove bean pods, scraping pulp and seeds into the cream. Cool.

2. Add remaining 3 cups cream to the cooled mixture. Mix well.

3. Churn-freeze.

Yield: ½ gallon

New Year Meringues

  6 egg whites, at room temperature
  ½ teaspoon salt
  ½ teaspoon cream of tartar
1½ cups sifted sugar
  2 tablespoons powdered instant coffee
  ¼ teaspoon almond extract
  1 quart ice cream

1. Preheat oven to 275 degrees.

2. Cover 2 cookie sheets with baking parchment. Using an 8-inch-long bell pattern, trace 2 bells on each piece of paper.

3. Beat egg whites until frothy. Sprinkle with salt and cream of tartar; continue beating until stiff but not dry. Combine sugar and instant coffee; gradually beat this in, adding almond extract with the last of the sugar. Continue beating until sugar is dissolved and meringue stands in stiff peaks.

4. Using the plain round tube of a pastry decorating set, place rims of meringue on all 4 bells about ¼ inch in from the edge. Fill in 2 of the bells solidly with meringue, and again outline all 4 bells with meringue to give extra height.

5. Bake until surface is dry, about an hour. Remove from paper with spatula. Put a hollow meringue on top of a solid meringue, sticking them together with water. Arrange bells on a platter and fill centers with ice cream.

Yield: 6 servings

Biscuit Tortoni

  2 teaspoons unflavored gelatin
⅔ cup light corn syrup
  2 egg yolks
¼ teaspoon salt
  1 teaspoon vanilla extract
  3 tablespoons cream sherry

  1 cup heavy cream, whipped
¼ cup chopped pistachio nuts
   or almonds
½ cup vanilla wafer or
   macaroon crumbs

1. Soften gelatin in ¼ cup cold water. Heat corn syrup to boiling and stir into gelatin.
2. Beat egg yolks until very light and add syrup mixture gradually, beating constantly. Cool thoroughly, add salt and flavorings, and fold in whipped cream. Add nuts.
3. Turn into small fluted paper cups or into an ice cube tray. Dust top thickly with crumbs.
4. Freeze without stirring until firm.

Yield: About 14 small cups

Watermelon Sherbet

  1 cup sugar
  1 cup light corn syrup
  1 tablespoon grated lemon peel
 ¼ cup lemon juice
2½ cups finely chopped watermelon pulp
  2 egg whites, beaten

1. Set freezer control for fast freezing.
2. Boil sugar and 1 cup water until syrupy, stirring until sugar is dissolved. Cool.
3. Add corn syrup, lemon peel and juice, and watermelon pulp.
4. Pour into freezing tray and freeze until firm.
5. Turn into a chilled bowl, break up with a wooden spoon, and beat with electric or hand rotary beater until free from lumps but still mushy.
6. Fold in beaten egg whites. Return to freezer tray and freeze until firm.

Yield: 6 servings

Coeur à la Crème

2 cups creamed cottage cheese
1 cup heavy cream
  Salt

1. Beat cheese to a smooth consistency while gradually adding the cream. Salt to taste.
2. Line with cheesecloth a heart-shaped basket (one that measures 4½ to 5 inches from point to point) and arrange cheese mixture inside. Stand on a plate in the refrigerator for 24 hours or longer to drain out moisture.
3. Unmold and serve, if desired, with fresh mint, fresh strawberries, and pineapple and sugar.

Yield: 6 servings

Pastries and Cookies

Pâte Brisée

   2 cups flour
 ¼ teaspoon salt
   3 tablespoons sugar
   3 tablespoons ice water
   1 egg yolk
 ¼ pound cold butter

1. Form a wreath of flour on a wooden board (or marble slab) with the center about 5 to 6 inches wide.
2. In the free space at the center, put the salt, sugar, and water. Mix with fingers until there is no trace of sugar or salt. Stir in the egg yolk. Mix well.
3. Add butter in small pieces. Work and mix until all liquid is absorbed. Work in the flour.
4. Form a ball. With the palm of your hand, press and flatten the ball outward several times. Form ball again and work the dough outward. Do this 3 times.
5. Flatten the ball to a thickness of about 1½ inches, keeping it round. Wrap it in foil and chill in the refrigerator for 2 hours.
6. Roll to a 12-inch circle. Fit into a 9-inch tart tin with fluted edge and removable bottom or 10-by-1-inch flan ring set on a baking sheet. Trim and prick bottom with fork.

Yield: 1 unbaked pâte brisée shell

Pâte Sucrée

 1½ cups flour
   1 egg
 14 tablespoons (approximately) lightly salted butter, at room temperature
   1 teaspoon grated orange peel
   5 tablespoons sugar
       Uncooked rice or beans

263

1. On a board or pastry marble, sift out flour in a ring. In the free space at the center, combine egg, butter, orange peel, and sugar into a soft mass. Then, working quickly and lightly with the fingertips, pull in the flour. Don't knead but work on the dough just enough so that it holds together in a ball.
2. Refrigerate immediately in a covered bowl for at least 2 hours. Put rolling pin in the freezer.
3. Preheat oven to 400 degrees. Grease the inside of a 10-inch flan ring and the center of a cookie sheet.
4. On a clean, lightly floured board or pastry marble, quickly roll out the refrigerated dough. Rotate the dough as you roll, sprinkling more flour underneath and on top of it to prevent sticking. Keep rolling until you have a sheet of dough about ⅛ inch thick.
5. With a metal spatula, work dough carefully away from board, slip both hands underneath and transfer to top of flan ring on cookie sheet. Press dough down inside ring and press against inner sides of ring. Run rolling pin over top edge of ring, cutting off excess dough hanging over sides. (This excess can be used to make cookies.) Reserve excess in refrigerator.
6. Gently push dough just up and over the top edge of the flan ring. Take an ample sheet of buttered foil, place it over ring (butter side down) and fill with uncooked rice or beans, arranged so as to keep dough from slipping away from sides of mold or rising off cookie sheet during baking.
7. Bake in center of oven for 8 minutes or until pastry has set. Remove foil and beans. Continue to bake for 10 to 12 minutes longer or until crust has just begun to brown.
8. Remove from oven. Unmold and slide crust onto a rack.

Yield: 1 Baked 10-inch pâte sucrée shell

Cookie Dough Pastry Shell

  1¼ cups sifted flour
⅓–¼ cup sugar
  ½ teaspoon baking powder
  ¼ teaspoon salt
  3 tablespoons shortening
  2 tablespoons butter, softened (approximately)
  2 egg yolks
3–4 tablespoons milk or water

1. Preheat oven to 400 degrees.
2. Sift together flour, sugar, baking powder, and salt.
3. Add shortening and butter and chop or rub into flour mixture until mixture resembles cornmeal.
4. Mix egg yolks with 3 tablespoons milk or water. Add to flour, blend, and stir until well mixed, adding enough additional milk or water to make a stiff dough.
5. Roll on a floured pastry cloth or board until large enough to fit into a 9-inch pie plate. Fit into the buttered pan without stretching. Trim edge and make a standing fluted rim. Prick in bottom of pan.
6. Bake on the lower shelf of oven until brown—about 25 minutes. Cool slightly and remove from pan. Let stand on a rack until cool.

Yield: 1 baked 9-inch pastry shell or 4 tart shells

Cornets

 2 egg whites
½ cup sugar
⅓ cup sifted flour
 3 tablespoons butter, melted and cooled

1. Preheat oven to 400 degrees.
2. Beat the egg whites until stiff, sprinkle the sugar over them, and fold it in gently. Fold in the flour and the butter in the same way.
3. Butter and flour a baking sheet and heat it in a hot oven. Drop the batter onto the hot sheet by tablespoons and spread it thinly. Bake for about 3 minutes, or until the wafers are golden brown.
4. Quickly take wafers from sheet with spatula; roll while still warm into cones. If they cool and become too crisp to roll, return to oven briefly. Place on cooling rack to crisp.

Yield: 14 to 16 cornets

Danish Pastry

PASTRY

½ teaspoon salt
¼ cup sugar
½ pound plus 4 tablespoons
   butter
½ cup milk, scalded
1 package dry-active yeast or 1
   cake compressed

¼ cup lukewarm water (about
   110 degrees)
1 egg, beaten
3 cups sifted flour
   (approximately)
Oil

GLAZE

1 egg, beaten
¼ cup milk
1 teaspoon sugar

1. Add salt, sugar, and 4 tablespoons butter to scalded milk. Cool to
   lukewarm.
2. Sprinkle or crumble yeast into water and stir until dissolved.
3. Combine milk and yeast mixture and add egg.
4. Add and stir in about half the flour. Beat until smooth. Add and
   stir in enough additional flour to make a soft dough.
5. Turn out on a floured board and knead until smooth and elastic.
   Place in an oiled bowl, oil surface of dough, and let stand in a
   warm place (80 to 85 degrees) until double in bulk.
6. Punch down and refrigerate 1 hour.
7. Roll dough into a rectangle about ½ inch thick. Dot ⅔ of the
   dough with 5⅓ tablespoons of remaining butter. Fold unbuttered
   third over middle third and remaining buttered third over
   double layer. This makes 3 layers.
8. Repeat Step 7 twice. Refrigerate whenever dough and butter are
   too soft for easy handling. Chill the finished dough 30
   minutes or overnight.
9. If dough has chilled overnight, let stand at room temperature
   until soft enough for rolling. Roll and shape as suggested
   in following directions or as desired.
10. Preheat oven to 400 degrees.
11. Place on oiled baking sheets and let rise until double in size.
12. To glaze, brush with a beaten egg which has been blended with
    ¼ cup milk and 1 teaspoon sugar.
13. Bake until well browned—about 20 minutes.

Yield: 12 to 16 pastries

HOW TO SHAPE DANISH PASTRIES

COCKS' COMBS: Roll dough to ¼-inch thickness and spread with a paste made by creaming together equal measures of butter and sugar. Cut into 4-inch squares. Place a spoonful of desired filling across center of each square, moisten edges, fold into rectangles, and press edges to seal. Cut 4 or 5 deep slashes in sealed edge. Let rise, brush and glaze, and bake.

SPANDAUERS: Role dough to ¼-inch thickness, spread with paste made by creaming together equal measures of butter and sugar. Cut into 4-inch squares. Place desired filling in center. Fold corners to center and press down. Let rise, brush with glaze, and bake. Drop a teaspoon of jelly in center of each.

FILLED TRIANGLES: Roll dough to ¼-inch thickness. Spread with desired filling and fold in thirds, like a letter. Cut into 4-inch squares and then cut each square into 2 triangles. Let rise, glaze, and bake.

FILLED ROUNDS: Cut large rounds of dough which has been rolled to ¼-inch thickness. Place filling across center, pick up outer edge of rounds, and pull together to overlap, join at center. Press to seal. Let rise, apply glaze, and bake.

CHEESE FILLING

1 cup cottage cheese, sieved	1 tablespoon butter, melted
1½ tablespoons flour	½ teaspoon vanilla extract
1½ tablespoons sweet or sour cream	3 tablespoons currants or raisins
2 eggs, separated	½ cup chopped blanched almonds
½ cup sugar	

1. Mix cheese, flour, cream, egg yolks, and sugar. Add butter and vanilla and mix until smooth. Add currants or raisins and almonds.
2. Fold in stiffly beaten egg whites.

Yield: 2 cups

PRUNE FILLING

1 cup pitted prunes, cooked and drained
½ cup apricots or raisins, cooked and drained
½ cup dry bread or cake crumbs
¼ cup honey

1. Grind or chop the prunes and apricots or raisins.
2. Add crumbs and honey.
3. Heat, stirring constantly, until well blended. If too thin, add more crumbs; if too thick, add lemon juice.

ALMOND PASTE FILLING

  8 tablespoons butter
½ cup sugar
  1 cup ground almonds

1. Cream together the butter and sugar.
2. Add and blend in the almonds.

Hamantashen

POPPY SEED AND HONEY FILLING

  2 cups poppy seeds
  1 cup water or milk
½ cup honey
¼ cup sugar
    Pinch salt
1–2 eggs

1. Scald poppy seeds in water or milk, drain, and pound or grind.
2. Cook together, stirring, all ingredients except eggs until thick.
3. Let cool. Add eggs, beating in thoroughly. If the addition of eggs thins out filling excessively, return to heat and cook over low heat, stirring constantly, until thick.

COOKIE DOUGH

⅔ cup shortening (approximately)
½ cup sugar
  1 egg
  2 cups sifted flour (approximately)
  3 tablespoons water or milk
½ teaspoon vanilla extract

1. Preheat oven to 350 degrees.
2. Cream shortening and sugar. Add egg and cream well.

3. Add flour and water or milk and vanilla alternately, using enough flour to make a soft ball. Chill thoroughly.
4. Roll and cut into 2- to 4-inch circles. Place a ball of filling on each and bring edges up to form a flat triangle. Pinch edges together to seal.
5. Bake on a cookie sheet greased with shortening until brown, about 10 minutes.

Yield: About 24 small pastries

Soft Molasses Cookies

1 cup shortening	2 teaspoons baking soda
1½ cups molasses	2 teaspoons ground cinnamon
¼ cup sugar	1½ teaspoons ground ginger
4 cups sifted flour	½ teaspoon ground clove
1½ teaspoons salt	1 egg

1. Melt shortening in saucepan large enough for mixing cookies. Stir in molasses and sugar; cool.
2. Sift together flour, salt, soda, cinnamon, ginger, and cloves. Add a small amount to molasses mixture and mix. Beat egg into molasses mixture.
3. Add remaining flour mixture, blending until smooth. Chill dough about 2 hours.
4. Preheat oven to 350 degrees.
5. Shape dough into 1¼-inch balls. Place on greased cookie sheets about 2 inches apart to allow cookies to spread during baking.
6. Bake for 15 minutes.

Yield: 4 dozen

Madeleines
(French Tea Cakes)

4 eggs, at room temperature
¼ teaspoon salt
⅔ cup sugar
1 teaspoon vanilla extract
1 cup sifted flour
8 tablespoons butter, melted and cooled

1. Grease well and flour pans for 4 dozen madeleines. If only half this many pans are available, cut the receipe in half and make the second batch after the first one is completed. This is because the butter, on standing, settles to the bottom and causes a heavy rough layer. Place racks near the bottom of the oven and preheat oven to 400 degrees.
2. Beat the eggs with the salt, adding sugar gradually, until the mixture stands in very stiff peaks. Add vanilla.
3. Sift about ¼ of the flour at a time over the egg mixture and fold it in until no flour shows.
4. Add the butter about a tablespoon at a time and fold it in as quickly as possible. Fill the prepared pans about ¾ full, place in oven immediately, and bake until brown, about 10 minutes.

Yield: 3½ to 4 dozen madeleines

Swedish Cookies

3 eggs, beaten
3 tablespoons heavy cream
6 tablespoons sugar
1 teaspoon salt
4 cups flour (approximately)
    Shortening for deep frying

1. Combine eggs, cream, sugar, salt, and flour. Use enough flour to make very firm dough.
2. Roll out dough very thin. Cut into diamond shapes with a cookie cutter with 2-inch sides. Cut a small slit in center of each diamond and draw 1 point of the cookie through it.
3. Heat shortening to 350 degrees.
4. Fry the cookies in it for 30 seconds to a minute or until golden brown. Drain on absorbent paper. Sprinkle with granulated sugar.

Yield: About 3 dozen

Fried Desserts

Beignets Soufflés

 4 tablespoons butter
¼ teaspoon salt
 1 teaspoon sugar
½ cup flour
 2 eggs
½ teaspoon vanilla or lemon extract
　Oil for deep frying
　Confectioners sugar

1. Put ½ cup water, butter, salt, and sugar in a saucepan; bring to a boil. Remove from heat, add flour.
2. Cook over very low heat, stirring, until mixture rolls away from sides of pan without sticking.
3. Add eggs one by one, mixing well after each addition. Add the flavoring.
4. To cook, fill a tablespoon full of the mixture and slip half of it off into deep hot (370 degrees) oil. Then slip off other half of mixture. Make 2 beignets from 1 tablespoon.
5. When beignets are browned, remove from the oil. Drain well. Place in hot serving dish, sprinkle with confectioners sugar.

Yield: 6 servings

Strufoli

 2 cups sifted flour (approximately)
¼ teaspoon salt
 3 eggs
 2 cups shortening or salad oil
¼ cup sugar
½ cup mild-flavored honey
　Pine nuts
　Colored candy sprinkles

271

1. Place 1½ cups flour and salt on a board. Make a well and crack the eggs into it. Use a spatula and mix, adding enough additional flour to make a fairly stiff dough.
2. Using half the dough at a time, roll on a floured board to ¼-inch thickness. Cut into ¼-inch strips. Roll each strip of dough with the hands to form a rope. Arrange several of these ropes side by side and cut into ¼-inch thick pieces. Place these separately on a floured board or tray.
3. Heat shortening or oil to 350 degrees in a deep saucepan. Carefully lower the squares by spoonsful into fat and fry, stirring constantly, until light brown. Remove with a slotted spoon and drain on absorbent paper. Keep warm.
4. Mix sugar and honey in a large skillet. Cook over low heat, stirring constantly, to consistency of a heavy syrup, about 5 minutes.
5. Add fried dough and toss to coat each piece with syrup.
6. Shape into a mound (or other desired shape) on a platter and sprinkle with pine nuts and sprinkles.

Yield: 8 servings

Chremselach
(Passover Dessert)

14 tea matzohs	¾ cup chopped nuts
7 eggs, separated	Oil for deep frying
1¼ cups sugar	4 cups foamy lemon sauce
1 teaspoon lemon peel	(optional) (see page 303)
½ teaspoon salt	Confectioners sugar
⅛ teaspoon grated nutmeg	(optional)
1 cup matzoh meal	

1. Soak the matzohs in water until soft. Squeeze out the excess water. Add the egg yolks, sugar, peel, salt, nutmeg, matzoh meal, and nuts to squeezed-out matzohs.
2. Beat the egg whites until stiff, but not dry, and fold into the matzoh mixture. Drop by tablespoonsful into the oil heated to 365 degrees. Fry until golden, turning once. Drain and serve with the foamy lemon sauce or dust with confectioners sugar.

Yield: About 6 dozen

Aunt Mary's Apple Fritters

4 or 5 ripe eating apples
Oil for deep frying
2 cups flour
2 eggs, separated
1 tablespoon dark rum
¼ teaspoon salt (approximately)
1 cup milk (approximately)
Confectioners sugar

1. Peel and core the apples. Slice them into rings about ¼ inch thick.
2. Heat the oil to 375 degrees.
3. Put the flour in a mixing bowl, make a well in the center, and add egg yolks.
4. Add rum and salt to flour-egg mixture and mix well with a wooden spoon.
5. Pour milk gradually into mixing bowl, stirring so that dough does not form lumps. Mix well.
6. Beat egg whites until they have formed stiff peaks. Fold them into the dough. If the dough seems too thick as you begin to fold in the egg whites, add a small amount of milk to loosen it up.
7. Coat the apple rings with dough and fry them until they are golden brown in the deep fryer. Turn each ring once during frying.
8. Drain the fritters on paper, sprinkle with confectioners sugar, and serve while still hot.

Yield: 4 servings

Pompushkes

1 cup cottage cheese
1 cup grated apple
2 eggs
1 cup sifted flour
1½ teaspoons sugar

¼ teaspoon ground cinnamon
¼ teaspoon salt
1 teaspoon baking powder
¼ cup sour cream
½ cup shortening

1. Combine cottage cheese, apple, and eggs in a mixing bowl. Beat with a rotary beater until well blended.
2. Mix and sift flour, sugar, cinnamon, salt, and baking powder. Stir into cheese mixture. Add sour cream and mix well.
3. Heat shortening in a heavy skillet. Drop cheese batter by tablespoons into hot fat. Fry over medium heat 3 minutes or until golden brown. Turn and fry about 3 minutes longer to brown other side. Drain on absorbent paper. Serve hot with sour cream, honey, or a mixture of cinnamon and sugar.

Yield: About 15 medium-size pompushkes

Fruit Desserts

Platanos Maduros en Paila
(Caramelized Plantains)

2 cinnamon sticks
6 cloves, roughly broken
3 tablespoons sugar
1 cup boiling water
1 ripe plantain
1 tablespoon butter
¼ teaspoon salt
1 teaspoon oil

1. Combine cinnamon, cloves, and sugar in boiling water.
   Leave at full boil for 5 minutes.
2. Meanwhile, carefully peel ripe plantain and cut in half. Then
   slice the halves in half, lengthwise.
3. Off heat, add butter, salt, and oil to sugar mixture, while
   mixture is still hot. Let butter melt and stir to blend in.
4. Arrange plantain pieces in a small skillet. Strain sugar mixture over
   them.
5. Bring sugar mixture to a boil. Cover and cook over medium heat,
   or enough heat to maintain a vigorous, but not rolling boil.
6. After roughly half the volume of the sugar mixture is gone,
   reduce heat, uncover, and turn plantains.
7. Continue cooking slowly until sugar mixture has been reduced to
   a small amount of syrup and plantains have picked up a light
   caramel coating. Serve hot.

Yield: 2 servings

Pancakes with Apple Meringue

    4 tablespoons butter
    1 pound apples, peeled, quartered, and cored
    2 tablespoons granulated sugar
    1 tablespoon plus ½ teaspoon lemon juice
12–14 Hungarian pancakes (see page 189)
    2 egg whites
    5 tablespoons confectioners sugar

1. Melt butter in a heavy saucepan. Add the apples and sprinkle with granulated sugar. Cook, covered, for 30 minutes, over very low heat; stir often.
2. When the apples are cooked, mix in 1 tablespoon lemon juice and mash the apples with a fork, to make a spreadable but lumpy sauce.
3. Preheat oven to 300 degrees.
4. Make the pancakes. As each one finishes cooking on the second side, flip it out into a deep, buttered 8-inch baking dish (round heatproof glass is good). Spread each one with some of the applesauce. Continue this way until all pancakes and sauce are used. Leave the last pancake top plain.
5. Make a meringue: Whip the egg whites, confectioners sugar, and ½ teaspoon lemon juice until the mixture forms peaks.
6. Spread the meringue on top of the pancakes. Bake in the preheated oven for 15 minutes, or until golden brown.

Yield: 6 servings

Figs Flambé

2 1-pound cans figs in syrup
2 pieces crystallized ginger, very finely cut
½ cup light rum
    Whipped cream (optional)

1. Drain figs, reserving ½ cup of the syrup.
2. At the table, place the reserved syrup in a chafing dish and bring to a boil. Add figs, sprinkle with ginger, and heat thoroughly, turning the figs once. Set dish aside.
3. Warm the rum over the chafing dish flame. Add to figs and ignite. Serve figs hot with the rum-spiked syrup as a sauce. Top each portion, if desired, with a little unsweetened whipped cream.

Yield: 6 servings

Broiled Pears

    3 pears, peeled, halved, and cored
 1½ tablespoons lemon juice
    2 tablespoons butter (approximately)
 2–3 tablespoons brown or white sugar
    1 teaspoon or less grated lemon peel (optional)

1. Brush cut surfaces of pears with lemon juice and place in buttered pan.
2. Place a bit of butter in each cavity and sprinkle with sugar and lemon peel.
3. Broil about 4 inches from source of heat until browned. Serve as dessert or as a garnish for meat or poultry.

Yield: 6 servings

Poires Glacées

    6 ripe, nicely shaped pears
    2 tablespoons lemon juice
    4 cups dry white wine (approximately)
   10 ounces frozen strawberries, thawed
   10 ounces frozen raspberries, thawed
    1 cup heavy cream
   ⅓ cup confectioners sugar
   ½ teaspoon vanilla extract
 3½ tablespoons ruby port

1. Peel the pears, being careful to leave the tapered ends intact. As they are peeled, place in a bowl of cold water with the lemon juice added.
2. Bring the wine to a boil in a heavy nonaluminum saucepan or casserole that is just large enough to hold the pears in a single layer.
3. Add the pears and additional wine to cover and cook, covered, very gently 8 to 10 minutes or until the pears are tender but firm.
4. Remove the pears to a rack to drain and cool. (The cooking liquid can be boiled down with 1½ cups sugar to make a syrup for ice cream or fresh, peeled pears.)
5. Drain the strawberries and raspberries and puree the fruit through a fine sieve. Chill the puree. (The juice may be used in a fruit compote.)
6. In a chilled bowl, over cracked ice, beat the cream, sugar, and vanilla until it starts to thicken slightly. Beat in the port.

Place in the bottom of a chilled, flat serving bowl that will just hold the pears; chill.

7. Arrange the pears with tapered ends up. Spoon the puree over the pears and around the base of each one.

Yield: 6 servings

Rhubarb Crumble

4 ounces fine noodles
3 cups diced rhubarb
¾ cup sugar
¼ teaspoon ground cinnamon
4 tablespoons butter
1 teaspoon grated lemon peel
3 tablespoons flour

1. Cook noodles in boiling, salted water until tender. Drain and rinse.
2. Preheat oven to 350 degrees.
3. Arrange rhubarb in bottom of greased 1½-quart casserole. Arrange noodles on rhubarb.
4. Combine ½ cup sugar, cinnamon, 1 tablespoon melted butter, ¼ cup water, and lemon peel. Pour mixture over rhubarb and noodles.
5. Make a streusel topping by mixing 3 tablespoons butter, flour, and ¼ cup sugar. Sprinkle this topping over noodles. Bake for 35 minutes.

Yield: 4 servings

Fruit Dumplings

½ package dry-active yeast
2 eggs, beaten
1 teaspoon salt (approximately)
  Sugar
2 cups flour (approximately)
12 fresh plums, apricots, or apples, pitted or cored

1. Soften yeast in 1 cup warm water. Add eggs, salt, 1 teaspoon sugar, and flour and stir until blended, using enough flour to make a stiff dough. Let stand 10 minutes and knead until smooth and elastic. Let rise in a warm place (80 to 85 degrees) until double in bulk.
2. Turn out on a floured board, knead slightly, and roll into a sheet ½ inch thick. Cut into squares or rounds large enough to cover selected fruit.
3. Fill fruit cavities with sugar; apricots should be peeled. Chop tart cooking apples and sweeten to taste. Place whatever fruit is used in center of round or square of dough, bring up dough around fruit to cover it, and press dough to seal edges. Let rise until dough is somewhat light.
4. Drop into a large pot of boiling salted water and cook, covered, 15 to 20 minutes. The dumplings are done when they are light and spongy at the center (test by tearing one apart with 2 forks). Remove with slotted spoon. Serve hot.

Yield: 12 dumplings

Candy

J. Paul Getty's Chocolate Fudge

    4 cups sugar
    2 cups less 2 tablespoons milk
 1½ tablespoons cocoa
    1 teaspoon vanilla extract
    4 tablespoons butter

1. Bring sugar, milk, cocoa, and vanilla to boil in large saucepan, stirring with a wooden spoon. Boil for about 20 minutes, until mixture starts to thicken and granulate around the edge of the pan, at 238 degrees on a candy thermometer.
2. Remove from heat and cool to 110 degrees by immersing pan in cold water.
3. Add butter and beat hard with a spoon or electric beater until thick.
4. Pour into a buttered tin to a depth of about ¾ inch and leave to set until cool. (If it does not set properly, it has not been cooked long enough.)
5. Cut into squares before completely cold and hard.

Yield: 8 to 10 servings

Blazing Yule Log

LOG

    5 cups puffed rice
  ¾ cup sugar
  ¼ cup light corn syrup
  ½ cup strong coffee
  ½ teaspoon salt
    2 ounces unsweetened chocolate
    1 tablespoon butter

1. Preheat oven to 350 degrees.
2. Measure puffed rice into shallow pan. Heat in oven 10 minutes. Pour cereal into large greased bowl.
3. Combine sugar, syrup, coffee, and salt in a saucepan; bring to a boil. Add chocolate and continue cooking until a few drops in cold water form a soft ball (234 degrees on a candy thermometer). Add butter and stir until combined.
4. Mixing quickly, gradually pour cooked syrup over the puffed rice. With greased hands, shape the mixture to form a log about 12 inches long. Place on a baking sheet to cool.

MERINGUE "FLAMES"

2 egg whites
¼ cup sugar
¼ teaspoon vanilla extract

1. Preheat oven to 350 degrees.
2. Beat the egg whites until stiff but not dry. Add the sugar a tablespoon at a time, beating after each addition. Add vanilla.
3. Spread the meringue across the top of the log, making peaks to resemble flames. Bake about 10 minutes or until meringue is browned.

Yield: 8 to 10 servings

Molasses Taffy

1 cup granulated sugar
1 cup brown sugar
2 cups light molasses
6 tablespoons butter (approximately)
¼ teaspoon salt
⅛ teaspoon baking soda
Cornstarch

1. In a heavy 4-quart saucepan, cook sugars, molasses, and ¾ cup water, stirring until sugar dissolves. Continue cooking to 265 degrees on a candy thermometer (hard but not brittle in cold water), stirring occasionally. Lower heat toward end of cooking and stir almost constantly to prevent scorching.
2. Remove from heat and add 4 tablespoons butter, salt, and soda,

stirring only enough to mix. Turn into 1 or more buttered
pans to cool. As edges cool, fold them toward center.
3. When candy is cool enough to handle, gather it into a ball
    and pull, using fingers, until rather firm and light yellow in
    color. If it sticks to fingers while pulling, dust them lightly
    with cornstarch. Stretch into a long rope on a buttered surface
    and cut into pieces with scissors. Wrap immediately in wax paper.

Yield: 1¾ pounds

Pulled Mints

1½ cups sugar
  2 tablespoons light corn syrup
     Butter
 ¼ teaspoon oil or essence of peppermint

1. Mix ½ cup water, sugar, and corn syrup in a 1-quart saucepan.
    Cook over low heat, stirring constantly until sugar is dissolved.
    Cover and cook 3 minutes. Remove cover and cook without
    stirring to 260 degrees on a candy thermometer or until a
    small amount of mixture forms a hard ball when tested
    in very cold water. During cooking, remove sugar crystals from
    side of pan with a fork covered with damp cheesecloth.
2. Pour into a buttered pan and let stand until cool enough to
    handle. Put oil or essence of peppermint into center of the
    candy; fold over corners.
3. Pull candy with fingers until it has a satinlike finish and
    light color. Pull into long strips, ½ inch in diameter.
    Cut into ½- to 1-inch pieces.
4. Place candy pieces in layers in a pan or bowl, separating the
    layers with wax paper. Cover. Store overnight or until mints
    become creamy.

Yield: About 12 ounces

Holiday Striped Taffy

  2 cups sugar
½ cup light corn syrup
    Few drops oil or essence of peppermint
    Few drops red food coloring.

1. Cook sugar, syrup, and ½ cup water in a 1-quart saucepan to 268
   degrees on a candy thermometer (firm ball—almost brittle in
   cold water), stirring until the sugar is dissolved. Pour into
   2 greased pans to cool.
2. When cool enough to handle, add a few drops oil or essence
   of peppermint to each pan and a few drops red food coloring
   to one pan. It is easier for two people to pull the candy, but
   if one works alone, set one pan aside where it will not cool too
   rapidly. Fold edges toward center, remove from pan, pull
   with fingertips until candy is almost firm. Stretch it into a rope
   on a greased surface. Then do the same with the reserved candy.
3. Twine the ropes together to give a striped effect. Stretch
   into a long rope ½ inch in diameter and cut with scissors
   into 1-inch lengths. For canes, cut longer pieces and shape
   each into a curved-handle cane. Wrap each piece in waxed
   paper and store in a tightly covered container.

Yield: 1 pound, 2 ounces

Icing

Apricot Glaze

3 tablespoons apricot jam
1 tablespoon dark rum

1. Heat jam until it thickens slightly.
2. Add rum off heat and apply immediately to cake.

Yield: Glaze for 1 10-inch cake layer

Crème Pâtissière

¼ cup sugar
2 tablespoons flour
1 teaspoon cornstarch
1 cup milk, scalded
2 egg yolks, beaten
½ teaspoon vanilla extract
¼ cup heavy cream, whipped

1. Mix sugar, flour, and cornstarch. Add scalded milk, stirring, and return to saucepan. Cook, stirring, until the mixture boils.
2. Add milk mixture to the egg yolks, stirring constantly. Return to saucepan and cook over the lowest possible heat, continuing to stir, until the mixture is thickened. It must be the consistency of a thick mayonnaise.
3. Add the vanilla and cool. The whipped cream is not folded into the crème until just before using.

Yield: About 1½ cups

Crème Frangipane

1 egg	3 tablespoons butter
1 egg yolk	(approximately)
¾ cup sugar	1 tablespoon vanilla extract
½ cup flour, sifted	½ cup macaroon crumbs
1 cup milk	1 teaspoon butter, softened

1. With an electric beater, blend egg and yolk in a bowl. Then slowly beat in sugar and continue beating until mixture lightens in color and has thickened. Then beat in flour.
2. Boil milk in a saucepan and beat into egg-sugar mixture. Pour mixture into clean saucepan or top of double broiler. Stirring with a whisk, cook over simmering water until mixture begins to coagulate. Lower heat and beat vigorously for 3 minutes while flour cooks through. Don't worry if a small amount of custard burns at the bottom of the pan. Just don't use it.
3. Stir in the butter, vanilla, and macaroon crumbs, and cool. Run a spoon coated with softened butter over top of custard so that a skin does not form while it cools.

Yield: About 2 cups

Chocolate Whipped Cream Filling

3 ounces semisweet chocolate
1 cup heavy cream, whipped

1. Place chocolate and 3 tablespoons water in a small pan, over low flame. Stir until chocolate melts into water and mixture is smooth. Start with 3 tablespoons water and add more if necessary for smooth texture.
2. Cool, but do not refrigerate. Combine with whipped cream.

Yield: Filling for 1 10-inch layer cake

Liqueur Cream

⅓ cup flour
⅔ cup sugar
¼ teaspoon salt
2 cups milk, scalded
4 egg yolks
3 tablespoons liqueur, brandy, or rum
½ cup heavy cream, whipped

1. Sift together flour, sugar, and salt.
2. Add milk, stirring, and cook in the top of a double boiler over simmering water, stirring until thickened. Cover and cook 10 minutes, stirring occasionally.
3. Beat egg yolks slightly. Add some of the hot mixture while stirring. Return to double boiler and cook, stirring until thickened. Cool.
4. Add liqueur, brandy, or rum, and fold in whipped cream. Chill thoroughly.

Yield: About 3 cups

NOTE: *This is a sauce for fruit, cooked or raw, pudding, or cake.*

Chocolate Icing

4 ounces semisweet chocolate
6 tablespoons unsalted butter

1. Soften chocolate in a double boiler over simmering water.
2. Add butter to chocolate. When butter melts, stir it into chocolate until mixture is smooth and all lumps have disappeared. If icing is too thick to pour, add more butter. If it is too loose, add a small amount of chocolate. It should coat the spoon heavily and drip slowly off.

Yield: Icing for 1 10-by-2½-inch cake

Chocolate Icing I

  2 egg yolks
1½ cups sugar
  ½ cup milk
  4 ounces unsweetened chocolate
  4 tablespoons butter
  1 teaspoon vanilla extract

1. Heat egg yolks, sugar, and milk without boiling, stirring occasionally for 5 minutes.
2. Melt chocolate and butter over hot water. Add to eggs, sugar, and milk; add vanilla; beat until thick.

Yield: About 2 cups, enough for 1 8-inch cake that is 4 inches high

Chocolate Icing II

1½ cups sugar
  ¼ teaspoon cream of tartar
  6 egg yolks
  ¾ pound unsalted butter, at room temperature
  6 ounces sweet chocolate, melted
  2 tablespoons rum or 1 teaspoon vanilla extract

1. Boil sugar, ½ cup water, and cream of tartar to 232 degrees on a candy thermometer.
2. Beat yolks in electric mixer. Still beating, add syrup gradually and beat at high speed until thick and cool.
3. Add butter a little at a time and beat well after each addition, using medium speed.
4. Blend ¼ cup water with chocolate and whip into the frosting. Add rum or vanilla.

Yield: Icing for 2 9-inch or 3 8-inch layers

STOCKS AND SAUCES

Veal Stock

2 pounds veal shank
1 tablespoon butter
1 carrot, diced
1 medium onion, chopped
4 scallions, chopped
1½ cups dry white wine

12 quarts warm water
1 teaspoon salt
½ teaspoon dried thyme
4 parsley stems
1 bay leaf

1. Preheat oven to 450 degrees.
2. Have butcher cut veal shank (meat and bones) into sections an inch or 2 long. Put sections in a pan and brown them in the oven, about 1 hour, turning so that all sides brown but do not burn.
3. Meanwhile, heat the butter in a skillet and sauté carrot, onion, and scallions until carrots have softened and taken on a shiny color and onions are translucent.
4. Put meat and vegetables in a large, heavy pot. Cover and place over very low heat for 20 minutes. Uncover, add ½ cup wine, raise heat as high as it will go, and let liquid evaporate until meat juices in bottom of pot turn brown. Repeat this process twice, with ½ cup wine each time.
5. Add the warm water to contents of pot, bring to a boil, add remaining ingredients, and simmer, uncovered, for 5 to 6 hours. Add more water if needed.
6. Strain stock, cool at room temperature, refrigerate, and skim the resulting layer of fat off the top of the stock prior to using. Measure and make up to 3 cups with water if necessary.

Yield: 3 cups

Jus de Veau Lié

14 pounds veal shank, with
  bones
6 pounds veal shoulder
2 carrots
4 medium onions
2 medium leeks
½ small stalk celery
6 sprigs parsley

2 bay leaves
1 teaspoon thyme
2 cloves
1 tablespoon salt
3 strips pork rind, blanched
6 tablespoons arrowroot
½ cup madeira

1. Have the butcher cut the veal shank into as small pieces as possible. Cut meat away from bones.
2. Take roughly ⅔ of the shank bones and put them in a large stock pot. Tie up the meat from these bones with ⅔ of the veal shoulder into an easily manageable package and put it into the pot. Add hot water to cover, bring to a boil (straddling the pot over more than 1 burner will speed this), skim and add 1 carrot, 2 onions (quartered), 2 leeks, the celery, 3 sprigs parsley, 1 bay leaf, ½ teaspoon thyme, the cloves, and the salt.
3. Reduce heat and simmer very slowly for about 2½ hours.
4. Remove meat and bones from pot and discard. Strain liquid. Clean stock pot. Preheat oven to 450 degrees.
5. Cut the remaining carrot and onions into thick rounds and spread them over the bottom of the stock pot. Similarly, cover the bottom with the pork rind strips.
6. Cut remaining veal shank meat and veal shoulder into rough chunks. Arrange them in the pot along with the remaining bones.
7. Check volume of liquid produced at Step 4. Add water to it, if necessary, to bring the total up to 6 quarts. Pour 2 cups of this liquid into the stock pot and put stock pot into the oven. As soon as the liquid has completely reduced, add another 2 cups. Let it reduce completely as well. There will be a residue of fat at the bottom each time.
8. Remove stock pot from oven. Add to it the rest of the liquid from Step 4, and remaining parsley, bay leaf, and ½ teaspoon thyme. Bring to a boil, skim, and simmer partly covered for 3 hours. Skim occasionally.
9. Strain through a chinois or other fine strainer, having discarded bones and other solids. It is even better to lay a folded clean

dish towel over the strainer. Cool and refrigerate strained stock overnight.

10. Discard layer of fat that has formed on top of the stock. Reserve 1 cup stock and bring rest to a boil. Reduce to 2 quarts of liquid (or to 1 quart, if you want a truly lavish sauce base).
11. Dissolve arrowroot in cup of reserved cold stock and then stir mixture into hot stock. Simmer for 1 minute longer and pour through a fine strainer.
12. Pour madeira into stock and freeze in small containers.

Yield: A little more than 2 quarts

Vegetable Stock

¼ cup dried navy beans	2 sprigs fresh or ½ teaspoon
¼ cup dried green split peas	dried thyme
1 medium onion, sliced	1 bay leaf
1 carrot, quartered	3 whole cloves
½ stalk celery, chopped	⅛ teaspoon mace
1 bunch parsley	2 quarts water

Place all the ingredients in a kettle. Bring to a boil; simmer 3 hours. Skim well. Strain broth.

Yield: About 1½ quarts

Red Wine Fumet

2–3 pounds fish bones and	⅛ teaspoon dried thyme
heads, roughly chopped	Salt
1 large onion, chopped	Pepper
6–8 sprigs parsley	1 quart water
1 bay leaf	3 cups red Graves wine

1. Place all the ingredients in a large saucepan, bring to a boil, cover, and cook over medium heat for 30 minutes. Skim as necessary.
2. Strain the broth, discard bones and seasonings.

Yield: About 1½ quarts

Sauce Villeroi

4 pounds veal shank
1 chicken carcass, preferably
   raw, with most of meat
   removed
6 carrots
3 onions, peeled and stuck
   with 1 clove each
6 scallions
1 stalk celery
6 sprigs parsley
1 bay leaf

1 sprig fresh thyme or ½
   teaspoon dried
1 tablespoon salt
12 white peppercorns
½ pound butter
1 cup flour, sifted
2½ cups chopped mushrooms
   Juice of ½ lemon
5 egg yolks, lightly beaten
¾ cup heavy cream

1. Separate meat from veal bones, cut and break up meat and
   bones as much as possible, and submerge meat, veal bones, and
   chicken carcass in water to cover. Bring to a boil. Discard
   water. Rinse meat and bones and return to large pot. Add 5½
   quarts cold water. Bring to a boil. Skim carefully, and
   continue to cook over low flame for 5 hours, skimming
   occasionally.
2. Add to pot carrots, onions, the scallions tied with the
   celery stalk, parsley, bay leaf, thyme, salt, and 6 peppercorns.
   Continue slow cooking and skimming (adding more water to keep
   the level up to 4 quarts) for 3 more hours.
3. Strain into large bowls through a strainer lined with
   cheesecloth. Discard meat, bones, and vegetables. Let stock
   cool overnight. The next morning, remove and discard the layer
   of fat on top of the stock.
4. To make a pale roux, put butter in a heavy pot. Heat until
   foam dies down. Remove from heat, add flour, stir together with
   butter, and return to moderate heat. Stir occasionally and cook
   for 10 to 12 minutes.
5. Meanwhile, reheat, but do not boil, 3 quarts of stock. As soon
   as roux has cooked, remove from fire and whisk the hot
   stock into it. Return mixture to heat and bring to a boil,
   whisking constantly. Add 1½ cups mushrooms and simmer for
   30 minutes. Skim frequently and thoroughly.
6. Add an additional 2 cups of cold stock and remaining
   peppercorns, bring to a boil, then simmer until sauce is reduced
   to 2 quarts, skimming often. Strain through cheesecloth. You
   now have velouté, a basic white sauce.
7. In a heavy saucepan, combine 1 quart velouté, remaining 2

cups stock, ½ cup mushrooms, and lemon juice. Bring to a boil, stirring.

8. Combine yolks and cream. Whisk 1 to 1½ cups hot sauce into the yolk mixture. Return to the saucepan slowly and cook over high flame until the volume is reduced to 1 quart, whisking constantly.
9. Remove from heat, pour through a fine strainer, and whisk until cool. This is sauce allemande.
10. Place allemande in saucepan with 1 cup reserved velouté and remaining ½ cup mushrooms. Whisking constantly, reduce until sauce heavily coats the back of a wooden spoon. Strain and whisk until lukewarm and ready to use.

Yield: About 6 cups

NOTE: *Extra velouté can be frozen and used in other recipes.*

Sauce Poivrade

8 peppercorns, crushed
½ cup white vinegar
1 cup jus de veau lié (see page 292)
2 tablespoons red currant jelly

1. Mix together peppercorns and vinegar and cook until reduced to ¼ cup.
2. Add jus; simmer slowly for 30 minutes. Stir in jelly. Strain.

Yield: About 1 cup

Francatelli's Venison Sauce

2½ tablespoons port wine
1 cup red currant jelly
   Small cinnamon stick, bruised
   Thinly pared peel of a lemon

Simmer all ingredients together for 5 minutes, stirring. Strain into a hot sauceboat.

Yield: About 1 cup

Béchamel Sauce

   2 tablespoons unsalted butter
   3 tablespoons flour
1½–2 cups milk
   ¼ tablespoon salt
     White pepper

1. Melt butter in a saucepan. Add flour, mix with a wooden spoon, and cook over low heat until mixture is smooth. This happens quite quickly and browning should not be allowed to take place.
2. Heat milk in a saucepan and whisk gradually into flour-butter mixture over low heat until sauce has thickened. Stop adding milk when desired thickness is reached. Be sure any lumps have been whisked smooth. Add seasonings.

Yield: About 2 cups

Ragú Bolognese
(Meat Sauce)

   1 tablespoon butter
   ½ cup fresh ham or pork butt, diced (about 3 ounces)
   1 onion, finely chopped
   1 carrot, finely chopped
   1 stalk celery, finely chopped
   ½ pound ground lean beef
   ¼ pound chicken livers, chopped

   3 tablespoons tomato paste
   ¾ cup dry white wine
     Salt
     Pepper
   ¼ teaspoon grated nutmeg
1½ cups beef stock or water
   1 cup heavy cream (optional)

1. Heat the butter in a skillet. When it has foamed, add the ham or pork butt and brown lightly.
2. Add onion, carrot, and celery. Brown them.
3. Add ground beef and brown thoroughly, turning with a spatula.
4. Add chicken livers. Sauté for 2 or 3 minutes. Then add tomato paste, wine, and seasonings.
5. Add the stock or water, cover, and simmer over very low heat for 30 to 40 minutes.
6. If you want greater smoothness to your sauce, stir in the heavy cream just before serving, off heat.

Yield: 6 servings, or enough for 1½ pounds of pasta

Salsa di Noci
(Walnut Sauce)

1 cup shelled walnuts
¾ cup fresh parsley leaves
¾ cup olive oil
2 tablespoons grated parmesan cheese
3 tablespoons butter, melted
   Salt
   Pepper
3 tablespoons ricotta cheese

1. To peel and skin walnuts: Immerse in boiling water. Remove from heat and, as soon as nuts are cool enough to touch, begin removing skins. Leave the unskinned nuts in the water. If you remove them from the water all at once, they will be much more difficult to skin. A nut-pick is helpful in this. You should end up with about ¾ cup.
2. Grind walnuts and parsley together in an electric blender.
3. Add remaining ingredients to blender jar and blend at high speed until smooth.

Yield: 4 servings, or enough for 1 pound of pasta

Sauce Trainiera

1 cup olive oil
¼ cup capers, drained
5 cloves garlic, finely chopped
2–3 tablespoons chopped fresh ginger
   Hot red pepper flakes, to taste
   Salt
   Pepper
1 teaspoon oregano

Combine all ingredients, stirring and tasting as you go.
Let sauce rest for approximately 30 minutes before serving.

Yield: 4 servings, or enough for 1 pound of pasta

Hot Oyster Sauce

1 pint small oysters
1 small onion, grated
2 tablespoons butter
2 tablespoons flour
½ cup dry white wine
½ teaspoon salt
  Pepper
2 tablespoons lemon juice

1. Drain oysters, reserving liquor.
2. Sauté onion in butter about 1 minute. Add flour and blend well.
3. Add oyster liquor, wine, salt, pepper, and lemon juice and cook, stirring, until thickened.
4. Add oysters and cook, stirring, until edges curl. Do not boil.

Yield: 4 to 5 servings, to accompany sliced turkey or broiled fish

Tomato Sauce

1 pound tomatoes, peeled and sliced
  Salt
  Pepper
3 shallots, finely chopped
1 teaspoon brown sugar
1 bay leaf
½ cup vegetarian brown sauce (see page 299)

1. Place tomatoes, salt and pepper to taste, shallots, brown sugar, and bay leaf in a saucepan. Bring to a boil and simmer until tomatoes and shallots are well cooked.
2. Remove bay leaf and press through a food mill or sieve. Add brown sauce and reheat.

Yield: About 1½ cups

Piquant Sauce

¼ cup vinegar
 1 medium onion, finely chopped, or 2 shallots, chopped
 1 cup veal stock (see page 000) or brown gravy
 2 tablespoons chopped sour pickles
 1 teaspoon chopped parsley

1. Cook vinegar and onion or shallots until liquid has been reduced to 2 tablespoons.
2. Add stock or gravy and boil slowly 10 minutes.
3. When ready to serve, add the pickles and parsley.

Yield: About 1¼ cups

Scallion Sauce

½ bunch scallions
 3 tablespoons imported black (thick) soy sauce
 4 tablespoons white vinegar
 4 tablespoons sugar
 1 teaspoon salt
 2 teaspoons five-taste spice powder

1. Chop scallions crosswise into rings about ⅛ to ¼ inch thick.
2. Combine scallions in a bowl with all other ingredients.

Yield: About 1 cup

Vegetarian Brown Sauce

2 tablespoons flour
 2 tablespoons butter
 1 cup vegetable stock (see page 293)
   Salt
   Pepper

1. Preheat oven to 450 degrees.
2. Place the flour in an ovenproof skillet and brown in the oven. Stir occasionally and do not burn. It will take about 10 minutes.

3. Melt butter in a saucepan, add the flour, and cook 5 minutes. Gradually stir in the vegetable stock; bring to a boil. Season with salt and pepper to taste and simmer 4 minutes.

Yield: About 1 cup

Cumberland Sauce

1 orange
  Boiling water
2 tablespoons red currant jelly
  Cayenne to taste
⅛ teaspoon dry mustard

1. With a swivel-bladed potato peeler remove the colored skin from the orange and cut into thin slivers. Cover with boiling water and let stand 5 minutes. Drain.
2. Mix peel with the juice of the orange and the remaining ingredients in a saucepan. Bring to a boil, stirring.

Yield: About ½ cup

Mayonnaise

3 egg yolks
3 cups salad oil
  Juice of 3 lemons
  Salt
  Pepper

With a wire whisk break up the egg yolks in a bowl. Pour in the oil very slowly, drop by drop, beating constantly. After you have incorporated all the oil, very slowly add the strained lemon juice, salt, and pepper.

Yield: 3 cups

NOTE: *One of the most important factors for the success of this dish is that all the ingredients should be at room temperature.*

If the oil and eggs separate, it is very simple to save it. Begin again with 1 egg yolk, and, instead of oil, add the separated mayonnaise to it very slowly, beating constantly.

Aïoli

6–12 cloves garlic, peeled and finely minced
    4 egg yolks
    1 tablespoon rapidly boiling water
   ½ tablespoon or more salt
      Pepper
 1¼ cups peanut oil
    1 cup olive oil
    1 tablespoon or more lemon juice

1. Place the garlic in a large mixing bowl and add egg yolks. Start beating with a wire whisk, a rotary beater, or electric mixer. Add boiling water rapidly, salt and pepper to taste.
2. Add peanut oil, drop by drop, until more than half of it is added. The peanut oil and olive oil may then be added in increasing quantities. Beat in lemon juice.

Yield: About 2½ cups

Rouille

   ¼ cup chopped red pepper, simmered until soft in salted water
    2 small red chili peppers, also simmered in salted water until tender
    1 medium potato, peeled and cooked in chicken stock
    4 cloves garlic, mashed
4–6 tablespoons olive oil
      Salt
      Pepper

1. Mash together both kinds of peppers, potato, and garlic in a mortar with a pestle or in an electric blender.
2. Into this mixture dribble olive oil as for mayonnaise, beating or blending until you achieve a smooth, but not a loose, consistency. Add salt and pepper to taste.

Yield: About 1 cup

NOTE: *You can make rouille as hot as you like by adjusting the amount of chili peppers. More bell pepper will darken the sauce's color. Serve it with Artichokes Croisette (see page 4) or as an accompaniment to most fish courses.*

Carly's Salad Dressing

½ cup peanut oil
½ cup vinegar
¼ teaspoon dry mustard
¼ teaspoon curry powder
½ teaspoon sugar
Juice of ½ lemon

1 tablespoon ketchup
1 clove garlic, crushed
Salt
⅛ teaspoon worcestershire
sauce
Tabasco

1. Mix together all above ingredients, in order, tasting as you go along. If the end result tastes too much of vinegar and lemon juice, add more oil gradually to correct.
2. Just before serving salad, mix well again with a fork, pour over salad, and toss salad.

Yield: About 1 cup

Grand Marnier Sauce

4 egg yolks
½ cup sugar
¾ cup heavy cream
½ cup milk
2 tablespoons vanilla extract
4 tablespoons Grand Marnier

1. Beat egg yolks with sugar in top of a double boiler until well blended and light.
2. Add cream and milk. Heat mixture in a double boiler over simmering water until it coats a wooden spoon. Too much heat will curdle the yolks. Stir constantly during thickening process. If a small amount of "scrambled" egg appears in the bottom of the pan, it can be strained out later.
3. When mixture has thickened, add vanilla and finish with Grand Marnier. Pour over dessert.

Yield: About 2 cups

Foamy Lemon Sauce

1 tablespoon potato starch
1 cup sugar, or to taste
  Juice of 1 lemon
2 eggs, separated

1. In a saucepan, mix the starch and sugar together. Gradually stir in 1½ cups water. Add the lemon juice and the yolks, lightly beaten.
2. Bring to a boil, stirring, and cook 1 minute. Beat the egg whites until stiff, but not dry, and fold into the hot mixture. Chill and serve cold.

Yield: About 4 cups

Eggnog Sauce

1 egg
½ cup confectioners sugar, sifted
2 tablespoons rum
¼ cup heavy cream, whipped

Beat the egg until thick and lemon-hued. Gradually beat in confectioners sugar. Add rum and fold in whipped cream.

PRESERVES, RELISHES, AND GARNISHES

Imogene Wolcutt's Cranberry Conserve

4 cups cranberries
2 cups raisins
4 tablespoons chopped orange peel
1 tablespoon chopped lemon peel
2 tablespoons lemon juice
½ cup orange juice
6 cups sugar

1. Mix all the ingredients together in a heavy kettle. Let stand for 30 minutes. Bring to a boil and boil vigorously 10 minutes.
2. Lower the heat and simmer until mixture thickens.
3. Pour into hot sterilized jars and seal.

Yield: About 6 pints

Glazed Apple Rings

½ cup sugar
  Juice of ½ lemon
¼ cup water or cider
¼ cup applejack or cider
4 cooking apples, peeled, halved, and cored

1. In a skillet, boil the sugar, lemon juice, and water or cider, stirring until sugar has dissolved.
2. Add applejack or cider, lower heat, and when simmering, add apple halves. Cook, turning carefully, until apples are just tender.
3. Cool apples in syrup. Pour remaining syrup over apples.
4. Serve with ham.

Yield: 8 servings

East Indian Apples

1 cup sugar
2 tablespoons curry powder
1 tablespoon finely chopped onion
¾ teaspoon salt
4 tart apples, peeled and cored

1. Place 1 cup water, sugar, curry, onion, and salt in a saucepan over low heat, stirring until sugar is dissolved.
2. Add apples, stem ends down. Cover and boil gently about 5 minutes.
3. Turn apples carefully, bringing stem ends up. Cover and cook 3 minutes longer or until apples are easily pierced with fork but still hold their shape.
4. Remove apples from sugar mixture and place in a dish.
5. Continue boiling sugar mixture 3 to 4 minutes or until it forms a thick syrup. Pour over the apples.
6. Serve hot or chilled with lamb, chicken, duck, or ham.

Yield: 4 servings

Spiced Peach Pickles

32 medium peaches (approximately)
 3 whole cloves for each peach
 3 teaspoons whole allspice
2¼ cups unsulphured molasses
1⅓ cups sugar
 1 cup water
 3 cups white vinegar
 4 cinnamon sticks

1. Remove skins from peaches and leave whole. Drop into cold salted water (1 tablespoon salt to 2 quarts water) to prevent discoloration. Rinse fruit before cooking.
2. Stick 3 cloves in each peach.
3. Tie allspice in a clean, thin cloth bag and add to remaining ingredients, except cinnamon, that have been mixed together in a large enamel, aluminum, or stainless steel pot. Boil about 3 minutes.

4. Drop in only enough peaches at a time to fill 1-quart jar. Cook until tender. Pack fruit and cinnamon (1 stick to a jar) into hot, sterilized jars.

Yield: 4 quarts

Spiced Baked Rhubarb

1½ pounds rhubarb
    Butter
¾–1 cup sugar
  2 1-inch pieces cinnamon stick
  3 whole cloves
  1 teaspoon grated orange or lemon peel

1. Preheat oven to 400 degrees.
2. Cut rhubarb into 1½-inch pieces and place in a buttered casserole.
3. Add remaining ingredients and mix with rhubarb.
4. Bake until tender—about 20 minutes. Serve as a relish with pork, veal, or chicken, or in pudding (see page 253).

Yield: 6 servings

Kachumar
(Indian Hot Relish)

32 medium onions, finely chopped
 3 medium tomatoes, finely chopped
 4 tablespoons finely chopped fresh coriander
 1 fresh green chili (or more if extreme hotness is desired), finely chopped
   Salt
 3 tablespoons white vinegar

Combine all ingredients. Refrigerate overnight. Stir the next morning, refrigerate, and serve that evening.

Yield: 8 servings

Sherry Jelly

  2 envelopes (tablespoons) unflavored gelatin
  1 cup boiling water
  ¾ cup sugar
  ¼ teaspoon salt
  ½ cup orange juice
  2 tablespoons lemon juice
1½ cups cream sherry

1. Soften the gelatin in ½ cup cold water. Add the boiling water, sugar, and salt and stir until the gelatin and sugar are dissolved.
2. Cool and stir in the orange juice, lemon juice, and sherry. Pour into individual molds and chill until firm.

Yield: 6 to 8 servings

Hot Lemon Pickle I

1 pound lemons, quartered
3 tablespoons salt
4 tablespoons crumbled red chilies
4 tablespoons dry mustard
  Pinch of asafetida
3 cups sesame oil

1. Roll each ¼ lemon in salt and place in a 1-quart jar. Close jar and let stand 4 days.
2. Add chilies, mustard, and asafetida.
3. Heat sesame oil. Cool and add to lemons.
4. Close and let stand in the sun (or in a warm place) for 4 days. It is then ready to serve.

Yield: 1 quart

Hot Lemon Pickle II

1 pound hot green peppers
  Juice of 4 pounds lemons
6 tablespoons salt

1. Cut peppers into pieces and put in a 1-quart glass jar. Add lemon juice and salt.
2. Close the jar and let stand in the sun (or in a warm place) for 4 days.

Yield: 1 quart

Sweet Chutney

      2 pounds apples
   2½ cups sugar
      1 pound seeded raisins
      3 red chilies, crumbled
      2 cloves garlic, minced
      1 tablespoon minced fresh ginger
     ½ teaspoon salt
      1 cup white vinegar

1. Peel and core the apples and chop coarsely.
2. Combine all ingredients in a pan, simmer gently, and stir occasionally until the chutney thickens.
3. Put into jars and, when cool, cover tightly.

Yield: About 5 cups

DRINKS

Spanish Hot Chocolate

    2 cups milk
    2 cups light cream
    ¼ teaspoon grated nutmeg
    1 tablespoon butter
    8 ounces semisweet chocolate
    3 tablespoons sugar
    ½ teaspoon salt

1. In a saucepan, combine the milk, cream, nutmeg, butter, chocolate, sugar, and salt. Place over low heat and stir with a wooden spoon until chocolate melts.
2. Remove from heat and beat with a rotary beater until foamy. Return to the heat and bring to a boil, stirring constantly.
3. Beat again until foamy. Return to heat, and beat twice more.

Yield: 4 servings

Syllabub

    1¼ cups sugar (approximately)
    2 cups dry white wine, chilled
    5 tablespoons grated lemon peel
    ⅓ cup lemon juice
    5 egg whites
    3 cups cold milk
    2 cups cold light cream
       Grated nutmeg

1. Stir ¾ cup of the sugar into wine. Add lemon peel and juice. Let stand until sugar dissolves.
2. Beat 4 egg whites until stiff. Gradually add to them remaining ½ cup sugar, continuing to beat constantly. Reserve.

3. In a punch bowl, combine milk and cream. Pour in wine mixture. Beat until frothy with a rotary beater. Taste. If not sweet enough, stir in an additional ¼ cup sugar.
4. Top punch with spoonful of remaining egg white, beaten. Sprinkle with nutmeg.

Yield: 16 ½-cup servings

NOTE: *Perhaps this is not so much a drink as a dessert. It actually stands midway between the 2 categories.*

Gogol-Mogol
(Milk Cocktail)

1 egg yolk
1 tablespoon sugar
¼ teaspoon salt
3 drops vanilla extract
1 cup milk

1. Beat egg yolk slightly, add sugar, and continue beating until frothy and lighter in color. Add salt and vanilla, mix well, stir in milk, and stir again.
2. Put mixture through a sieve, pour into tall glass, and serve.

Yield: 1 serving

Churchill Downs Mint Julep

1 tablespoon sugar (or more to taste)
1 tablespoon chopped mint leaves
Shaved or crushed ice
1–2 ounces Kentucky bourbon whiskey
1 small bunch fresh mint
2 drinking straws, cut short

1. Place sugar and chopped mint in a small crockery bowl. Bruise the leaves well with a muddler or back of a wooden spoon until mixture forms a paste. Add 1 tablespoon water and continue stirring. There should be a thick green syrup by this time.

2. Fill a metal cup (special julep cups are sold for this purpose)
   ½ full of crushed ice. Add the mint syrup and bourbon. Fill glass
   with crushed ice. Slip bunch of mint into the ice and beside it
   the straws, which should be no taller than the mint. Lift cup onto a
   tray, being careful not to touch the sides with the fingers, and
   put into the refrigerator to frost. This will take from a half to a full
   hour. Serve as soon as frosted.

Yield: 1 serving

Thomas and Jeremiah

   3 eggs, separated
   1 teaspoon sugar
   1 teaspoon ground cloves
   1 teaspoon ground cinnamon
  ¼ cup light rum
  10 jiggers (about 2 cups) bourbon whiskey
  10 jiggers (about 2 cups) hot, strong coffee

1. Beat yolks until thick and light. Stir in sugar and spices.
2. Beat egg whites until stiff. Fold into yolk mixture. Stir in rum.
   Let mixture stand overnight under refrigeration.
3. At serving time, put a tablespoon of the mixture in each of
   10 4-ounce demitasse cups or small mugs. To each cup, add a
   jigger (1½ ounces) bourbon and a jigger hot coffee. Stir.

Yield: 10 servings

Two Soviet Cocktails

Krasnyj Mak
(Red Poppy)

 1 ounce ruby port
⅓ ounce strawberry syrup
⅔ ounce cognac

Combine all ingredients in a cocktail shaker, shake well, and serve in a liqueur glass.

Yield: 1 serving

Mayak
(Lighthouse)

1 tablespoon sugar
1 ounce green or yellow chartreuse, chilled
1 egg yolk
1 ounce cognac, chilled

1. Frost a wine glass with the sugar by wiping the rim with a damp cloth, then dip in sugar and shake off excess.
2. Carefully pour in the chartreuse. Then lower the egg yolk on top of the chartreuse with a spoon.
3. Pour the cognac in slowly, down the side of the glass.

Yield: 1 serving

INDEX

A Note About the Editor

Raymond Sokolov ate his first meal in the summer of 1941 and proceeded to gain thirty pounds before his eighteenth month. He went on to refine his appetite in a home devoted to cooking of an international flavor, especially Eastern Europe and northern Mexico. After studying Greek and Latin at Harvard and Oxford, he worked for *Newsweek* as a correspondent in France and also as a cultural writer in New York. A closet foodie during all these years, he came out professionally at the *New York Times* as food editor in 1971. He has published many cookbooks, including *The Saucier's Apprentice, Fading Feast, The New Cook's Cookbook* and *The Jewish-American Kitchen.* His history of the post-Columbian migration of ingredients around the world is *Why We Eat What We Eat.* Since 1974, he has been the food columnist for *Natural History Magazine.* He is currently the editor of the *Wall Street Journal's* Leisure and Arts Page.

Mr. Sokolov has two sons and lives with his wife, a museum curator, in New York City. His hobby is tossing the caber.